# PUSHING THE LIMITS

*SUNY Series in Educational Leadership*
*Daniel L. Duke, Editor*

# PUSHING THE LIMITS

## The Female Administrative Aspirant

SAKRE KENNINGTON EDSON

*State University of New York Press*

Published by
State University of New York Press, Albany

© 1988   State University of New York

For information, address State University of New York
Press, State University Plaza, Albany, N.Y., 12246

Library of Congress Cataloging-in-Publication Data

Edson, Sakre Kennington, 1946-
    Pushing the limits.

    (SUNY series in educational leadership)
    Bibliography: p.
    Includes index.
    1. Women school administrators—United States—
Longitudinal studies.   2. Sex discrimination against
women—United States—Longitudinal studies.   I. Title.
II. Series.
LB2831.62.E33   1987   371.2'0088042   87-1893
ISBN 0-88706-556-2
ISBN 0-88706-557-0 (pbk.)

10 9 8 7 6 5 4 3 2 1

To C.M.

# Contents

# Preface

I would be less than honest if I did not report there were times when I despaired of ever completing this manuscript. Perhaps that is one of the pitfalls of a longitudinal study. More likely, juggling babies, data, intermittent financial backing, household chores and mounds of typing just got to me on particular days. I often feared the information I had to share would become outdated before I could get it into print, or public schools would change and women would reach parity with male administrators in the field—all rendering my book too late to be of help to anyone. But at various gatherings over the years, I would meet one more stranger who would assure me otherwise. After hearing about my work, someone would tell me about another woman's administrative application being discounted merely because of her gender. Apparently the echoes of, "we just couldn't go with a woman," have yet to subside in the public school system. Although I was always saddened to hear such tales, they spurred me on to finish. This is the story, then, of women all over the country in search of school districts willing to "go with a woman."

# Acknowledgments

To Pat Schmuck, who first introduced me to this topic and who remains, to this day, a role model for women in administration, I give my continuing love and respect. I am deeply grateful to the Ford Foundation for funding the original data collection and specifically to the Program Officer, Terry Tinson Saario, who in 1980 believed this was a story that needed telling. I also wish to thank the Northwest Women in Educational Administration for financing the update of these administrative aspirants, as well as Terri Williams and Phyllis Wells for their typing assistance. To John Packard, Lois Patton and Dan Duke, my appreciation for collegial support at critical junctures. And finally, to all who gave me encouragement along the way—especially the women in the study—I offer heartfelt thanks.

# Acknowledgments

# Introduction

I remember being told: "Oh, don't you know that women don't want to be school administrators? Just look at how few apply for or hold administrative positions nationally. That just *proves* they don't want those kinds of responsibilities!" I do not know how many times I had heard this kind of reasoning when I began research on female aspirants in educational administration nearly a decade ago. Because women are underrepresented, people assume they are either unsuited for school management or they do not desire those careers. Literature on educational administration proclaimed it, both female and male educators believed it, and consequently, even some female administrative aspirants internalized it. At the very least, aspirants should have been alerted by their own ambitions that such assumptions were wrong, that something—some piece of the puzzle—was missing. In my own experience as a staff member of an educational equity leadership project and as a doctoral candidate in educational administration in the 1970s, I knew and continually spoke with numerous women in my own state and elsewhere who wanted such positions of authority. Except for the infrequent accounts of a handful of women who "made it" prior to affirmative action, however, female aspirants remained all but invisible.

I began to realize the missing part of the puzzle was that no one talked to these women about their lives, their work experiences or their career aspirations. Without this information, people assume women lack such aspirations, and nothing could be more misleading. In truth, these suppositions are potentially lethal to the many women who *are* pursuing school management careers.

In the 1970s, some researchers began to question the underlying assumptions about women in the field. In a study of male and female teachers in New England, Diaz found a higher level of motivation among women than men and noted the difference between women's aspirations and their representation in the administrative ranks. She concluded such evidence indicated, contrary to popular belief, that women *do* aspire to administrative careers.[1] In an extensive case study of one female principal, Ortiz and Covel concluded: "Women have the same career ambitions as men, but they do not have the same opportunities."[2] Women and

1

minorities are held back, Valverde determined, not by lack of aspirations, but by "faulty characteristics" subconsciously or consciously ascribed to them—characteristics that are assumed to predict failure as school managers.[3] With such emergent evidence, some called for longitudinal studies to "focus on the needs of present and potential women managers, investigating the means by which their success can be brought about."[4] "Ideally," they reasoned, "these studies will be longitudinal so as to pick up changes in career strategies and to determine the interaction between effective strategy and organizational situation."[5] Larwood et al. suggested careful tracking of individual women over a five to ten-year period of their careers to better understand some of these concerns.[6]

Following these leads, I began a longitudinal study of women actively pursuing administrative careers to understand more fully their motivations and to share those insights with other aspirants who might be feeling isolated and invisible in the world of educational administration. I wanted to move away from the old questions of why women did not want to be school administrators—a question which gave far more predictable answers—to the more personally relevant question of why *do* women want to become school leaders? After many years of studying female aspirants, I confess to a curiosity about what motivated these women as well as to an astonishment that they could keep going in the face of all the well-documented barriers against women in education.[7]

The information presented in this study should assist aspiring women to make informed career choices about whether or not to go into this field. In addition, the descriptive data should be valuable to those studying or training administrators, those hiring within the field, and those minorities—both female and male—seeking top leadership positions in educational administration. Finally, the data provides important parallels for women and minorities in professions outside the field of education where gender-specific divisions continue to flourish.

Public school management is one of the many professions in this country that underutilizes its pool of potential female candidates. Hiring statistics of those in school leadership positions underline this fact. At the onset of this study, women held a mere two percent of the nation's superintendencies, only nine percent of the assistant superintendencies, and just sixteen percent of the principalships.[8] In a 1981 survey of school district hirings, the Office of Minority Affairs of the American Association of School Administrators concluded: "Besides the previously known statistics that white males predominate in school administration, it may be noted that white females come second, although far behind in numbers . . . . White females and other minorities, whether male or female, are underrepresented in their relation to their numbers in the American population."[9] Finally, Weber et al. noted the percent of both elementary and secondary female principals dropped sharply after 1948.[10] Although more recent figures show slight improvements, affirmative action programs apparently failed to produce the increases anticipated and hoped for in the 1970s.

Despite these figures, women continue to seek administrative careers.[11] Who are these women, and how do they remain interested in a field with a reputation for barring women? How do they view administration and incumbent administrators, and what impact, if any, has affirmative action had on their own ambitions and careers? To answer these and other questions, I studied 142 women across the country who actively sought at least a principalship in the public school system. This book represents two phases of research: the initial data collection in 1979-1980, and a career update in 1984-1985. Another follow-up is planned for 1990.

Individuals from a network of organizations and groups throughout the United States nominated potential female administrative aspirants. These individuals shared a commitment to promote quality administrators in public education and were members of such groups as state administrative organizations, leadership programs, state departments of education, sex-desegregation centers, as well as female superintendents within the states visited. From lists of potential aspirants, the 142 cited in this book agreed to participate in a study expected to last at least five years or more. At the beginning of the study, each aspirant actively sought management careers in at least one, if not several, of four ways: by taking administrative certification classes; by enrolling in doctoral programs in educational administration; by working in an entry-level administrative position (such as an assistant principal); and by applying and interviewing for administrative posts.

These 142 women do not statistically represent a national cross-section of female administrative aspirants, nor do their stories provide us with a composite or "typical" portrait of women advancing in the field.[12] In addition, the life of an individual aspirant is lost in a study that examines stages, refections and concerns of a larger group. The reader, therefore, will not be able to trace and compare an individual respondent's observations on topics such as marriage, administration and discrimination. Given these limitations, the data does provide a glimpse into the lives of some female aspirants and what they face in the field today. The qualitative details of their lives suggest an alternative way of viewing issues in educational administration. Their stories give texture and color to the quantitative data most often relied on in other studies, as well as offer a way of identifying with individuals throughout the country who seek administrative jobs and who wrestle with the demands of the work once employed. In short, their descriptions serve to highlight the immense complexity of issues and concerns that women face when making administrative career choices.

Data collection began in 1979-1980 with mailed questionnaires and face-to-face interviews. The questionnaires asked roughly fifty questions about the women's backgrounds, opinions and plans. The interviews, usually conducted at the respondents' homes or work sites, lasted approximately one hour and were recorded on tape for later transcription. Patterned after the style used by Studs Terkel, the interviews began with the opening question of "How did you get interested in administration?" and then followed the lead of whatever the women wished to reveal. Questionnaires and interviews yielded two distinct types of information: the questionnaires provided evidence concerning issues identified and studied by academicians interested in educational administration; the interviews generated information from the aspirants' points of view—the voices often missing from other studies. During the 1984-1985 school year, I sent a career update questionnaire to each woman to ascertain her progress and to learn about her current opinions of the field.

Because of the personal nature of the reported data, the women in the study remain anonymous. I identify quoted materials in terms of the aspirant's position and region of the country where she resided. I include these labels to enable others in similar locations and situations to compare experiences. I use lengthy quotations not only because I believe the women are their own best storytellers, but because I want the readers of this book—some whose experiences and opinions may differ from these women—to draw their own conclusions.

Any research that relies heavily on selective, self-reported information is subject to challenge—this study is no exception. But in asking my respondents questions, I felt duty-bound as a researcher to listen to their answers and to respect their points of view. This book seeks to *describe* their reasoning, not to *critique* that reasoning. At times I knowingly editorialize; however, I have tried to remain faithful to what the women have to say and to present both the usual and the unique in their experiences.

The book has five parts. The first covers career stages common to most aspirants (such as schooling, interviewing and mentoring), but from a female perspective. In the second part, women reflect on marriage and family (and how both shape single *and* married aspirants' lives), as well as on current administrators. Because women have special problems working in an all-male profession, the third part describes their concerns about discrimination in the workplace. The fourth part presents the goals and expectations expressed by the respondents at the beginning of the study (1979-1980), followed by information from the career update (1984-1985) on their levels of advancement and their advice to other aspirants. In the afterword, I reflect on both the study and the profession of educational administration today as they relate to female educators.

I am frequently asked what common patterns, if any, I found among these women. To address this point, I must also answer those who would ask how this book fits into feminist scholarship. To my mind, the questions are closely linked. Today, there is a growing body of work that is labeled "feminist scholarship." In a recent book, DuBois et al. give a strict definition of feminist scholarship as research that has a "recognizable feminist analytical perspective on the oppression and liberation of women."[13] If that was the only definition of feminist research, this book is clearly not "feminist." But the authors offer a broader interpretation when they conclude that research which addresses "the complex reality of women's experience and situation,"[14] and which is committed to working "on women's behalf,"[15] also fits within the confines of feminist scholarship. These two concerns guided this study of female aspirants.

As a result, the book is about women—some of whom consider themselves feminists and some of whom do not. What they share in common is not the same perspective on oppression or liberation, but a similar goal and determination to succeed as administrators. They openly share their hopes and dreams for the future, their varied training and work experiences, and their candid thoughts about what it is like to work towards a position typically viewed in this society as a man's. Despite diversity in age, race and geographical setting, these individuals have one thing in common: They want the chance to be school leaders at some point in their careers. Although most acknowledge barriers that militate against such goals, they are confident in their ability to overcome them. In some instances, they are expanding their internal, self-imposed boundaries, as well as their notions of what is possible for women in general. In other cases, they are fighting external limitations in their own districts, as well as those in the broader society. They are not willing to sit back while others formulate school policy, nor do they take for granted traditionally-held beliefs that men are the ones who should be making those decisions. In case after case, these women believe *they* are the best choices to be the future school leaders of America. Whereas books in the past document the plight of women—sometimes as passive victims of a patriarchal society—more and more accounts portray women actively confronting these same realities with a conscious sense of personal agency. My intention in writing this book is to highlight these women in education and, in doing so, I am satisfied that this book has a place in the evolving body of feminist literature.

It is impossible to assess whether the assertiveness of these 142 women to "push the limits" I have just described will affect the reality of who gets selected for the highest levels of school management over the next decades. With prepared, experienced and willing female leadership available, will hiring practices begin to reflect a change only hinted at in the 1970s? Will the division between what is now considered men's and women's work recede or dissolve completely? Will competent individuals—of either gender and of all races—be allowed to engage the difficult problems facing the nation's schools today? The 142 voices heard in this research resonate as one toward working for change. They hope to see hiring statistics reflect their aspirations and to see the myths about women not wanting top-level positions laid to rest. What began on my part as incredulity—about the

motives and reasons why these women persist—has given way over the
years to admiration for their steadfast durability. These women remain
hopeful about the field, and from that hope, I derive mine.

# *Part One*

## Stages

# 1 Deciding

I began to think of administration because of the tedium of daily classroom work—everything always the same. It was getting to me. I thought that instead of being at the bottom working with a small group of children, I might have some things to offer at a higher level in education. As a teacher, I was just one of the herd, and I felt I should and could do better than that.

(Assistant Principal, Southern metro)*

RESEARCH ON WOMEN in the field of educational administration leaves little doubt about difficulties women face when seeking administrative careers. A plethora of literature documents various reasons why women might not wish to go into school management.[1] Why, then, do so many women make such a career choice? They are not uninformed, for the realities of who gets hired in the field are too obvious and the articles and books about hiring barriers too prevalent. Despite these realities and barriers, the women in this study continue to pursue leadership positions in public schools. Why would female educators even *want* to confront such obstacles? Why would they challenge the accepted convention that men manage and women teach? What could possibly be motivating them? These questions provided the impetus for this project.

From various regions of the country, 142 women responded to my inquiry about why they sought administrative roles. Without hesitation, nearly seventy percent of the women simply say they want the professional growth and challenges inherent in school administration. Coupled closely with this declaration, sixty-six percent believe they will be good administrators once hired. And third, a little over half (fifty-three percent) plainly

---

*Quotations note the position, region and locale of each woman at the time of the initial interviews. Since all of the respondents represent pre-principalship candidates, those noted as "new" or "recently hired" principals are those who had not yet started those positions when interviewed.

9

want to do something more positive for children in schools than they presently see being done. The typical issues of increased salary or heightened prestige seldom figure into these women's thoughts and, unlike ten years ago, few women say they just "fell into" administration.[2] As these women speak about their plans and hopes for an administrative future, the key word for them is challenge.

*The Need for Change*

Some women seek administration because they want a change in their work situations. Educators who begin in classrooms or in counselling offices generally view administration as the logical avenue for professional development. Unless thwarted later in this effort, few women seem to consider career options outside of education. A teacher articulates this perspective:

> I went into administration because I knew I wanted to do more than teach. As a teacher, you could move laterally, but the tasks and responsibilities would always be the same. Taking on more meant an upward movement into administration. But I knew I wanted to do something in my field of expertise, not just move into business administration, for example. I had been trained in education, and it was in this field that I wanted to do more.
>
> (Midwestern suburb)

Whether it is the time, money and effort put into their formal education, or whether it is the more intangible connection of wanting to serve others (a phenomenon closely tied to feminine roles in this society), these women are reluctant to turn their backs on the field of education. Two students in the study exhibit this hesitancy:

> About five years ago, I was unhappy and frustrated as a teacher. I knew I needed to do something else. I considered changing fields or going into business, but that wouldn't be using my two previous degrees to their best advantage. I decided administration was a place where I would have more opportunities, so I came back to school in that area.
>
> (Midwestern city)

> I chose education over business, because I had trouble envisioning myself having loyalty to a corporation. I need to be committed to what I am doing for the sake of people. I also get bored once I've mastered something. Education provides a variety of things to do and a lot of mobility. Business might have been fun for a short time, but I couldn't stay with "Ma Bell" or Sears very long.
>
> (Southern city)

Boredom with classroom routine also influences their quest for change. "A lot of my motivation for entering administration," states another student (midwestern city), "is the continuous growth and change involved in being an administrator. I cannot stand to be stagnant." The need for variety often intensifies after working a number of years in the classroom. "I definitely felt the need to try something else after nine years in the classroom," explains a coordinator (southeastern city). Many of these long-time educators entered teaching because it was one of the few occupations open to women who wanted or needed work, and the hours meshed well with marriage and raising families. Initially, these women did not think in terms of long-range goals, or even of a career; however, after years of classroom routine and a growing skepticism concerning women's roles that accompanied the women's movement, many began reconsidering their earlier career choices. For some, the realization is surprising:

Maybe ten years into teaching, I said to myself: "Hey, wait a minute! Is this really what you want to be doing for the rest of your life?" The women's movement helped me to question the traditional female role. I wasn't particularly dissatisfied, but as I looked into the future, I had some questions. I realized that I didn't want to be sitting in some primary class grading papers for ten more years. The next step seems to be into administration.

(Teacher, Northeastern rural)

For others, the incentive to look beyond the classroom door comes from someone else. A teacher describes what happened when her principal approached her about moving into administration:

It dawned on me that I might be teaching until I was sixty-five if I didn't take his lead and get a little ambitious. Even though I enjoy the kids, I think you can stagnate in the classroom after a while if you don't move on.

(Southern suburb)

She is now working on her administrative credentials to expand her options. Another teacher recounts coming to a similar decision after seven years of coaching:

When I began coaching, it was all I ever wanted. But I deal with a lot of administrative tasks—budgets, planning, facility maintenance and working with other faculty. About the time I was beginning to feel my wheels spinning, my female principal brought up the idea of administration to me.

(Southern rural)

External encouragement at a critical moment is all that many female aspirants need. A new principal (western metro) describes the catalyst provided by her superintendent: "I knew if I taught one more year of Cortez coming to the new world I would die. At that point he suggested I try looking beyond where I was at the moment." She took it from there.

For those who lack such encouragement, another stimulus to consider administration can be the opportunity to move to a slightly different position. In many cases, the new job does not even need to be out of the current building or district, as this informant (now a district planner) explains:

> I was really bored with the classroom situation. It just wasn't challenging me anymore. Then I got the chance to be a resource teacher, and that gave me the opportunity to work with staff, volunteers and parents, as well as students. I realized then that I wanted to move towards those different, challenging opportunities.
>
> (Southern metro)

Jobs as resource teachers, counselors or coordinators often give female aspirants the extra perspective that enables them to see beyond their current situation. Though perhaps obvious to others, the thought that there might be other options is new to many of these women. As in the case of the coach whose responsibilities spilled over into administrative tasks, a small glimpse of the whole school or school district may be all that is needed. Given a broader perspective, many women automatically consider school management.

The women just described did not initially think beyond the teaching role when they entered education. Those individuals who decide to move into administration late in their careers, however, are only a portion of those in the study. Many others speak of entering education fully aware that they plan on moving beyond the teaching role sometime in their careers.

> This is my ninth year in education. I really have to say, that from the very beginning, I just knew I wouldn't stay a third grade teacher for twenty years. I knew there would be other positions I would be interested in.
>
> (Director, Midwestern suburb)

> I'm the kind of person who just doesn't want one thing in life. I've always been a leader, and I'm not the type to just teach year after year. I decided after my first year of teaching that there was something else I was going to do, and that something else was administration.
>
> (Teacher, Northwestern city)

Ever since I got into education, I could not see teaching the rest of my life. I knew there had to be something else. I would never go back to the classroom now.

(Supervisor, Southern rural)

These three exemplify women who think about work as a career and who have early visions of going beyond the teaching role. Although some did not initially contemplate the specific administrative positions they wished to attain, they clearly thought of management as the next step.

An early interest in administration often accompanies an image some women have about the way public schools could (and by inference, should) be run. Their sense of urgency about this mission propels them to think more about the future than, perhaps, those who only entered education because it was an "open field" for women. In addition, an early interest in administration often coincides with the positive assessment women make about their own potential as managers. They believe they have something more to offer public schooling than remaining in the classroom or the counselling office.

I'm not particularly interested in moving up the line for the sake of moving up the line. I'm not interested in power, prestige or status. I want to go somewhere where I can do something important in terms of helping children's education. I want to be in a position of authority where I can make some changes.

(Student, Western metro)

Certainly schools are not what I would like them to be, and yearly things seem to be getting worse. To tell you the truth, I want out of the classroom. I love the educational process, however, and I want to be involved as an administrator.

(Acting Assistant Principal, Southern metro)

I had the feeling I could do the counselling job backwards and forwards with my eyes closed for the next thirty-five years. But I also thought I could do more, and the place to do more is in administration. I think I have some visions for education, but I need some years of experience to implement those visions.

(Student, Southeastern city)

Women such as these realize that to influence education in the way they envision, they will need administrative titles.

Other women seek change and challenge in their work settings because of personal crises, such as divorce. They may not necessarily be bored in the classroom, but their personal problems may precipitate a re-evaluation of their professional goals. For these individuals, such exper-

iences prompt an earlier reassessment of their future than might otherwise
occur.

> The reason I went for the coordinator's job was I felt I needed a
> challenge. After my divorce, I was so devastated I just went through
> the teaching day, putting in a minimum of effort. I thought: "Is this
> how you are going to spend the rest of your life?" I knew I needed more
> than that.
>
> (Specialist, Western suburb)

> They offered me a job as a half-day assistant principal because of my
> rapport with children. I had thought about administration, because I
> knew I didn't want to leave this earth just being a teacher all my life.
> But then I was in the middle of a divorce, and I needed the extra money
> they gave me as an administrator.
>
> (Teacher, Midwestern city)

> I told everyone I was only going to teach ten years, so I wouldn't get
> complacent and stuck. Then I got divorced, so I started looking
> around. There wasn't anything else I was dying to do, and I couldn't
> quit my job at that point. My principal suggested I get certified to
> become a principal.
>
> (Newly Hired Principal, Northwestern suburb)

Although maintaining a job (and even the hope of an increased salary for
some) becomes critical for divorced women, the underlying concern they
share with many in the study is the desire for an alternative to teaching. For
women going through divorces, the decision to seek management positions
fulfills the practical, as well as the personal, needs they face.

In deciding to seek administrative positions, these women do not
denigrate the important work of teaching. One teacher (midwestern metro)
states: "I hate to say I feel like I want to do more than *just* teach, because
teaching is so important. But I just don't want to teach forever *myself*."
Most praise the hard work teachers do, but in the end they find the role too
confining for themselves. Whether the aspirant thought of administration
when first entering education or whether it came to her later in her career,
the desire for challenges and growth is foremost. They believe that
boredom and stagnation will not only hurt them personally, but will
eventually affect their performance in the classroom as well. A student
(midwestern city) sums up these concerns: "I believe you have to stir
yourself up and try something new from time to time in education, or you
tend to go very stale."

*Assessing Personal Abilities*

In addition to the desire for change and challenge, a second major reason women work toward administrative careers is their strong belief in their own abilities. As noted earlier, those who enter education with administrative careers in mind have usually reached this conclusion after assessing their capabilities. Others, however, come to realize their competencies only after many years in the system.

> After teaching for a few years, it dawned on me that the person in charge sets the tone for curriculum, discipline or whatever. Instead of just affecting the lives of the children I saw each year, I could affect many, many more children if I were in charge. And things would go the way *I* wanted them to go.
>
> (Assistant Principal, Western metro)

> I was a counselor, and after six years, I felt frustrated by not being in a position to make decisions that would affect a greater population of the school. Counselling is such a one-on-one, band-aid kind of thing. I wanted to be in a position to make policy and to create a positive climate in a school. Counselling skills seem necessary in administration, so it seemed like a natural step for me.
>
> (Newly Hired Principal, Northwestern city)

> After being a coordinator for six years, I started thinking if I really wanted to get things done I needed to be in some *other* kind of administrative position having more contact with teachers and children: something like a principalship, a directorship or a superintendency—something with a *real* job description to go with the work.
>
> (Student, Midwestern city)

After an initial passage of time in entry-level positions, these women begin reassessing their personal abilities. When a discrepancy arises between where they are and where they want to be, many realize that all they lack are the proper credentials to back up their skills and experiences.

> There are major problems in public school classrooms, and I'm interested in solving them. I don't see teaching as an avenue to doing that. Realizing that frustrated me, so I began to pursue a Ph.D.
>
> (Student, Southeastern city)

> After being in guidance for four and a half years, there were so many things that I had to check out with the administration before I could do them. I couldn't make any of the decisions I felt capable of making

myself. So that's when I started taking classes for my principal's certification.

(New Assistant Principal, Midwestern suburb)

By returning to graduate school in administration, aspirants often reap unexpected benefits. Not only do their horizons broaden, but many find graduate programs the perfect testing ground for their administrative aptitudes. Two women highlight the effect of returning to school:

After taking administrative classes, I got more and more interested in administration. I could say to myself: "I enjoy teaching, but I am glad to be doing this as well." I began to paint the field of education with a different brush, so to speak, by studying administration.

(Student, Northeastern rural)

In beginning my Master's program, I became increasingly aware of my own potential in making some kind of influence on the educational setting. I had some very definite feelings about how things should be handled in particular situations. I was told it didn't matter what I thought; after all, I was only the teacher. That was the straw that broke the camel's back as far as my developing an interest in administration. Although teachers have the bulk of responsibility for these kids, we don't make the decisions. I have the ability to make those decisions, and I want to be part of it.

(Teacher, Midwestern metro)

Whether reassessment comes through years of experience as an educator or because of returning to a university, these women begin to realize that their abilities should qualify them for management positions. When this occurs, the classroom often appears too small an arena for the ideas and dreams they are eager to implement.

I wanted more than the classroom. I wanted to make some decisions that would influence policy. I want to be in a positions so I can say more than just "these are the things we need to do." I want to follow through on them.

(Counselor, Southern metro)

Over and over, these women tell of their desire to influence and change public schools. Notably absent from their explanations are the commonly held notions of why individuals pursue leadership positions, namely: the need for personal prestige and status. These women desire power, but not personal power. They simply wish to influence the educational environment of children in a positive way.

I'd like to be in a position to take care of the problems and have a little authority. To be blatant, I'd like to have some power to put new ideas into action. Otherwise, it's just me as a teacher fighting the whole school.

(Student, Northwestern city)

There are certain things teachers and schools should do with kids. We have them such a short time, and there's so much we've got to do with them. I'm not so idealistic anymore; I know that change comes from the top, principal to teacher, not the other way around. That's where I need to be.

(Teacher, Midwestern rural)

Frequently a feeling of powerlessness coincides with the frustration female aspirants experience when seeing inadequate administrators already *in* positions of power. In such cases, many women feel compelled to become administrators:

My God! Here I am taking orders and directions from people I feel are incompetent. I know I could do a better job. I could effect more change for kids as an administrator. Basically, I am fed up with my lack of power, lack of challenge and the underutilization of my own abilities.

(Assistant Principal, Northeastern suburb)

When comparing their own skills with incumbent administrators, women come to realize their own potential and skills—perhaps for the first time.

I have been exposed to some administrators who have done an extremely poor job. I think that gave me a lot of incentive to go for their jobs. I thought I could do much better than they were doing. I certainly would like the opportunity to try.

(Teacher, Southern suburb)

For those women who always knew they would go into administration when they entered education, their assessment of current managers only reinforces their initial goal. A newly hired principal recalls:

When I decided to go for the principalship, I looked around at the kind of principals there were. I thought: "Lord, I can do at least as well as they are doing. If *they* can do it, *I* can do it."

(Northwestern suburb)

In every region across the country, women believe they *can* do the job better than many current public school leaders.

*Caring about Students*

A third motivating reason women mention for aspiring to administrative careers is a concern for children in the public school system. Here, women emphasize children's needs rather than their professional career goals. One student contemplates this concern shared by so many in the study:

> My interest in becoming an administrator is not just to say I'm an administrator. It's to help the students learn more and to help teachers teach better. There's not much difference in the money, so I'm not going for that. And I don't see teaching as a low prestige job, so it's not for the prestige. My concern for kids is the main aspect.
>
> (Southern city)

Women realize that without administrative authority, they will never wield the power necessary to help individual students in American schools.

> I really enjoy young kids, and each time I go back to school for additional training it has been with the motivation to increase my involvement and my influence. I don't mean influence in a negative or power way, but as a positive influence to bring about change for kids.
>
> (Student, Midwestern city)

A preoccupation with the needs of students and a disavowal of interest in administrative status seem to stem directly from the criticisms female aspirants have about current public school managers. They contend that many school administrators fail to display sufficient concern for students and are all-too-often motivated by personal power needs. Perhaps the strongest expression of this sentiment comes from a specialist:

> I'm sorry, but most of these male administrators are just jocks! They don't know anything about public relations or faculties or curriculum. And *kids*? You never hear them mention kids! That's why I want to be an administrator.
>
> (Northwestern town)

Certainly some individuals—both female and male—attempt to enter administrative ranks with less-than-noble intentions. But the predominant belief that emerges from the wide range of women interviewed is a sense they need to be more dedicated and more clear about what they want to achieve in the field than the average male candidate. To succeed in administration, they report, it is not enough to be average and female: women must be superior. By virtue of their gender alone, female aspirants challenge the rules of the game just by asking to play. But the stakes—the

future of American schools and students—are too important for these
women to ignore and cannot dissuade them from seeking their goals. A few
women, mostly divorced, admit to wanting the higher salaries available to
some administrators, as does this assistant principal who was at the top of
the teachers' pay scale:

> I have to be honest in saying the difference in pay between teachers and
> administrators made a big difference to me. When I came to this
> position, my salary went up $5000 from Friday to Monday.
>
> (Southern metro)

She proved the exception, however, as most women in the study contend
that children, not money, is the critical issue. In the words of a teacher:

> I'm not in it for the money or the vacation. I end up working or going
> back to school during vacations anyway. The kids are the important
> part.
>
> (Southern suburb)

*Summary*

A need for change and challenge, a positive assessment of management
potential, and an overriding concern for children's welfare propel the
women in this study to become school leaders. Despite a long history of
gender-specific work within the educational profession, these women no
longer accept the traditional view of men's work and women's work.[3]
Whether early in their work lives or after years of accumulated experience,
these women begin to move away from the classroom toward management. Although they value the teaching role, they believe they can
accomplish more in an administrative role. A teacher concludes:

> If I taught the rest of my life, it wouldn't be the end of the world. But
> it's not my ultimate goal. I want the challenge, the creativity, the
> excitement and the power of being an administrator. I want to channel
> my enthusiasm into a positive improvement of education, ultimately
> helping children. After all, that's what it's all about anyway.
>
> (Western metro)

# 2        Graduate School

I was on a university campus all last year and
thoroughly enjoyed the break from the
school building. I would recommend it to
anyone who can afford it. It's just delightful
to learn there is weather outside all year
long!

(Teacher-Administrator,
Midwestern suburb)

IN CHALLENGING THE TRADITIONAL work roles so prevalent and
accepted prior to the advent of affirmative action in 1972, female educators
in this study believe advanced graduate degrees in administration are
necessary for their career success. Women's expectations for themselves
and for their careers underwent a metamorphosis in the 1970s. I remember
being encouraged to apply for a doctoral program in educational
administration in the mid-1970s because the "time was right for women in
administration," or so said the program director. Faced with declining
enrollments, many graduate programs opened their doors to qualified
female students, patently courting their applications and student credit
hours. The gender composition of students in educational administration
programs across the country reflected important shifts.[1] As a result,
the percent of all doctorates in educational administration and supervision
earned by women increased from fourteen percent in 1976 to thirty-seven
percent in 1982.[2] For some women, this new-found acceptance at the
university level gave them the impression that society as a whole and
school districts in particular were now receptive to female administrators.
As many women in this study are finding out, such is not always the case.
Yet, in a time when sex-segregation and discriminatory hiring practices are
still the rule in education, graduate programs provide a tempting
alternative for female aspirants. They hope another degree will make them
more acceptable to hiring committees or, at the very least, will provide
them alternative credentials to compensate for the lack of administrative
experience so typical of female candidates.

Nearly all of the women in this study possess at least one Master's
degree, and eighty-one percent have (or are earning) the necessary

administrative credentials for their planned career moves. Whether full or part-time students, most of these women continue to work on certification and/or higher degrees concurrently with maintaining jobs and families. Although the lure of pay incentives from districts willing to financially reward hours beyond a Bachelor's degree may motivate a few of the women, most return to school for other reasons. Three explanations characterize their interest in graduate work: first, graduate programs provide opportunities for professional stimulation and for exploring future career possibilities; second, returning to school offers aspirants a means of changing the direction of their lives, particularly in the case of divorced women and those whose children are leaving home; and third, advanced administrative degrees enhance their future employment possibilities in a way deemed necessary for a field where gender still figures strongly in hiring practices.

*Challenges*

Women cite the promise of professional growth and challenge as the main reason they return to graduate school—the same reason they gave when explaining their initial interest in educational administration. According to the women interviewed, administrative certification and graduate degrees come second in importance: their primary concern is to remain professionally alive. As one teacher explains:

> Being a teacher, you're not exposed to anyone else in education. You're in the classroom, not learning anything new. I have always loved going to school, so I take a course each quarter to keep up in the field and just to be around other adults. I really think teachers and administrators need constant professional growth.
>
> (Southern metro)

Stated more bluntly, another teacher (northeastern metro) relates: "I went back to school because I was bored and wanted something else to do; I found it worthwhile." One recently promoted assistant principal (northwestern metro) indicates that her administrative degree program revitalized her career: "It's easy to slack off and not continue achieving. Being involved in a Master's program and an internship has given me a lot of zest."

In addition to providing professional stimulation, graduate school also furnishes a training ground for women considering administrative careers. Many benefit from meeting other aspirants and enjoy the exposure to administration as a field of study. One teacher-turned-student declares:

> My program gave me a whole new outlook on my future and what I

could do. It brought me into a new life, and I began to see the principalship in a new way.

(Southern rural)

Through graduate programs, many women get their first glimpse of how their own capabilities compare to those of other aspirants in the field. As they assess their goals and abilities, many experience a growing sense of excitement about school administration. As a rural southern teacher concludes: "I realized I was just as capable as the next person; in fact, as capable as some of the current male administrators in my district!"

*Changing Directions*

A second reason women give for returning to school centers around stages in their own personal lives. For women going through significant alterations in their lives (such as divorce or grown children leaving home), university life provides a new focus for their energies. Although many married women juggle employee, wife and mother roles with those of being a student, divorced women in this study approach school with slightly different agendas. The upheaval of divorce brings new demands and new possibilities to their lives. A specialist describes the changes in her life:

> Before our divorce, my husband had been encouraging me to go back to school. But we were actively involved in church, and I was already trying to be a wife, mother, full-time teacher and housekeeper. I didn't see how I could go to school as well. Then when my husband left me, my whole routine changed. Suddenly the house wasn't as important as it used to be; the ironing wasn't always caught up all the time. I felt better about letting some things go and doing some things for myself. Getting my Master's was a way of getting into circulation a bit and a way of meeting people. It's a lonely world after you've been married such a long time. It's like getting back into the world, and you don't quite know how to do it.

(Western suburb)

For divorced women, time to focus on their own personal needs and goals often creates a new sense of well-being, as an assistant principal (southeastern city) attests: "For the first time I felt comfortable about being able to go to school myself, and I could see where my future might lead." Others express a new, almost urgent sense of determination when explaining their reasons for returning to school following a divorce. Another assistant principal (southern city) states: "I got into my certification program while holding a full-time job and going through a tragic, sad divorce; but I was determined to give myself some new professional options." For these women, returning to school not only provides a way "back into the world," but, for some, it serves to reinforce their determination to actively reshape that world.

Although women experiencing the "empty nest syndrome" do not express the same intensity or urgency that many divorced women do, they do go through a similar period of refocusing their priorities. As Sheehy notes in her book about such "passages," this is a period of "self-declaration" for these women:

> It is not through more caregiving that a women looks for a replenishment of purpose in the second half of her life. It is through cultivating talents left half finished, permitting ambitions once piggybacked, becoming agressive in the service of her own convictions rather than a passive-agressive party to someone else's.[3]

This is not an easy transition for some women. One assistant principal recalls how she faced this particular phase in her life:

> When my nest was empty and all of the kids were gone, I was very blue. The focus of my life had been removed. My husband was away a lot on business, and I decided I had to do something to fill my time. I considered bridge, alcohol and having an affair! My fourth idea was to go back to school for a Ph.D. It wasn't anything like a warm child, but it filled my time.
>
> (Southern metro)

As children begin their own lives, mothers feel free to concentrate on themselves, perhaps for the first time in years. For example, an assistant principal explains how emancipated she felt when her son entered the service:

> Once I was assured this was what he really wanted, I felt this was the time for me to make my move. If he had wanted to go to college, I would have held back again on my desire to return to school. *His* schooling would have taken priority over mine.
>
> (Northeastern rural)

With this new-found freedom, women often find returning to graduate school an appealing option.

### Added Insurance

A third reason women give for electing to go to school for higher administrative degrees (particularly in the case of doctoral degrees) stems from their perception that women must be better qualified than men even to be considered as serious administrative candidates. Eighty-seven percent of those questioned concur in this belief. A student (southeastern city) strongly states: "I don't think I have a prayer of a chance of getting into administration as a woman unless I have a doctorate." Although an assistant principal (southern city) admits that no one indicated she needed a doctorate to succeed in the field, she notes: "I have the strong impression my doctorate added some force to my whole resumé." When female candidates compare themselves with male peers, the need for higher degrees appears obvious.

> Where a man with a Master's would be acceptable, we have to go for a doctorate. If we don't over qualify ourselves, we won't get in the door. And women *definitely* have a harder time just getting in that door.
> (Teacher-Coach, Southern rural)

Some women only suspect they need more credentials than men; others cite concrete evidence to support their beliefs. They are told outright by personnel directors or superintendents that higher qualifications are a fact of life for female aspirants. A student relates:

> My personnel director told me straight out that the best avenue for me to achieve my administrative goals would be to get a doctorate. He said women needed that edge because "everything else ain't equal."
> (Midwestern town)

Some administrators admit that a doctorate sometimes determines whether a woman gets an interview (or job) or whether her application is set aside. Because of these disclosures, many women believe they have no alternative, as this assistant principal asserts:

> One friend of mine was recently hired as an assistant principal, and the superintendent clearly admitted she would not have even been considered except for her doctorate. Even though the male candidates did not have doctorates, she would not have even been interviewed without one! I, too, see the doctorate as something I simply have to have to accomplish my next move.
> (Northeastern metro)

Along with improving their chances for administrative employment, most women contend a doctorate will give them increased credibility once they are hired—particularly with established male executives. A specialist (northwestern town) assumes once she has her degree, the men "will have to listen." A doctoral candidate (southeastern city) agrees: "You can't be ignored with a doctorate; for women, it gives us a little something most male administrators don't have and can't ignore." Most of those questioned cannot envision how this "little something" might backfire: rather than increasing their credibility in a positive fashion, women holding advanced degrees may prove threatening to those men who already view their positions in jeopardy. This double bind, unique to female (and minority) candidates seeking leadership roles in male work arenas, remains unresolved.

### Campus Experiences

Whether for professional growth, life refocusing, or added career insurance, women who return to graduate school assess their campus experiences very differently. Some are pleasantly surprised about the value and challenge of their administrative coursework. These individuals, who often remember irrelevant teacher education classes with contempt, anticipated a similar experience with administration classes. One student was "amazed" at how good her program turned out to be:

> Ten years ago, education courses were terrible, and I learned absolutely nothing from them. Anything I know about teaching I learned in the classroom, not from courses. I expected this year in administration classes would be a year of killing time. But I have found the classes excellent—both in content and presentation. When I go back and talk with my principal now, there is nothing he can throw at me that I haven't had experience with, and that gives me a lot of confidence. The professors work us to death, so being a principal will be a snap in comparison.
>
> (Southern city)

Another student, who expected her classes to be "terrible," reports:

> The professors are bright and articulate. I brought a certain cynicism to my studies, based on past exposure to university professors whom I felt couldn't even make it down to the faculty lounge in a public high school without help. But my program offers a nice mix of practical common sense and experience, plus the theoretical research background to make it provocative.
>
> (Northeastern rural)

A supervisor (northeastern metro) summarizes the general feeling of the women who are pleased with their programs: "I was astounded at how much I learned in the program and how much I didn't know about what a principal actually does." These informants see a direct link between the amount of challenging coursework and their satisfaction with the program: institutions that demand a lot of work, also earn respect.

Not all women who return to campus have such positive experiences. One group of female students found their programs to be "worthless" and a "waste of time." Because many women enroll in graduate programs to determine whether administrative careers are right for them, finding administrative classes with little content or depth is frustrating. One student (northwestern city) complains: "My classes are so vague that I can't get a good idea of whether I want to be an administrator or not!" For women in entry-level management positions already, the work often seems shallow and useless. One assistant principal says she feels "blue" whenever she thinks of her graduate training:

> I need about six more hours, but I keep putting it off. Because my program is so boring, I have to gear up for it. I've only had one or two interesting courses in all. Maybe if I was coming right out of the classroom, it would be alright. But as a practicing administrator I find it all so irrelevant.
>
> (Southern city)

Unsatisfied students on campuses with highly reputable programs in educational administration feel doubly cheated. One student laments that in her poorly run program, even the professors lose interest:

> Our program has lost a lot of professors over the last few years. And although we get the important theoretical orientation we need, we get very little of a practical nature. Nevertheless, the program has a wonderful reputation! I keep wondering what the *other* programs look like if this one is supposed to be so good!
>
> (Western metro)

Clearly, those attending schools with reputedly superior programs feel defrauded if the expected results fail to materialize.

What constitutes a good program in the eyes of these women? The debate of what is most important—a theoretical framework or practical experience—continues in administrative circles. In this study, there are proponents of both sides. Many hope to find a program that gives them enough practical experience to determine the extent of their interests and competencies in management. A teacher (midwestern suburb) notes that her classes "piqued my interest in administration and have helped me become increasingly aware of my own potential, as well as my desire to be influential in educational settings." Another student concurs:

> I still have lots of doubts since returning to school, but I am no longer doubting *why* I am doing this. I can't say for certain that I'll be sitting somewhere someday as a principal, but I can't say that I won't either. The more courses I take, the more confident I feel that I can do a good job.
>
> (Northeastern rural)

In valued classes, female students explore leadership styles, meet practicing administrators in the field, attend administrative conferences (often for the first time), practice interviewing for potential jobs, as well as learn how to think critically about important educational issues, trends and innovations. In a program where they experience some of the everyday issues principals face, they gain an appreciation of the job and develop an ability to critically judge the performance of administrators "back home."

Contact with other students provides another attraction for women entering administrative programs. As might be obvious, this is particularly important to rural women who feel isolated or to older women who believe they lack the necessary professional contacts to break into management late in their careers. Many describe the benefits of going back to school not in terms of the quality of classwork, but in terms of the stimulation they receive from other students. A teacher describes these relationships and their importance to her:

> I enjoy the inspiration and encouragement of other students. I am a senior citizen in most of my classes, but it doesn't seem to matter. The relationships in graduate school transcend age, and I have made some friends I will probably have for the rest of my life.
>
> (Southeastern rural)

In addition to intellectual stimulation, student relationships help to establish professional networks that maintain themselves long after students have left college campuses. One student (southern metro) describes her participation in a training program for people interested in administration as "priceless." She now has a network spanning five states and hopes it will develop into a source of job opportunities for her. Exposure to other students in a campus setting can also provide women with significant role models. One female student notes:

> When I was working on my Master's in education, I met some people who were getting their certification. I had never thought of that before, and I realized it would be stupid not to add the extra [certification] hours to my own program.
>
> (Northwestern city)

Because of these positive role models, many women begin to think about administrative careers for the first time.

*Internships*

Graduate programs with practicum or internship experiences yield valuable insights into administration for all aspirants. Women, however, realize they benefit in a special way, for these practical experiences may provide the only means of getting in the otherwise closed door of school leadership. Female interns not only gain useful knowledge, they also acquire familiarity and visibility in the school system where they intern. For others, this may be the only true administrative experience they will have to put on their resumés. Also, women interviewed in districts with programs especially designed for female aspirants feel particularly optimistic about their chances of getting hired in school management.

Internships allow a trial period for aspirants to view the field and to weigh the possibilities of administrative careers. As one teacher (north-eastern rural) predicts: "My internship will provide me with an opportunity to actually picture myself as an administrator." Another student (southern city) agrees: "So much hinges on this internship as far as helping me decide which way I want to go in administration." Because they need to evaluate administrative careers, many respondents choose university programs based on the strength of their internship program alone. A student states:

> The strongest point about my program was the possibility of doing a practical internship. I wanted to see how I might fit into administration and whether, in fact, it was for me. An internship provides that opportunity.
>
> (Western metro)

Women frequently use practicums to garner experiences and skills in areas of school management unknown to them. One teacher (southern suburb) expresses her excitement about the opportunity to explore every aspect of administration, "from maintenance to personnel evaluations to school community relations." Likewise, a minority teacher (midwestern city) gained her first exposure to an all-black group after teaching in an all-white student body, finding "children are children." For women with limited means of exploring administrative work in their own districts, internships in other districts furnish them with a chance to gain the necessary experience elsewhere.

> I'll have to commute, but I'm looking for an internship in a system that's more agreeable to having a woman in the district. Here, they don't want a female administrator.
>
> (Student, Northeastern rural)

When women take an active role in shaping their internships and when their building administrators are supportive of those attempts, the internship can prove invaluable. Not all principals, however, actively back their female interns. As one teacher (northwestern suburb) explains: "Internships are not always a positive experience; much depends on how helpful your principal is." Women who fail to earn the support and encouragement of their building administrators find practicums defeating. One teacher, thoroughly frustrated with her internship, offers an example:

> The internship was really no training at all: board meetings, take home exams with no feedback, trips to maintenance, and a few speakers. The big deal was I got to spend one whole day—one—in a building! It was mostly busywork. I outlined some of the things I wanted to do, such as evaluating teachers, but all I ever got from my principal were things a secretary should have done.
>
> (Teacher, Southern metro)

Whether through luck or persistence (or both), women who have positive internship experiences often remember the time as a turning point in their careers. Two women share their insights:

> My interest in being a specialist declined when I did my internship. I've worked with my principal on budgets, and analyzed our school population and grounds maintenance schedules. I found administration more challenging and interesting than I had previously thought. Now I am working towards a principalship.
>
> (Head Teacher, Western suburb)

> While supervising teachers, I missed interacting with the kids. So I interned in two schools as a part-time administrator. After that, I only became more hungry for an administrative job.
>
> (Assistant Principal, Southeastern city)

For these women, internships helped to clarify their interests and served to focus the direction of their future work. In addition, practicums give school districts an opportunity to see women in administrative roles and to assess their potential. One new assistant principal attributes her promotion to her practicum performance. In her words, it was "a real educational experience":

> There were bomb threats, fires set, racial problems and a teachers' strike! One of the reasons I am here today is because the principal saw how I handled things. He felt there wasn't much else that could go wrong in a school that I hadn't already handled!
>
> (Midwestern suburb)

In some districts, internship experiences do not figure prominently in hiring decisions; however, many believe they would not have gained entrance into the field—or at least not as quickly—if they did not have them. Others realize internships have limited value in districts that will not consider hiring a woman over a more experienced male. Because of great variance, women considering internship programs need to be realistic about the outcomes in their own districts. If, on the other hand, districts raise women's expectations by providing or requiring practicums and internships, they need to genuinely assess how these experiences will be weighed when selecting entry-level administrators.

### Special Concerns

Female students completing internships and administrative coursework face unique problems in universities. A major concern is how to balance the student role with other roles as employee, wife and mother. Undoubtedly male aspirants experience similar role conflicts, but few seem to return to graduate school without the benefit of a wife at home to manage the house and children. Most of the women in this study add the student role *on top of* their homemaking and parenting concerns. A recently promoted principal expresses her frustration:

> It was a hassle being a full-time wife, mother and administrator, as well as going to school. My goodness! The work I could have done if I had had the full year free to be a student! But you learn to piece it together as best you can. You can never divorce yourself from the fact that you are a mother: when it came to taking a course or depriving the children, then I didn't take the course.
>
> (Southeastern city)

A concern for their children, especially, runs through many of the women's stories. Another principal outlines the conflicts:

> I was much older when I got my degree. All through my education, it's been a hassle. I have had to be mother and wife, and at one time, I was my husband's bookkeeper and secretary as well! I started school when the kids were seven and eight, and it was a slow, slow process—taking three hours here and six hours there.
>
> (Midwestern metro)

Although some aspirants have husbands who shoulder the housework and cooking on a temporary basis while they return to school, most report that this is more the exception than the rule. In general, as long as home routines remain somewhat constant, women experience support from their families. An assistant principal (midwestern suburb) says her schooling does not affect her family one way or the other, "because I've been going to school so long—forever, it seems—that they are just used to it." Such experiences get built into the fabric of family life. Some women find that by actively enlisting their families in the pursuit of their goals, they reduce friction between family and school demands. One divorced assistant principal describes her summer on campus:

> I was the only one there, alone and with two children. My attitude with the children was this was an adventure (living away from home for the summer), and while Mommy had a goal and would be very busy, we were a team that needed to work together. It was a stressful program and a hectic period. But as one of my professors would say: "If you can't handle this, you shouldn't be an administrator." And I agree. At one point I got sick and my doctor wanted to hospitalize me. I said, "No way! I'm a graduate student!"
>
> (Southern city)

The determination and tenacity this woman displays illustrates the commitment many in this study have towards completing their graduate work.

Closely related to family responsibilities, another issue of concern to female graduate students is the distance many of them must commute to attend accredited programs in educational administration. One new principal explains the difficulties:

> I knew some people who had gotten their credentials, so I knew it was possible to teach full time, take care of the kids and house, *and* go to school. But I had to commute one hour and fifteen minutes one way (one night a week) with two other gals just to *get* to school. Then I had to live on campus five weeks one summer to complete the degree.
>
> (Northwestern suburb)

A specialist, who has no children, reports similar conflicts:

> My husband supports my going to school. But my main difficulty is I can't get the certification I need here. I have to go away and live at school. This is the first summer in five that I haven't been away from home. But you know you have to do it, no matter how many other responsibilities you carry.
>
> (Northwestern town)

Women in rural areas of the country suffer the most in terms of limited school opportunities. A teacher (southern town of 600) says, "I want to get my doctorate, but we need to move to a bigger city for me to do that." Although men in rural and small towns also experience frustrations about commuting, the diversified roles women play—specifically the mother role—makes their plight especially stressful. Not only must they contend with long distances, but commuting makes their stays on campus intermittent and short, severely curtailing the benefits and opportunities available to full-time students. Although a teacher (southeastern rural) enjoys her program, she contends: "Since I am on campus so little, I can't get to know the other students or professors like I'd like." This is a point worth contemplating, for others in the study emphasize the importance of personal contacts made on campus. The loss of potential encouragement, sustained stimulation, influential role models and professional networks is impossible to calculate. Some districts, sensitive to travel issues, bring university classes into their districts; however, these arrangements seldom provide contacts with new individuals outside the work setting. Ultimately, unless a woman happens to live in an area where institutions are plentiful, she ends up adding travel time and an isolated student existence to the other daily concerns of her life.

Although surprisingly few women consider money as critical as some of the other concerns, a few find financing their graduate education difficult. Where families are less than supportive of the aspirant's goals, the issue of graduate expenses may create additional problems. One student (midwestern city) found a way around her husband's objections by financing her schooling from her own retirement fund, calling it "investing in herself." Exploring grant possibilities provides another option for solving monetary difficulties, as a new principal relates:

> I would like to do my doctorate, and I know there are some grants floating around. As a minority maybe I'd have an advantage. But how do you get access to hearing about such things?
>
> (Southeastern city)

By being on campus only part-time, these women often fail to hear about the grant and scholarship opportunities that full-time students hear of through campus newspapers, department meetings and university publications. Likewise, in contrast with full-time students, they are less apt to be recommended by their professors for available assistance because of their part-time status. As previously noted, however, most of the women interviewed report that financing their advanced training is less of a problem than commuting and juggling family responsibilities.

Although determined to complete their graduate schooling, respondents often express dismay at how long it takes them to complete administrative coursework. As one full-time teacher (midwestern suburb) reflects, "Sometimes it seems like I'll never get my certificate; it's slow going when you work full-time." This is particularly frustrating when they compare their progress with their male counterparts.

> My assistant principal is finishing up his doctorate. He and I began together, but he—being male—was able to steadily complete his degree, while I just took a course now and then. He's taking a leave to finish up now.
>
> (Supervisor, Southeastern city)

Clearly male graduate students experience their own frustrations. But women's roles as mothers and wives take precedence over their needs for further schooling in a way not experienced by most men: men do not have to justify further schooling, because it is *expected* they will advance in the field. For women reaching beyond the teaching role, this is not the case. Many of those interviewed laugh and say, "If only I had a wife . . . ." They believe that if they did, they would not only complete their schooling more easily, but be further up the career ladder.

For women who surmount problems of getting to campus, a whole new set of challenges await them. Most institutions offering educational administration programs have a history of all-male student bodies. Since the 1970's, however, more and more women have sought and gained admission to graduate programs. Several of the women studied share their experiences in administrative programs undergoing transition:

> When I started the program, the department was all male. I was one of only two female students. This year there are four or five more, so someone is encouraging women.
>
> (Student, Southeastern city)

> There are more women than men in my classes, but that's relatively new. I think, like me, some women are just beginning to realize their potential, so there are women in their thirties and beyond in the classes now. The men, by and large, are younger than the women.
>
> (Teacher, Midwestern metro)

> In some of my classes, the ratio of men to women is fifty-fifty. In some, there are more women than men. I'm amazed! I thought I was going to be a pioneer, but I'm not pioneering anything. Even the profs admit that a roll call five years ago would have been predominately male.
>
> (Teacher, Southern suburb)

Although some schools now have a large percent of female students, it is still a relatively new phenomenon. These programs make an important difference to women considering administrative careers. "Once I was on campus, I saw all kinds of people aspiring to administration," notes a teacher (western suburb). She concludes: "The women were bright and energetic, and if *they* were interested in the field, *I* was. It made me feel like the field was open to anyone." Although caution should be used in equating this new openness on campuses with a general receptivity to women in the field, clearly the increased support and visibility of women on campus is important to female aspirants.

Many women find the added numbers of women in administrative classes help to counterbalance some of the negative aspects of being female

in a male university setting. One student reflects on the status of female
administrative students:

> What I need to capture for you is the *mood* on campus. When I first
> came here, I was a very lonely female graduate student. In the last two
> years, more women have come in, and they have gotten together to
> share concerns about the program. If I had it to do over again, I wish I
> was coming in now—after all the initial struggling and complaining.
>
> (Southeastern city)

A more detailed account comes from a teacher:

> We did a presentation in one class about women and minorities in
> administration. We put a lot into it, but the men just went to sleep. That
> made me mad. One guy said, "I'm so tired of all of this—women, women,
> women. I have to get where I am the hard way, but you just get your
> jobs because you're female." At first I thought I was the only one sensi-
> tive to all of this, but other women shared similar feelings with me.
>
> (Midwestern suburb)

Because of their small numbers in most programs, these women come to
rely upon each other for the support and encouragement necessary to
maintain their nontraditional career goals. Being a minority is never easy,
but these women contend that sharing with other women improves the
climate in graduate school.

> I feel outside of the networks for finding out about jobs, and I find that
> this isn't unusual when talking to other women. I don't have a mentor
> at the college level; the protégés, chosen by faculties dominated by
> men, are all other men.
>
> (Coordinator, Western suburb)

As this woman points out, not only are the students mostly male,
most (if not all) of the professors are male as well. A student (midwestern
city), who said she did not experience any negative male-female conflicts in
her classes, *did* state that the male faculty issue is significant: "We have two
female professors; one new this year. I am looking forward to my first class
with a woman, given that all my advisors are male." An assistant principal
(southern city) believes women have been "accepted as equal aspirants in
administration, but we have no female faculty." A district office administrator bluntly states:

> When I went back to school, the faculty was dominated by Caucasian
> men over fifty. They didn't have a minority professor in the whole

school of education. And a woman? Are you kidding?

(Western metro)

A few women said they had contemplated leaving graduate school because of the negative experiences they had with male professors. A lead teacher explains:

> I thought about quitting the program, despite the ramifications for my career. The male profs are something else! They seem threatened by my assertiveness in class; apparently I talk too much. The whole experience has been pretty negative.
>
> (Southern metro)

Others describe incidents where male professors tried to convince them to drop their administrative career goals because they are women. A teacher gives one such example:

> The department chair was very disappointing. He told me I didn't belong in administration, because I was married. He said, "You can't maximize on two competing roles." He didn't think I could manage a family role and a professional role at the same time. We obviously had different perceptions about what I was capable of doing or of what I *should* be doing!
>
> (Northwestern metro)

A student reflects on a similar experience:

> My advisor has been awfully discouraging the whole time I've been here. He constantly says I'm young and I don't know what I'm doing. He puts down women just enough to discourage them. He calls all women "girls," whether they're twelve or eighty. And he tends to attribute certain behaviors to us because of our sex, not our abilities.
>
> (Western metro)

Whether consciously or not and whether directly or indirectly, some male faculty members negatively affect the lives of their female students. An assistant principal recalls her graduate experiences:

> Five years ago I went to the university to talk about becoming an administrator, and the department head's advice was to take Curriculum and Instruction courses and rethink my goals! He thought it was just a whim on my part, and that made me mad.
>
> (Southern suburb)

Despite her professor's subtle discouragement, this woman's anger propelled her forward. In other situations, respondents say attempts to dissuade them from their aspirations are more direct and hostile. In a midwestern city, females are repeatedly told they are not welcome in leadership classes because they are "second-class citizens," and women in other parts of the country report hearing similar derogatory comments.

How individual women adjust to each graduate program is obviously a personal matter. Some are assertive, as this student was when she tried to discuss sexist language used in her classes:

> Two professors said they were aware of the sexist comments in administrative classes, but were "trying to not do it." But one man said, "But most of my students are male!" I almost fell out of my chair, realizing how little he knew what the implications of his statement were.
>
> (Midwestern metro)

One new assistant principal tries to handle the problem with humor:

> A lot of the college folks are supportive, but once-in-awhile they slip and say "we want you guys to do such and such." I say, "Can I, too?" We tease a lot.
>
> (Northwestern town)

For other women, the lack of sensitivity and support shown by male professors is not a teasing matter. A district program planner recalls her stay on campus:

> The good old boys' system was very prevalent at the university, even with the professors who *said* they were supportive of women. I don't believe their heart was truly in it though. I heard such things as "such and such a district isn't ready for a woman yet." I just don't think that is the proper attitude for a professor to take who is placing qualified administrative candidates. The issue is one of qualifications, not sex. If these people don't push, some districts will *never* be ready. You can't do it on your own as an applicant. It's so frustrating to find your support at the university dwindle away when it comes to actually apply for jobs.
>
> (Southern metro)

She elaborates by adding:

> Women were encouraged and groomed to go into administration here. But when it came time to recommend someone for a position, none of the professors recommended these women. Their names never came up. One of my professors asked me at a social gathering why I hadn't

applied for a certain job. I told him I hadn't heard about it. He said, "I recommended two or three people just this morning, so they still might be interviewing." I wanted to say, "Didn't you recommend me?" Supposedly we have a group of strong, qualified women at the university, and there is an affirmative action program. But the bias in the department is very, very obvious. I don't think the professor I just mentioned was at all aware of what he was doing, because he thinks of himself as supportive of women as a group.

(Southern metro)

For women wooed onto university campuses with the idea that the "time was right for women," these mixed messages are doubly defeating. They question what will happen when they graduate. Will male professors support and promote their female students? One student ponders this question:

My advisor's attitude is: "We place our people." But the established network around here is the old boys' network and, indeed, the male students are placed. Since I'll be one of the first female graduates, we still don't know what will happen to female students.

(Southeastern city)

Many will not learn until *after* graduation whether the limited support they have received from professors will extend to helping them secure administrative positions. While women realize that many of their male professors are forced to accept them as students, they resent men described as "blockers" or ones "who should have been buried ten years ago." One assistant principal (southern metro) notes, "In order to keep their enrollments up, male professors have to change their thinking; but they don't like it at all."

Several express hope that incoming female faculty members will be more understanding of women's administrative aspirations than male faculty have been in the past. Although having a female professor does not guarantee that the status of female students will change, the informants remain hopeful: perhaps she will be more understanding of the load female students bear at home, perhaps she would be sensitive to the difficulties females have when aspiring in the field. These are the hopes, and for some, at least, the hopes are realized. One student (northeastern rural) describes one of her classes with a female professor: "The issue of women in administration comes up in her classes where it didn't in others; usually the topic is relegated to chit-chat outside in the halls." To any serious female candidate, being "relegated to chit-chat" could be damaging. A department chair (southern rural) underscores how class discussion about the problems women face in the field validate her administrative aspirations, for her female professor is "very concerned about women's goals."

Although female faculty members may provide aspirants with positive role models and may promote a non-sexist climate in the classroom, their ability to significantly influence the careers of female aspirants remains circumscribed. Many of these new female professors on campus lack the administrative backgrounds of their male colleagues, which may adversely affect their credibility on campus as well as their power to aid female administrative candidates in securing administrative positions. In the meantime, however, the overriding concern of the informants is to "shake the mentality" on campuses, as one student (southeastern city) states, and to push for recruiting more female faculty members.

Not all the women questioned view the hiring of female professors as a critical issue. Many have had positive experiences with male professors and acknowledge some men make extra efforts to insure equality of treatment in course content, as well as in classroom environment.

> Our professor invited three principals—one female—to come and talk to our class. He paid careful attention to the issues, emphasizing the characteristics needed for administration, not one's sex.
>
> (Student, Midwestern city)

Women frequently cite these men as being important mentors in helping them make decisions about entering administration. In many ways, university professors act as gatekeepers to the profession. Respondents universally praise those male professors with a sensitivity to see beyond today's stereotypes and biases and with an ability to see management potential in an individual who happens to be female. All over the country, these men are remembered for their help and fairness:

> While I was talking to the professor about my husband's certification, he said he thought *I* would be an interesting candidate. They had no women at the time, but he convinced me to come and take a course. I had never thought of administration before.
>
> (Assistant Principal, Southern metro)

> The Dean of the department and two professors (one male and one female) have played a significant part in encouraging me to go into administration. They all felt I would make a good administrator.
>
> (District Program Planner, Southern metro)

> One of my professors wrote on my paper: "You are spinning your wheels in the classroom. Why don't you go for a doctorate in administration?" So I began looking into it.
>
> (Newly Hired Principal, Northwestern suburb)

When encouragement to pursue administrative careers is followed by an equal commitment to inform women about job opportunities and to promote actively their candidacies, women feel satisfied with their relationships with male professors. Currently, however, only thirty-seven percent of those in the study find male faculty members helpful as sources of job information. Female aspirants realize the ultimate responsibility for getting a job rests on their own shoulders. Yet, in a field that has failed to hire many women in the past, faculty support and promotion remains critical. For those lucky enough to have this encouragement, the future looks entirely different, as two women relate:

> I will be registering at the placement center this spring. I feel fortunate that they seem so knowledgeable about openings in the field. I do think I will hear about the jobs and think I have an equal chance to get my foot in the door for an interview. Then it will be my responsibility to take it from there.
>
> (Student, Midwestern city)

> My professors are very supportive and want to see women move into administration. They are helpful with job placement because they think women will bring more humanity into the schools. That's a sad statement about male administrators, but I'm glad they justify women in administration for helping kids rather than because of some constitutional amendment.
>
> (Teacher-Intern, Southern suburb)

### Doctorates

Despite different concerns and diverse experiences with administrative programs, women generally agree that a doctorate in administration will help them secure management positions. Many articulate the benefits they expect from a doctorate, as this coordinator explains:

> Getting a doctorate—especially one from a prestigious school like mine—is definitely important for me. Eventually I want a superintendency, and a prestigious degree gives me crucial access to a network throughout the U.S. If you're looking for a job at the national level, you not only need skills, but the right degree.
>
> (Northeastern metro)

A student concurs:

> The additional knowledge gained from a doctorate is important, but more than that it's the contacts you make while getting the degree. As a woman, you need those contacts to get into this field—especially with the old boys' network. Getting a doctorate doesn't make you an old

boy, but it gives you a way of chiseling into that network. I've found other women who agree with me.

(Southeastern city)

Although women in some districts do not regard a doctorate as a necessary qualification for female candidates in administration, most others do. This is especially true for younger women and women without prior administrative experience. One assistant principal discloses:

> At twenty-nine, I don't feel I have a chance of getting a principalship before I'm thirty-five without a doctorate. And to be honest, I'm not willing to stay an assistant principal that long!

(Northeastern suburb)

A student adds:

> There are a few of us who have chosen a doctorate as a vehicle for getting into administration. For myself, I hope it will help. It's not going to get me a job, but it may be an asset. As a catalyst for growth, it may assist me in entering administration.

(Midwestern city)

Another woman (northeastern town) calls a doctorate a "ticket into administration." Although most believe that a doctorate *is* going to help them, others are skeptical:

> My anger about how slowly I am advancing in administration comes and goes. I don't think conditions have changed much while I've been at school, but maybe a doctorate will help me. It would be a real shame to go through this personal sacrifice of getting a doctorate, only to find out it didn't help me. Now, you talk about anger—that's when I'd *really* be angry.

(Student, Southeastern city)

For many women, getting higher credentials and degrees represents a risk, both personally and professionally. But because of hiring biases in public school administration, women do not see many other choices. Fully eighty percent of the women interviewed believe they have to be better than men to get hired, and they view a doctorate as one way of gaining that edge. As a department chair notes:

> My goal is to get my doctorate. By then I will have two or three more years of experience as a department chair, as well. With all that, I should be able to go anywhere, and there shouldn't be any excuses not to hire me.

(Northwestern metro)

Respondents who now hold doctorates in administration—roughly eight percent of the group in the study—confirm the validity of its significance. They found their degrees important, not only in helping them in securing a position, but also in providing them greater job mobility. A newly hired assistant principal attests to the value of her degree:

> I can go to Timbuktu or anywhere because I have all my credentials. I think that's an added asset. And now I don't have to be within commuting distance of a credentialing institution like so many other aspirants.
>
> (Northwestern town)

## Summary

Whether for personal or professional reasons, the women in this study turn to administrative programs in an effort to advance their careers. There seems to be no general pattern of when a woman returns to school; much depends on her family situation and how many roles she is able to handle at one time. But because many of these individuals already know they want more out of their careers, further graduate work seems a given. Some overcome high personal costs to return to school. Once on campus, some find negative experiences with largely male professors and male peers. Few women find it easy to tread this path to career advancement. One assistant principal (southern metro) confides, "There were some rough years— working, going to school and raising a family—but once I get going on something, I follow through to the end." Her determination is typical of the women studied. However and whenever possible, these aspirants continue to work hard at fitting graduate work into their busy lives. Most seem to thrive on the challenges of the programs, and the contacts they make at universities hold the promise of ongoing support and help in finding jobs once they graduate. Most of all, these women trust that their extra schooling will help them surmount some of the barriers they face in attaining leadership roles. In a field where male superintendents may not even have a doctorate, requiring doctorates of women for entry-level administrative positions raises some questions. For those who lack administrative experience, perhaps the recommendation to pursue higher credentials and degrees is legitimate. But when inexperienced men are hired before those women with years of school management as assistant principals, for example, perhaps these women have cause to raise more than questions. In the long run, those who hire will determine whether graduate administrative degrees compensate for the lack of practical administrative experience.

# 3  Interviewing

> Job hunting can be frustrating, but I'm sure
> it's frustrating for anyone. You just can't
> give up. It's terrible to get calls all the time
> saying, "Well, you missed again!" But if
> you're that sensitive, you shouldn't be in
> administration anyway. If you can't take the
> crap, you'd better not be in the game,
> because it's still pretty rough out there.
>
> (New Principal, Northwestern town)

FOR FEMALE ASPIRANTS, attempting to enter the managerial ranks
of most professions is a little like visiting a foreign country: the people
often look, speak and act differently. Education is one of those professions
that has traditionally barred women from its upper echelons. As Grambs
observes, "There is obviously a clear pattern of sex assignment by
occupational levels in the educational establishment."[1] Arguing the
corporate world is much the same, Harragan notes that the women who
succeed under these circumstances are those who persist and who strongly
believe in the direction they are moving.[2] If the women in this study have
anything in common aside from gender, it is their persistence in seeking
leadership positions. Fully sixty-five percent describe themselves as
"extremely interested" in obtaining management positions in education,
and to do so, they know they must learn to interview well. At the onset of
the study, thirty-two percent of the women were in the process of applying
for various administrative openings and many were actively interviewing.

During the interview process, informants often come face-to-face
with how few women actually get hired in school management. They may
be one of few women, if not the only one, to apply. The selection committee
or school board they face is likely to be all or nearly all male. Under such
conditions, Grambs contends men continue to control the selection
process by typically choosing other men for key positions.[3] In 1975,
Schmuck found "about half of the time screening committees were all men,
and in the remaining cases there were one or two women on the
committees."[4] Though the composition of committees and school boards
may have changed somewhat over the past ten years, their propensity to

hire males has not. Half of the women studied agree that there is now at least some encouragement for women to apply in school management, but seventy percent still believe most school board members—those with the final veto power—prefer hiring male candidates. Despite this double message of encouragement and selection bias, women know they must continue interviewing to advance in the field. "A good interview is a two-way conversation, one in which you, as the applicant, can find out about an organization and a possible job at the same time they are finally finding out about you," notes Lee.[5] She admonishes female aspirants: "Passive patience and the hope that your good qualities will outshine those of all the other hopefuls are not enough."[6]

Although women in this study are actively pursuing administrative jobs, many have little or no previous interviewing experience. One assistant principal (northwestern city) considers she did well in her interview for her current position given she had "never interviewed for a job before." In her first teaching position, she was placed midyear through the university placement office, without a formal interview at the school. Many other speak of entering the administrative interviewing arena nearly as blind as this woman. The experience of one teacher is not atypical:

I interviewed with the assistant superintendent of personnel for this administrative position. I hadn't been to an interview for fifteen years, so I really didn't know how to let him know I was good without asking him to just take my word for it. I think I did fine in the interview though. He asked me some good questions about building a discipline model, dealing with parents and with unpleasant situations, and evaluating teachers. I only had five hours of certification, so I didn't know much about any of it then.

(Southern suburb)

Because they lack knowledge about interviewing, many women approach the process as a learning experience. A student explains:

One interview I had was extremely threatening. It was pointed out to me later that I had been naive, because the interview was *supposed* to be threatening. It was a deliberate attempt to keep me ill at ease to see how I'd function under pressure. Even though I didn't get the job, it was quite an experience. I hadn't interviewed in a long time, so I learned a lot.

(Midwestern city)

### District Variations

The process of interviewing varies greatly from district to district across the country. In some areas, interviews are short and informal. "I applied for a resource position once," recalls an administrative assistant (southern city), "and had about a five-minute interview!" In other districts, however, the procedures are formal and lengthy. A newly selected principal describes her interview:

> I applied for a job in a nearby state to get back into the swing of things. I had to submit a paper before the interview on a topic of my choice, as well as send in two questions pertinent to anyone entering administration. Then I had an essay exam at the interview. There were eight people on the interviewing team. It was a careful and candid interview, and committee members recorded my responses in their notebooks. There were two and a half hours of twenty-five questions, then a break. Then twenty-five more questions, another break and so forth. I really felt good that they put so much into it.
>
> (Northwestern town)

Although some report that the procedural complexities relate to the level of the position sought, others did not find this true. Some women interviewed all day with several groups of people for a principalship (as described above), while others only met briefly in informal sessions with the superintendent. In most cases, however, the days of a casual talk with one administrator before filling a position is a thing of the past. Recent hirings are more apt to involve a committee, usually drawn from administrators, teachers, school board members and community people.

### Practice Interviews

Many report feeling puzzled with how to handle committee interviews. For example, a supervisor (southeastern city) recalls one interview she had with six people: "I knew all of them, but not one of them cracked a smile at me. I just tried to forget it and to do my best." An assistant principal describes her interview:

> I thought my interview went well, but sometimes you can't tell because you don't know what the interviewers are looking for. The team came from administration, teachers, parents, a community person and a student. I answered the questions as honestly and competently as I knew how, without pulling any punches. I used old-fashioned, every-day English—rather than philosophical jargon— to give them their answers.
>
> (Southern metro)

Being subjected to pressure and scrutiny from colleagues can be nerve-wracking for any aspirant, but women experience added pressure because of their lack of interviewing experience and their scarcity as administrative candidates. "A woman in a male profession," observe Patterson and Engelberg, "is forced to be self-conscious, burdened by the feeling that she is 'on.' She must calculate the impression she is making *and* counteract possible wrong assumptions about and misperceptions of her by others" (emphasis added).[7] To counterbalance this problem and to gain a certain level of comfort with the interviewing process itself, many informants choose to practice interviewing. "Even if I don't get a position this fall," states a teacher (midwestern metro), "I'd like to have some interviews just for the experience." An assistant principal recalls an interview she had for a job she knew she would not get:

> They needed to hire another minority, but I applied anyway just to have the chance to interview. I needed to see how interviews went and to meet the people interviewing. I knew them, but they didn't know me. It was a good opportunity for them to see there was a female out there with the extra hours of certification to qualify for that job. It was pretty rare then.
>
> (Southern city)

Sometimes these attempts to gain experience, confidence and exposure prove problematic for women. Describing some negative repercussions, a department chair relates:

> I interviewed for a principalship this Spring with the approval of my principal. We talked prior to it about the advantages of my interviewing, but not about the disadvantages. Some women were jealous, saying: "What makes you think you are qualified for this job?" The men were also jealous because I had finished my program before they had.
>
> (Northwestern suburb)

Although negative reactions may arise when practicing interviews, these must be weighed against the gains of familiarity, visibility and comfort with district procedures. One student describes the dilemma and her own resolution:

> I have an inner feeling about which jobs to apply for, even though I've been told to apply for everything that comes along. I would not want to interview for a job I was not really interested in; it would be a waste of their time and mine.
>
> (Southern city)

On the other hand, women less sure of their interviewing skills and of what they face as administrative candidates view this predicament differently.

If I was going to interview again, I'd get a bunch of friends together
and have them question me, so I could practice and prepare. I'd like to
be less ruffled, than I was in my last interview—especially with sexist
questions. I was once asked if I could handle budgets, and I have a
degree in business administration *and* I am a bookkeeper! The
innuendo was: How could I—a woman—handle all that money? I
think practicing with some friends would help.

(Specialist, Northwestern town)

*Gender Bias*

As the last informant indicates, the issue of sexism and blatant bias against
female candidates often surfaces during interviews. Several women offer
examples of how they see the interviewing process affected by gender
issues:

After our individual interviews, the applicants (fifteen men and two
women) were brought together by the personnel director, which was
very strange. He wanted us to know we were all well-qualified, and he
wanted us to know who the board had chosen. I was their first choice,
he said, and he asked everyone in the room to give me the support I was
going to need. That had never happened before. I hate to think it, but I
believe it's because I'm a female in a secondary position. They assumed
I'd need more help than a man.

(Secondary Supervisor, Southern rural)

I tried for a principalship in a vocational education school, and even
though I was better qualified than most of the men there, being female
kept me out. I was interviewed, but I know it was just a courtesy
interview. They were not going to place a woman in a school with a
majority of male faculty. Realistically, I know many men have a very
difficult time dealing with a female supervisor. Despite my seniority as
far as years in the system, and a Master's in the field to back up that
experience, in the end I am still female. I really felt that was why I
didn't get the job.

(State Department Coordinator, Northeastern metro)

After my interview, there was a big hassle with the board over the
interview process. The newspaper referred to me as "that woman" and
talked about the low morale in the school because they had taken so
long in the deliberations over me. "Surely it would be difficult for 'that
woman' to function there now," they wrote.

(Assistant Principal, Midwestern suburb)

Of particular concern to many women are the questions interviewers ask that are unrelated to the job or its requirements, making an interview "illegal" according to the respondents. A new principal describes the kind of questions she hears in interviews:

> This year I had only one legal interview. They ask: "What does your husband think of your moving? What are your babysitting plans? How do you relate to men? Can you work with men?" It's a downer to go to these interviews and get asked the same illegal questions. After awhile you really get tired of it.
>
> (Northwestern metro)

Many reach a conclusion similar to this person:

> I want to have a couple of interviews and find out what the process is like and what the expectations are. I'm always asked how I will handle boys in the sixth grade who are as big as I am and twice as strong. I find that question so irrelevant. Women have been managing kids all their lives. It astounds me that people still ask that.
>
> (Assistant Principal, Northeastern rural)

Some conclude that experiencing many interviews is the only means of keeping perspective. A new principal offers this advice:

> I don't want to be negative, but I think women should be prepared for hard interviews. Until the men interviewing wise up, the little innuendos will probably continue to creep into women's interviews. It's a dumb, silly game. Some men seem to think women are taking over the world now that they interview for administrative positions. It's sad that men are that discouraged by female candidates. But women have to persist anyway.
>
> (Northwestern suburb)

Experienced interviewees appear to gain confidence from fielding these questions over and over. Remaining calm is a necessity, claims a teacher:

> When I interview for practice, I get the comments I've gotten all my life: "Well, you've got two things going for you—you're black and you're female." They never mentioned anything about my brains! I hear this all the time from men, and from some women as well. If I get hired because of quotas, that's not my problem. Once I'm there, I'll prove I'm competent.
>
> (Northwestern suburb)

Some choose to meet these comments head on, as these women describe:

Most of the questions at my last interview were directed towards being a woman. For example: "What would happen if you were told you got the job because you were a woman?" The principal told me outright the only reason I got an interview was because I was a woman, but I responded: "If that's the reason I get the job, then that's the reason. But if I *do* get the job, I'll do my damnedest." I didn't get the position, but another woman did. Later my superintendent encouraged me to keep interviewing and say the same things next time in response to those sexist questions.

(Teacher, Northeastern rural)

During the interview I was asked over and over whether I was going to be able to handle night time activities with the other administrators. And I said: "That's my problem. I'm applying for the job, and I'm ready to accept what I have to do or I wouldn't be here." They also wondered what my husband thought. I said, "I'm here; leave it at that." They seemed to have no problem with my answers.

(Administrator-Teacher, Midwestern suburb)

I was interviewed once and asked point blank if I planned on having babies. They didn't want anyone who was going to have babies! Apparently, they thought they shouldn't bother with a woman if she planned to leave. I mentioned this in another interview, and a man said, "That's illegal." Then he proceeded to ask me about my recent divorce and whether that had changed my values. I said, "Hey, you are doing the same thing!" He offered me the job, saying I was the "gutsiest" woman he had ever met.

(Resource Teacher, Northeastern rural)

Others diplomatically seek to redirect inappropriate or illegal questions back to the job requirements, as this assistant principal details:

I had to swallow a lot of pride in the interview, I tell you. I was asked how I thought I'd do as an administrator, being female, unmarried and "looking the way you do. Are you going to have trouble with the boys?" I tried to answer tactfully and not to push people into a corner. I was asked whether I intended to marry and how that would affect my career. Would I get pregnant and leave? I told them I had no immediate plans and tried to relate everything back to the job. I truly believe some people are unaware of the legal ramifications of the questions they ask. I could have sued, but if I intend to have an administrative career I'm going to have to compromise. You have to give and take; otherwise, you don't belong in administration where give and take is a daily thing.

(Midwestern metro)

Illegal questions, such as those reported above, persist in all areas of the country. They are the rule rather than the exception. While women express frustration at repeatedly hearing the same questions, they understand the concerns behind the challenges. They realize many people still think women do not know about the demands of management work and believe women do not view administration as a permanent career. Because women understand these concerns, however, does not mean they accept the assumptions. Female aspirants know what administrative work entails, and they are willing to take on those responsibilities. Aspirants believe that screening committee members —particularly school board members and community people—seem unaware of the depth of this commitment. They contend school boards and communities often lag behind some male administrators who have come to accept female colleagues. A number of women share examples of this problem.

> Whenever I am in interviews with lay people on the committee, they ask illegal questions such as, "How are you going to manage your own children?" They are difficult questions to answer. I just say I have managed so far and I have no reason to believe I cannot continue to do so
>
> (New Principal, Northwestern rural)

> I've gotten some very sexist questions from male community members during interviews. For example: "How are you —at 5'2"—going to handle our two competing football quarterbacks having a fight in the hall?" There are a lot of questions about my size and my strength.
>
> (Student, Southeastern city)

> I applied for an assistant principalship, and I think there was no question I was the first choice of the superintendent and principal. But when I met the school board, there was a different flavor to the interview as compared to the one with the administrators. Board members were very concerned with discipline, and I think it would be fair to say they didn't perceive a woman as being an effective disciplinarian. They hired a 6'4" male who projected the image more than I could. They also asked some inappropriate questions in the interview about my kids and my husband, but I responded politely. I told them my husband was supportive of my application, and they could check with my previous employers regarding my track record on completing my commitments. I understood their concerns, but they were not valid ones.
>
> (Assistant Principal, Northeastern suburb)

In other areas of the country, women report the problem of bias in interviewing extends beyond school board and community members to include incumbent school administrators. In many districts, male administrators still refuse to see women as legitimate candidates for school leadership—despite all the legal guidelines and affirmative action programs. A lead teacher describes a problem with her personnel director:

> As a rule, I don't think personnel directors take women applicants seriously. They ask incredibly unprofessional questions which are hard to tolerate. I think they have interviewed too many women in the past who view the profession as something less than a career. These directors don't understand the women who *do* see education as a career. I don't think it's deliberate, they're just not used to it. But then again, maybe it's just threatening to them to see women aspiring.
>
> (Southern metro)

Whether the discrimination is conscious or not, the consequences of assuming all women have the same aspirations or that women today seek the same limited career goals as those in the past, restricts opportunities for upcoming female aspirants.

### Tokenism

A direct result of inaccurate thinking about women in the field is that applications from female candidates are frequently not taken earnestly. Although they may get called for interviews, respondents claim that affirmative action quotas—not their qualifications—are the reason for the invitations. Even under such contingencies, some women willingly accept these interviews to gain experience.

> I'm not bitter or anything, but I was interviewed a couple of times as a token woman. I know that for a fact, because one position was already filled before they interviewed me. I knew it, but applied anyway for the sake of getting some interviewing experience.
>
> (New Principal, Midwestern suburb)

Others get angry when they realize their applications are not taken seriously:

> When we moved here, I knew it was going to be hard to get into administration. But I didn't know *how* hard! I was interviewed for one assistant principalship and even though I was there all day long, it was very evident that I was just a woman applicant they had to see. During my interview, the secretary came in and said, "Mr. So and So is here." Everyone just got right up and left. I was very angry.
>
> (Student, Southeastern city)

Another student (midwestern suburb) tells of an interview in a district that needed to show that they had some female applicants in their pool. She was obviously a token, she argues, because she had not even applied for the job—she was asked to apply. A newly hired assistant principal explains that "certain feeling" about tokenism women often have in their interviews:

> In one district, I felt I was their token women. The superintendent kept talking about how few women secondary administrators there were in the state and how I would "put them on the map" if they were to hire me.
>
> (Northwestern town)

Some women accept tokenism as a given when they try to break into a male profession, but other cannot. This is particularly evident in cases where women find themselves interviewing for jobs that are "wired," or where a candidate—often a male—is preselected. A student (southeastern city) notes how she got the sense that the committee's "minds were made up" in one of her interviews. When they hired the man she thought they would, she felt like she had been "slapped in the face." Another student tells this story:

> I interviewed with one principal who told me he would "put my hat into the ring with the others." I had already heard he had selected someone for the position and was just going through the formalities of interviewing. Although they said they needed a woman or a minority, the person they hired was neither—he wasn't even qualified for the elementary level.
>
> (Southern city)

Even before an interview, some administrators openly admit to female applicants that their minds are already made up, as one assistant principal (southeastern town) was told. Other women sense that the choice has already been made by the way the interview is conducted:

> As soon as I walked in the door for the interview, I knew I didn't have a chance. The school was in a traditional farming community, and the board had six men. They wanted an athletic director, and although I have ten years of experience in athletics, I felt discouraged. Even their body language told me they weren't listening.
>
> (Teacher, Northwestern city)

The interview was frustrating because they made me feel like they knew who was going to get the job and were just giving you some time. The questions were short, and there was no opportunity to elaborate

on anything. The only time I got to say anything was at the very end
when they couldn't stop me. I knew they weren't even listening.
                              (Secondary Supervisor, Southern rural)

### Other Hurdles

Unfortunately, tokenism is not the only problem women face when trying
to interview for administrative positions. A teacher (northwestern city)
complains that some jobs are still not properly advertised in her district,
and others talk of procedural irregularities that ensure that men, rather
than women, are hired. An assistant principal (southern metro) recalls
interviewing for a position, and the next day the paper reported that one of
the men on the interview team was hired! In the same area, a department
chair describes the elaborate procedure for filing an application in her
district, but concludes: "Supposedly you don't get hired unless you go
through all that, but we all know people who interview without completing
the required steps."

The biggest hurdle women face in interviewing situations remains
their lack of practical experience in the field. The problem is circular:
women are denied access to experience in the field because they are female,
and then they are told the reason they are not acceptable candidates is
because they do not have managerial experience. As one new principal
summarizes:

I had seven different interviews this summer and came in second on
several. I asked one person what I could do differently in my interviews
to make them better. He said the interview was excellent; they just
wanted someone with more experience. Back to the same old question:
How do you get the experience if you don't get the job?
                                               (Northwestern rural)

The experience criterion is particularly frustrating for women who
perform management tasks, but never get an administrative title. Often,
such women contend they do the job of their principals, for example, but
do not get the credit and the recognition they deserve. A counselor
(northwestern city) claims she performs the same duties as an assistant
principal, but is told repeatedly that she has no administrative experience.

These informants believe a major reason they cannot get the
administrative experience necessary to secure initial interviews is because
they lack the proper connections with current administrators in the field.
In administration, the network of contacts is mainly informal and, for the
most part, exclusively male. One teacher describes how she discovered this
informal system:

Most information about interviews in our district is communicated at ball games. At one game recently, someone asked me if I'd be interested in a particular school. I said, "Is this a joke?" He said, "No, they're getting rid of a guy. Are you interested?" When I said yes, I knew he'd be talking to someone, but I have no idea to whom. A week later, the rumor circulated that they were looking for an administrator in that school.

(Teacher, Northeastern metro)

Although this woman is partially connected to the network, most women are not. The consequences of being excluded are evident in hiring statistics. If an applicant knows the right people, everything—including the interview—can go more smoothly. As an administrative assistant concludes:

To be honest, the interview was easy. I spent only five minutes with the area superintendent. He chose me on my recommendations, saying if so and so thinks you are good, you must be. The right people and being in the right place at the right time help.

(Southern metro)

### Summary

Clearly, interviewing for jobs can be a frustrating experience for any applicant. But for female aspirants in educational administration, the interviewing process can be shaped by many factors revolving around the issue of gender. Whether there is tokenism, game playing and biased questioning, or whether the culprits are inexperienced community members or established male administrators, women learn through interviews that discrimination is a problem. In this study, many contend that the same kind of school managers are hired over and over in many of the nation's districts. As one of four finalists for a position, a teacher (southern suburb) reflects: "When I saw who they hired, I had to laugh. He was a carbon copy (although younger version) of the man who did the interviewing." Aspirants continue to hear statements like this one reported by a specialist (northwestern town): "Gee, you had the qualifications, but I just couldn't go with a woman." Until female candidates are taken seriously, female aspirants will continue to face added pressures as they prepare themselves for administrative interviews. Having the degrees and, in some cases, the experience to assume leadership roles is not always enough for women in the field. If interviewing *is* truly "a two-way process of selling and buying,"[8] as Settles concludes, then female aspirants have the difficult task of selling themselves in many districts reluctant "to go with a woman."

# 4    Mobility

> I don't especially want to leave this city. I've
> lived here all my life, and I've been happy.
> But if I must move to get a line position, I
> will. I could move anywhere in the state or
> even outside it, if the job offer was a fantastic
> one.
>
> (Department Chair, Southern metro)

MUCH OF THE CURRENT literature in educational administration
paints a portrait of the immobile woman, an individual limited in
administrative aspirations by family ties and responsibilities. "Women
more than men," Kanter concludes, "tend to be concerned with local and
immediate relationships, remaining loyal to the local work group even as
professionals, rather than identifying with the field as a whole and aspiring
to promotions which might cause them to leave the local environments."[1]
For example, Krchniak surveyed over 1300 female educators in Illinois
holding administrative certificates, but not employed in administration,
and found that seventy-eight percent were unwilling to relocate their
homes in order to obtain an administrative position.[2] In a study of female
superintendents, assistant superintendents and high school principals,
Paddock found that "less than half were willing to move to new districts
and only twenty-eight percent were willing to move to new states."[3]
Because administrators must be geographically mobile in order to move up
the career ladder, and because they know that in many cases "failure to
move means automatic forfeiture of the ball,"[4] female aspirants have been
urged to display a "willingness to move on the job."[5] Either the women in
this study are taking this advice or they never felt unwilling to move in the
first place, for seventy-five percent of the informants state they are willing
to move out of their districts to further their careers and thirty-nine percent
are willing to move out of their states. Minority, suburban, midwestern
and northwestern women are most willing of all to move for new job
opportunities.

*Meeting Career Goals*

Why are these female aspirants so willing to move compared with their more reluctant predecessors? The main reason appears to be their determination to excel in administration. Many realize they must leave the security of their current positions to achieve their goals.

> I was promised an assistant principalship next year, but because there is so much turmoil in our district I am not going to wait around for that opportunity. I'm going to be seriously looking around elsewhere. If I have to relocate in order to advance in educational administration, then I will move. I have discussed it with my husband and, although it might mean a commute for him if we move, he is willing. A couple of times in our marriage I have had to commute because of his job. So, if the best educational opportunity happens to be out of state, then I will go out of state and fly home every so often.
>
> (Counselor, Southern metro)

> I'd like to stay in this district because I know the community and the people, but I'm not limiting myself to this district. I would try for any available position within a given geographical region from my home.
>
> (Teacher, Western suburb)

While some of the women interviewed view relocating as an "adventure," others, especially those having trouble with promotions or facing limited opportunities, find moving to be the only option they have to keep their management aspirations alive.

> I was the fourth generation in my family to live in that ten-mile radius where I used to live. I really didn't want to explore the option of moving, but I was so discouraged at job opportunities there. When I finally accepted the fact that they were not going to give me a position and I would have to look elsewhere, my depression left. When I was offered the job here, I knew I had to move because administration is what I want.
>
> (Director, Midwestern suburb)

Because of the limitations or specific requirements attached to career advancement in particular schools or districts, many women must reassess their initial plans and goals. As they advance in the field, they must alter their feelings about mobility in order to move into leadership positions.

> In this district, you have to be a department chair before you move up in administration. Our chair is doing fine and is unwilling to give up the chair right now. So I am transferring to another school where the

chair is opening up, and I'll be interviewing for the position.
(Teacher, Northwestern suburb)

My husband teaches here, too, so it would be a big thing for us to move. But I might have to because there are only three high schools here. If I stay, I'll have to wait for someone to retire or move on.
(Assistant Principal, Northwestern town)

*Personal Costs*

When an aspirant is single or divorced, the issue of job mobility may not carry the same weight as for a married woman. Several single respondents explain how they feel about moving to a new job:

The last three years I only applied within a sixty-mile radius of my home, because I was married to a man who didn't want to sell the house and move. I recognized that severely limited my chances of getting a job, but I chose my marriage over my career. Now that I am single again, I will apply to different places—even out of state.
(Teacher, Northwestern suburb)

I would prefer not to move until my son gets out of high school. But if an opportunity came along that was good for me *and* my son, I'd probably move anyway. I have no qualms about relocating.
(Assistant Principal, Southern suburb)

I'm not married and have no children or ties to keep me here. I could always travel back to see my parents. So I can see myself interviewing in other states and if accepted, just packing up and leaving. If something comes up, I am going to jump at the opportunity.
(Teacher, Midwestern suburb)

Although single women seem open to future moves, they do admit to their own special concerns and insecurities. For these women, personal friendships may replace traditional support systems married women often have with their husbands and children. So even though single women express a willingness to move, they realize they do so at some personal cost. In other words, they cannot bring their support systems with them.

Married women must contend with whether or not they can move without negatively affecting either their husband's job, their children's schooling, or in some cases, their parents' or in-laws' well being, as these examples illustrate:

I interviewed for a position about four hours drive from here and ended up in an interesting female dilemma. I had just remarried and had joint custody of the kids and couldn't move. So I told myself I was just doing this for the "experience." But I became a finalist, and the job got more and more attractive. At the end I would have given my right arm for that job, but I could see even commuting would endanger my marriage and interrupt my son's high school experience. The job became a question for my whole family to consider.

(Student, Northeastern metro)

I've been recommended for some jobs out of the county and even out of the state, but I am not one who can pick up and leave my family. I am sort of like Ruth in the Bible as far as my husband is concerned. This is his home, so it's my home. Some of the job opportunities I heard of were just not in the right places, so I didn't apply.

(Assistant Principal, Southern metro)

I have to stay in this part of the state, because we have two widowed mothers to look after.

(Teacher, Northwestern city)

Whether because of family responsibilities or just because a woman is not "one who can pick up and leave" the home, the women who pass up such opportunities—even temporarily—suffer frustration.

My family has been supportive up to a point, but they don't want to move. They figure I should be patient, and that if I'm good enough, the district will find something for me. But so far, no one's retiring. As for commuting to a job, are you kidding? My husband would just remind me that *my* money is not putting food on the table!

(Assistant Principal, Southeastern suburb)

Fortunately for this woman, she was later promoted to a principalship in her district. But for many others similarly confined, the restrictions on their career options can be devastating, personally and professionally.

*Two-Career Families*

In earlier times when a woman chose teaching as a career, the issue of job mobility was of little concern. In fact, being a teacher afforded considerable job mobility. Whenever the family moved, she was usually easily hired in the new situation. But when women begin to seek management positions, their aspirations often conflict with family interests. The resulting "two-career family," as it is often referred to today, brings new pressures to bear on the institution of marriage. For some, resolution is easy, as in the case of one assistant principal (southeastern city) who relates: "I'm not as mobile as a lot of people, because I do have a husband

I'd like to keep!" But for others, the choices produce major conflicts between husbands and wives.

> I've already delivered an ultimatum to my husband. If my principal gets hired as superintendent and I am passed over again for his job, I am leaving whether my husband comes or not. I really did my best to make it here, because he wants to live in this town. But if they don't hire me for this opening, I'm leaving.
>
> (Teacher, Southern rural)

When both the wife *and* husband pursue career advancement in separate work settings, the possibility of having to move can generate much introspection. One student describes her thinking about the two-career family:

> I get very angry when people say mobility is the main thing and women have to be able to move. That's fine and dandy if, one, you're not married or two, if the marriage you have is not one where both people are trying to be individuals. But just as I wouldn't want to move merely because my husband told me to move somewhere, he doesn't want to move just because I might. The specifics would have to be negotiated in terms of where both of us were at the moment. My husband and I are clear that at some point I may have to move, and we will consider that when it occurs. But now there are no givens; either of us may move for the other's job. It's very complicated.
>
> (Northeastern metro)

For some couples, the wife's administrative aspirations may result in a "commuter marriage," in which dual residences are maintained. For others, the husband's career may be subordinated to allow the wife to accept a new career opportunity.

> My husband brought up our future plans, and we agreed that since we moved for his job the first thirteen years of our marriage, now we will move where mine is for the next thirteen. If he simply couldn't find a job and he had to move away, we would have two homes. We hope it won't come to that.
>
> (Student, Midwestern city)

> My husband *said* he would be willing to relocate and take a lesser job if I wanted to move. But if we have to seriously consider it, he might have some reservations. At least we are talking about the possibilities now.
>
> (Assistant Principal, Southern city)

Because of women's expanded career aspirations today, many families face the necessity of moving or of maintaining two households. Women in this study, all actively seeking career advancement, realize they must confront difficult questions about the implications future moves may have for their families. Will marriages survive a commuting situation? What happens to the children of couples who maintain two households? How will the relationships change if husbands limit their job opportunities and perhaps accept a primary parenting role for the first time in their lives?

Many women understand the fears their husbands now face, because they have personally encountered them before. A student comments on the uncertainties of a possible role reversal:

> Now we have the problem of two careers in the same household. We moved here because of my husband's job, even though I had an administrative job offer back home. If we went back for my career, it would be a step back for my husband's career and he would earn less. But he said he'd be willing to move if I couldn't get anything else here. In the past, it has bothered me that things have been cut out from underneath me when we moved for *his* jobs. So, in some ways, I would love to go back home.
>
> (Southeastern city)

Some women believe their careers threaten their husbands; however, they also mention their own repressed feelings:

> I think I could easily find a job down South where I still have contacts, but my husband is reluctant to move. As head of the family, he would feel threatened if I were hired more quickly than he was. But then he'd be in the position that *I* am here.
>
> (Teacher, Midwestern city)

The personal and career-opportunity costs that accompany moving to a new location—costs usually borne by female aspirants in the past—now squarely face their husbands. If men must limit their career aspirations, they may become as frustrated as this woman (southeastern city), who felt forced to return to graduate school when her husband changed careers: "I was an administrative assistant, and everything was going great in my district back home. Then my husband went back to school, and we had to move here." She found that her previous administrative experience did not qualify her for a similar position in the new district and, rather than go back into the classroom, she returned to school in an effort to salvage something from the move. She feels she is going backwards in her career in comparison with his.

*Summary*

Certainly the heightened aspirations of the women in this study bring up new concerns for marriage and family relationships. For some, commuter marriages may be the right answer; for others, alternating family moves for one and then the other spouse may prove the best solution. Without doubt, the married women in this study feel an added burden in trying to assess the importance of their own career goals and personal needs with those of their husbands and children. They realize there is an element of risk involved in the broadened horizons they now have for themselves. But for these women, the past decision of automatically putting their careers on hold for their husbands' jobs is just that—a thing of the past.

In a recent doctoral study of 199 female administrators, Crandall finds two patterns of mobility for women.[6] She describes K-12 district superintendents and assistant superintendents, along with middle and high school principals, as "career-bound," i.e., they are willing to move to new districts, to change responsibilities, and even to vary from administrative to nonadministrative activities (such as attending executive school board sessions when invited) to further their careers. On the other hand, she describes elementary district superintendents and principals, district office personnel and, to some extent, K-12 assistant principals as "place-bound"—individuals who wait "in the same district or position until the position they want comes along."[7] She cautions female aspirants to anticipate the consequences of their career moves if reaching the higher levels of school management is important to them.

Whether single or married, the issue of job mobility is central to the careers of aspirants and cannot be pushed aside with wishful thinking that success will come without moving. When asked to reflect back on their careers, forty-five percent of these women report being impressed with how far they have come. Over fifty percent, however, respond in terms of the future, rather than the past. For these women, past accomplishments are less important than understanding how far they still have to go. To achieve their goals, therefore, they must realize that moving is frequently a requirement for success in educational administration.

# 5 Role Models and Networks

> I did not have a role model in my own immediate area when I first began aspiring in administration. Even now, we only have one woman in an elementary principalship. It's so important to have men and women doing a variety of things not traditionally done: children need to see men teaching first grade and women being principals.
>
> (Assistant Principal, Northwestern town)

> In this state, it's hard to hear about job vacancies. We hear only district by district or through letters and networking. I don't know if I am having problems because I'm new to this state or because I'm not a male. There truly is a distinctive old boys' network here.
>
> (Student, Southeastern city)

WEBSTER DEFINES A MODEL as "a person. . . considered as a standard of excellence to be imitated."[1] With few women currently employed in public school management, female educators lack same-sex representatives upon which to pattern their career aspirations and goals. Without these standards of excellence, some women find themselves questioning not only their desire to be school executives, but their ability to perform competently should they be hired. "Lacking female administrators as role models, or lacking experience with them," explains Grambs, "reinforces the stereotyped notion that men are better principals."[2] Such misperceptions narrow career options for women and limit the views of those hiring administrative aspirants. For those few women unaffected by such constricted thinking and who feel confident about their administrative skills, the pursuit of administrative employment can be lonely. Although more women are joining the professional ranks, Wolman and Frank conclude: "Most fields will continue to be dominated by men for some time, and a woman may find herself the only female in her working group, both as she goes through school, and as she takes on a job."[3]

Reflecting back on their educational pasts, women in this study know the lack of role models is a long-standing problem. Some recall seeing female elementary school principals as they were growing up, but even in these positions—once predominantly female—women are no longer as visible as they once were.[4] Most of the women interviewed contend they have no female role models at their work site. Although these women are determined to achieve their career goals, the effect of never seeing a female educator in a position of authority significantly shapes the timing of their plans and, presumably, their entry and advancement in the field. Because they saw no female principals, some did not consider administration an option until late in their educational careers. One counselor (southern metro) comments, "I remember looking around as a young girl and not seeing any female principals or even a woman counselor with whom girls could relate—no women with influence or decision-making power." For some, the absence of female role models in schools was underscored at home. Nearly sixty percent of the mothers of these informants were homemakers.

> One of the things I have thought a great deal about is role modeling. I've never had a female role model I could look up to. My mother just graduated from high school and never worked outside the home. To have another woman to model oneself after is important for young and old alike.
>
> (Assistant Principal, Northeastern suburb)

In the past, women pursued educational careers because they dovetailed with family responsibilities. But perhaps more importantly, they chose these jobs because they lacked other employment opportunities. The possibility of careers in school leadership did not exist in reality, nor in the minds of many female educators.

If role models are representatives "of the others of the same kind," as Webster further elaborates,[5] then female administrative aspirants obviously lack adequate role models. A teacher describes the conflict many have in contemplating the future:

> I have always aspired to be more than just an elementary teacher, but I didn't know what else there could be. I have a vivid early memory of being impressed with a former principal and thinking that being a principal was interesting to me. But, despite my feminist awareness, I was still struck with the inappropriateness of a woman being in that role. All of the principals I had ever seen were fat, balding men. The

names or eye colors changed, but it was always the same guy.

(Northwestern metro)

Even though aspirants feel motivated to do more, the absence of other women in leadership positions hinders their thinking. When women add marriage to their work aspirations, their bewilderment multiplies. A student (northeastern metro) notes: "There are no role models for us at this point with regards to balancing career and marriage; it's very complicated." Again, there are few standards of excellence to imitate.

The end result of this confusion over roles and appropriate career ambitions for women is that the few who *do* break through the stereotypes to aspire to management positions often feel isolated. Many researchers find people who are alone in their work groups have difficulty being respected and listened to in the same way the others—usually the male majority—are.[6] In fact, the women who succeed in administration often do so without the same support and confidence men give each other in leadership areas. Without reinforcement, female aspirants often despair of ever gaining access to the field. A teacher-athletic administrator outlines this dilemma:

My principal wanted me to try for this training program in administration, but I'm not one for trying for something that I don't have a good shot at. I knew there weren't many female administrators, so I couldn't very well say to myself that I can be as successful as they are. There were no role models, and I probably wouldn't have even thought of administration if my principal hadn't suggested it.

(Southern rural)

The women in this study are highly motivated despite the lack of role models. As in the case of this last woman, it sometimes takes a male administrator to initiate and validate broadening their career horizons to encompass administration. If female models were available, it seems likely that these women would have considered leadership roles in the same numbers and at the same early points in their careers as their male counterparts. But as things stand today, women who pursue management realize they are still unique in the field. "I know I'm not typical of my peers, because I know of only one other woman trying to get into administration," admits a woman (northwestern rural) recently hired as a principal.

### Negative Examples

In districts where women actively seek role models—female *or* male—a negative assessment of an incumbent administrator can either reduce or reinforce their desire to become school managers themselves. Frequently, women in the study complain about the poor job being done by male administrators, as this newly hired principal explains:

> Sometimes I don't see the commitment to children in the male
> principal I work with. He is extremely affable, but at times he is unable
> to come through in a strong way when it's needed. The strength I
> expected in administrative role models just isn't there.
>
> (Western metro)

A department chair almost decided not to pursue management because of
the male role models in her district:

> I haven't been too impressed with the administrators in our district. In
> fact, I wasn't sure I wanted to be an administrator because of them. My
> male principal was not the type I could look up to or role model myself
> after. By watching him, I only knew what I *wouldn't* do!
>
> (Southern rural)

Aspirants typically say they have a clearer sense of what administration
should not be than what it should be by observing their present
administrator—even in the case of female administrators. An assistant
principal (southern city) who has three "assertive and bright" female
models that "keep her going," also notes that the remaining few women are
not "strong" or particularly helpful to other women trying to get ahead in
administration. In a midwestern suburb, a new assistant principal explains
that the school where she interned had a female assistant principal before
her whom "the teachers were unhappy with. She was ineffective and was
paper, rather than people, oriented." Finally a student (northwestern
metro) bluntly says she has yet to see a female administrator she would
"pattern" herself after.

Although negative administrative role models—both male and
female—dissuade some women from becoming aspirants, others find that
such examples intensify their desire to enter the field. When considering
their own skills, they feel motivated to replace those they believe are
incompetent. A student concludes:

> The role models that I have in administration have always been men.
> Mainly they have been jocks who are insensitive for the most part. I
> know I can do a better job than they can.
>
> (Western suburb)

This kind of assessment of incumbent administrators spurs many women
to choose management careers. Negative role models and the belief that
they can do a better job motivates many female aspirants to return to
graduate school and often provides them the necessary impetus to begin
interviewing.

*Female Pioneers*

Hopefully, public school administration will change as more capable women and men join management ranks and as women doing a good job gain recognition they deserve. Most of those in this study report they at least know of other female administrators, although twenty percent still have never worked with one personally. Seeing other women doing an excellent job in administration significantly influence aspirants' career goals.

> We had a female assistant principal at our school who was very, very professional. She was kind, fair and a good organizer. I like her humanistic style and will pattern myself after her.
>
> (Teacher-Administrative Intern, Southern suburb)

> The principal I work for is a strong person and very much a role model for me. She is very knowledgeable and has been in administration several years. It is definitely a plus to work for a strong female administrator.
>
> (Student, Midwestern suburb)

Being the first or lone female administrator in a district carries added burdens. The few who "make it" experience great pressure to do outstanding jobs—both for themselves and for those hopeful of following in their footsteps. One department chair describes the spotlight in which these women find themselves:

> We have one female principal at the high school level who is unique. She took the job when she was pregnant, and the school was in a *tough* neighborhood. She whipped that school into shape, took three weeks off to have her baby, and then was back on the job. The school never missed a lick. She had one of the biggest male chauvinists working for her, and now he puts the word "Saint" in front of her name and sings her praises. It helps having a woman like her as a secondary principal. It's just like any place else where a minority is breaking in: if the ones breaking in don't do a fantastic job, all of their failures will be magnified and their successes sloughed off.
>
> (Southern metro)

A specialist comments on the progress of the lone female administrator in her district:

> I'm optimistic, even though we only have one female in our district. She does a dynamite job and is on all of the committees. She is really coming through for herself and for the rest of us. I was afraid when she

was first hired, because she's the only female. But she is not crying or
falling apart, even though she is gentle. I guess it's a matter of time and
of people getting to know female administrators. It's too bad there's so
much pressure, but then any minority goes through it.

(Northwestern town)

Many women interviewed express pride, concern and gratitude towards
these path-breaking women. An assistant principal (midwestern suburb)
notes: "One thing that helped me was there was a competent black woman
in the district office before me." Many believe the field is now opening up
to women because of the good jobs the pioneers do.

When I first went to district meetings, I was the only woman. Then the
next year, there was another, and then another. After five years, it's
now almost fifty-fifty in the county. I think women doing a good job in
administration opened things up. If those first one or two women had
not done well, I believe the reverse would have happened: we would
still be pulling, prodding and pleading.

(New Principal, Southern town)

A new principal (northwestern suburb) sums up the feelings of many:
"There are some competent ladies in executive positions now. They give all
women a good name because they are not afraid to say where they stand.
Eventually, I hope to reach their status and rank."

As this woman undertakes her new administrative duties, she will
personally experience the pressures of being in the limelight. Women
occupying first or solitary entry-level positions share a common feeling of
isolation and bear the burden of being a responsible representative for
other women seeking similar placements. A new assistant principal
describes her feelings after being chosen for a job:

I'm nervous about being the first woman in administration in the
district, because I know people will be watching to see how I do. When
I was first introduced, some eyebrows went up, as if to say: "*That's* the
new assistant principal?" I want to do a good job, so it will be easier for
other women to follow.

(Northwestern town)

Another assistant principal echoes similar concerns:

I have a definite feeling of my obligation to other women coming after
me. I have heard some black people say the same thing. If I can do well
and establish a good reputation as an assistant principal, it will help
other women coming along. My female principal at the high school is

certainly doing that for me. Once a woman gets into a position, she must not forget other women.

(Southern suburb)

Others, however, dismiss the added pressure of being a pioneer that weighs on some aspirants. A new principal notes, "I don't feel embarrassed or that I won't do well if some other woman hasn't done well before me." But she is quick to add that she lacks many female role models and realizes that people in the district are watching her current performance—not as an administrator, but as a *female* administrator.

Whatever the additional pressures of being a role model, most women—because they suffered from the lack of role models themselves—willingly try to provide a positive example for others. Some minority women choose administrative careers largely because of the need for minority role models, as these women explain:

> One of the reasons I've gone into administration is to serve as a role model. As a woman of Mexican descent, I feel we need more role models—both male and female. When I was first encouraged to go into administration, I hesitated. But then I thought: How can I not practice what I preach? I must aspire to higher positions.
>
> (District Coordinator, Western metro)

> I got my administrative degree, and now I'm looking for an opportunity to use that knowledge and skill. So far, the opportunities haven't been there, but I still want to serve as a role model for women in administration sometime.
>
> (Counselor, Southern metro)

> My department head suggested administration to me, partly because of my interest in seeing women progress. She thought I could be of help to other women going into the field by role modeling for them.
>
> (Supervisor, Southern rural)

Like their nonminority counterparts, notes an assistant principal (southern city), these women believe they might have taken themselves "more seriously, sooner, if someone else had done so along the way." Because she believes role models are crucial in this process, she urges promising young teachers—especially minorities—to aim for school leadership roles. She concludes:

> I would like to help outstanding people along the way, because I think this is a whole new ball game for women. We need to learn to look beyond our own careers to the other women. We can't just do our own thing and say, "It's tough luck for you" to other women.
>
> (Southern city)

Students, as well as educators, benefit from positive female role models. Women in entry-level management positions report positive responses from children—both girls and boys. Seeing women in places of authority, these women argue, helps children expand their often limited horizons, as these stories illustrate:

> I think I do a lot of role modeling for my students. Many of them come from working class backgrounds, and their mothers have always worked. But dad was always in charge. So seeing me as an administrator changes many of their opinions about women's options. They don't have to be just factory workers, waitresses or even teachers. Teachers don't make that much money, and they somehow perceive that I do!
>
> (Administrator-Teacher, Midwestern rural)

> My students think it's exciting for me to aspire to administration. One third grader said she used to want to be a teacher, but after seeing me she thought she'd rather be a superintendent. I thought that was so neat. Of course, they get confused sometimes and want to know when I'm going to be president!
>
> (New Principal, Northwestern rural)

At home, some informants see their new roles in school management and even their heightened aspirations as beneficial for their own children. Some share the satisfaction they feel when their children (particularly daughters) express pride about their mother's work. A teacher (northwestern city) tells about her daughter's conversation with a friend: "My oldest girl told her friend I wouldn't be teaching long, because *I* was going to be an administrator! I hope my work has set a good example for my children's futures." Because of positive role models, daughters of these women may expand their own career horizons, and sons and daughters alike may come to expect that women will be a permanent part of public school management.

### Networks

To insure the visibility of female role models in administration, more and more women band together into networks of support and encouragement. The concept is not a new one in administrative circles—except in the case of female educators. For years, the "old boys' network" effectively served men in administration "through an informal and collegial exchange of names."[7] Now women are establishing similar kinds of networks through conferences, workshops, job banks and organizations designed especially for aspiring and beginning female administrators. Some are grassroots efforts with funding from local sources; others are organized under umbrella organizations, such as the Project AWARES (Assisting Women to Advance Through Resources and Encouragement) coordinated by the American Association of School Administrators (AASA) and initially funded by The Ford Foundation. For female aspirants, a connection with one of these organizations, or attendance at one of these gatherings, can prove pivotal to their careers. A teacher who attended one such conference relates:

> Ever since I attended a statewide conference for women administrators, I now know there are other women aspiring to administration. My only role model was so loud and aggressive that I felt negative about her. The conference confirmed for me that there were other women who could think and talk with intelligence who wanted to be administrators.
>
> (Northwestern rural)

Another woman, now an assistant principal (northeastern rural), tells how a group of women on a university campus influenced her: "I met some interesting and stimulating women who were an inspiration to me in establishing my career goals. They were role models of women who were making it."

One of the major benefits of banding together is to dispel the myth that women do not want to be school administrators. When a woman sits in a room with twenty or two hundred other women with similar interests, she no longer feels alone or strange; she realizes she is not the only one who thinks she can run a school. That experience, informants assert, is tremendously affirming. At a regional meeting for women in administration, a teacher-administrator (northeastern metro) discovered: "There were a lot of women out there getting ready for administration. Why not me?" A teacher in a support group (western metro) describes the impact of meeting upwardly bound women in administration: "This group is particularly important to me, because I see women who are actually making it." Another teacher (midwestern suburb) agrees: "We meet monthly and invite female administrators to talk to us. We share job information, but the main thing is the satisfaction of seeing all these successful women."

Many female aspirants view themselves as isolated from the field of administration, with little opportunity for feedback or support. So far, they have not been able to penetrate the traditional, informal systems of support available to most male candidates. A teacher who has attempted to break into the male network in her district concludes:

> Some people say we should infiltrate the male network and force them to include us in their informal meetings. My feeling is if they don't want you to know something, you're not going to know it. You can be

standing right in front of them, and they won't let you know.
(Northeastern metro)

Women already in entry-level management positions find they cannot break into the traditional male networks any more effectively than female aspirants. For these beginning female executives, new organizations and groups supporting women are a virtual lifeline. Within the encouraging environment of such groups, female administrators find they are not alone in the problems they face as school leaders—leaders who also happen to be female. One assistant principal comments on the importance of her local support group:

> The women hired this year get together as often as we can to discuss our problems and how we are handling them. It's really important to be able to talk to somebody, especially since I get no positive feedback on the job. The women's administrative group makes me realize I am not the only one in this situation, nor the only one fending for myself. There are some days I want to get away from my job. All I can think is, "God, I want to go home and have a drink!" Some days I might have three or four drinks to relax, and I never drank before I got into administration. But through my group, I've learned there are other women who have fallen into this pattern as well.
>
> (Midwestern metro)

Women like this one, as well as some men who do not fit into the mainstream of informal male networks, look to women's organizations to fill the void. Because traditional administrative support systems fail to serve all aspirants and practitioners in the field, the problem is particularly acute. As a student notes:

> Women cannot wait for somebody else to do things for them, they must do it for themselves. Napoleon said, "Ability is of little value without opportunity." And we must make our own opportunities. I think women must get together in some fashion and do something for women in the field.
>
> (Southeastern city)

Although some women are reticent to admit that there is a need for female networks, others reluctantly concede there are no alternatives. To secure administrative employment requires knowledge of job openings as well as active encouragement from those responsible for the selection process. In instance after instance, existing systems fail to promote women in the same way they promote men. A teacher-intern (southern metro) concludes: "I try to keep up a network, because a lot of hiring is very political: it's who you know and who you can manipulate—not qualifications—that counts."

When candidates are promoted for their skills and potential, not their gender, special female organizations may no longer be necessary.

### Summary

As more and more women assume leadership roles in education, the importance of role models (and the networks that now provide them) should dramatically change. Women may no longer need to concern themselves with debates about gender-appropriate behaviors or whether female school managers can be successful. In the future, the issue should be one of qualifications, skills and potential—not whether someone is male or female. Although role models will continue to be important, the emphasis will be on performance, not gender. When that day arrives, Speizer argues, the increased "number and diversity of women and minorities in work and educational settings might ease the burden on tokens and allow people to pursue their goals by trusting their own competence, unconcerned about whether they have a role model, mentor, or sponsor."[8] Until that time, however, women will undoubtedly seek out individuals and organizations that provide the standards of excellence and support needed to help them become the leaders of tomorrow. Women in this study do not fear success, as was once so readily accepted;[9] they fear never having the chance to try. If nothing else, aspirants in this study offer upcoming generations of school children a different view of administrators and provide positive examples for other women still waiting in the wings. As one teacher summarizes:

> I'm always dealing with family needs and those of career advancement. It's a never ending juggling act. But one day I'd like to be a role model for other women in similar situations. I'd like to tell them: "I did it, and so can you!"
>
> (Western metro)

# 6    Mentors

My principal is a mentor to me. In fact, he
first introduced me to the term itself. He is
the most significant person in terms of
pushing my career. Sometimes I think he is
pushing me too quickly, but he is always
supportive.

(Head Teacher, Western suburb)

TIED CLOSELY to the scarcity of female role models in educational
administration is the need women have of finding mentors. Because they
pursue management careers in a paradox of limelight and isolation and
because they often lack positive models to show the way, female aspirants
find the connection with an established sponsor in the field essential to
career advancement. Kanter defines mentors as "teachers or coaches
whose functions are primarily to make introductions or to train a young
person to move effectively through the system."[1] Likewise, Hennig and
Jardim argue that choosing the right mentor is synonymous with upward
mobility for men and women.[2] By sharing information that often bypasses
the formal hierarchy and by providing "reflected power" or influential
backing, mentors are invaluable resources for those seeking occupational
mobility.[3] Clearly all would benefit from this kind of encouragement and
sponsorship. For women who hope to be managers, however, locating a
mentor has added significance. As Kanter concludes, "If sponsors are
important for the success of men in organizations, they are absolutely
essential for women."[4] Although these studies describe the world of
business, women in educational administration find themselves in identical situations: mentors are essential to success.

Acknowledging this prerequisite, sixty-eight percent of the women
studied identified a mentor in their work settings—usually their male
principals. In a recent study of female administrators in Pennsylvania,
Pavan confirmed that male principals are most frequently mentioned as
mentors.[5] She explains that because "there are not enough successful
women to provide mentorship to young aspiring women, the job falls to
men willing to do it."[6] For those who find willing male sponsors, the road

72

to leadership positions is that much easier. But some women in the study, particularly older, established educators such as assistant principals, encounter difficulty gaining such support. Kanter believes the root of the problem is that men identify first with other men, not necessarily with competence: "Boy wonders rise under certain power structures. They're recognized by a powerful person because they are very much like him. He sees himself, a younger version, in that person... Who can look at a woman and see themselves?"[7] The problem seems circular in educational administration. Few men identify with women, however competent, and therefore few women are hired. By failing to hire women, female aspirants lack necessary role models and mentors, and men miss the opportunity of seeing women in leadership roles. As a result, few men identify with women as potential colleagues needing sponsorship.

*Male Sponsors*

Despite the problems of identifying and gaining the support of sponsors, most women know they *must* find mentors to succeed. A supervisor acknowledges the importance of mentors in her career:

> My male principal and assistant principal have pushed me many times when I didn't necessarily want to do something. They say, "Did you hear about this? We think you should apply." They want me to keep trying, even though they realize the situation is difficult for women in the field.
>
> (Northwestern town)

This woman feels particularly lucky that her bosses realize "there are only men and male voices at all of their meetings." Because men hold most of the positions of power in school management, encouragement from male colleagues is critical to female aspirants. A student describes how her male boss validated her need to change direction in her career:

> I think the most significant thing that happened [to push her into administration] was that I had a very close mentor relationship with an assistant principal at the junior high. He saw a lot of possibilites in me. My husband had encouraged me, but hearing it again and again from someone outside the family is different. When this assistant principal became the personnel director, he suggested I apply for his old job. At the time, it just blew my mind that anyone thought I was capable of being an assistant principal.
>
> (Northeastern suburb)

Many women report similar examples of male encouragement and explain that male mentors often aggressively catapult them into administration well before they may have envisioned such a career themselves. For these aspirants, the confidence of their sponsors outweighs the reality of how few women are hired in the field, and alleviates most doubts the aspirants may have about their own abilities to overcome these odds. Several women describe how their bosses' advice initiated career moves:

> I had never thought about administration until my principal pointed out that as a specialist I was really managing a part of the school. He thought I should consider a principalship, because I had organizational skills and could handle money, resources and people well. I looked into it right away. But I would never have thought of a principalship if he hadn't shown confidence in me and my skills in the first place.
>
> (Specialist, Western suburb)

> I got into administration because I was pushed. After fourteen years in education, I never really thought about administration until my principal made me department chair. I said, "No thanks," but he said I didn't have any choice. It was a headache, but I was challenged.
>
> (Assistant Principal, Southern metro)

Although spirited sponsorship also launches many men on their administrative careers, it appears doubly significant to women. In a field where few women hold leadership roles, female aspirants need extra encouragement in ways their male counterparts do not. Seeing few female leaders, they are less likely to automatically consider the option for themselves. If a woman independently decides on an administrative career, the support of a mentor validates her choice and keeps her going in the face of negative odds. An assistant principal (northeastern town) praises her sponsor for giving "lots of good feedback and support, which is what you need." Likewise, a teacher (northeastern metro) appreciates the backing she receives from a well-placed political friend who believes she is "capable of doing higher administrative jobs." She notes, "He tells me I have a lot on the ball, and that's important to me." Although a central office person (western metro) admits her boss had to "push, prod and pull me into getting my administrative credential," most women interviewed found their mentor's mere suggestion to consider administration sufficient impetus to begin pursuing that goal.

As women return to colleges and universities to update their credentials and work on advanced degrees, they often find their male professors a source of encouragement and support. An assistant principal (southern metro) credits her educational administration faculty with keeping her on target: "Every time I thought I just couldn't find the time to go on with classwork, they would call me at home, find me courses and get me back into school." Another assistant principal received similar support from her all-male advisors:

They work on getting a job for everyone coming out of their program—male or female. A lot of times I was frustrated over working full-time and taking nine hours. I just wanted to quit. But they'd say, "Wait a week more and think about it." By then, I'd get my strength back and plunge in again.

(Midwestern metro)

This kind of personal support from professors can provide the extra boost many female students need when simultaneously holding full-time jobs, meeting family responsibilities and taking college courses. But the question remains whether sponsorship at the university level is equivalent to that given at the district level. A teacher (midwestern metro) admits her professor gives her good recommendations, "but he isn't a good source of job information." A counselor (southern metro) describes how her professor promotes her at other colleges by saying, "Let's see if we can't help this person to advance." But many professors, like this one, only have influence in the collegiate world, and it is at the district level where jobs are announced and filled. Despite these limitations, professors often make important contributions as mentors by encouraging aspirants to look for positions in their own districts after leaving campus.

*Female Sponsors*

Although male mentors—both at the university and the district level—play a meaningful role for female aspirants, female sponsors can be especially important. As DiBella, Eckstrom and Tobias conclude: "For who, other than a woman, can better serve as a role model for another woman?"[8] As role model as well as mentor, women in leadership roles can offer something men cannot. When the women in this study talk about successful female administrators, their pride is evident. A teacher (northeastern rural) describes an assistant superintendent as both her mentor and her ideal: "She ranks at the top of all administrators that I respect. She has knowledge and the ability to apply that knowledge." In a western suburb, an assistant principal recalls one of her supporters:

I was very lucky to have a friend I taught with who was my mentor and my model. When she left here, she recommended me for her position and opened the door for me to be hired.

Another assistant principal (southern suburb) calls her retired female associate superintendent a mentor and "like a mother to me." She proudly adds that this retired educator is "one of the ones who sees me doing big things in the future."

If these successful female administrators are willing to support their colleagues, the outcome for female aspirants could be great. For example, several respondents named an assistant superintendent (western suburb) as being extremely helpful in getting other women up the ladder. A specialist in that district notes:

> Our assistant superintendent is very supportive of other women. She has a big job on her hands if she wants to get all of us where she wants us to be. She definitely has been a very positive influence on the women in this district.
>
> (Western suburb)

Conversely, when an established female leader fails to encourage female aspirants, the blow is doubly painful. A teacher describes her views:

> My experience with female administrators has not been positive, as far as them helping other people. From what I see, it's every woman for herself. The men help each other a lot more than the women do. I'd do better to attach my star to a couple of men who have power and could get me into the system. I can think of one female principal twenty miles away who wouldn't feel threatened by my aspirations, but she is the only one.
>
> (Northeastern town)

Among those in this study, the debate persists about why successful women fail to help other women in a similar quest for advancement (see Chapter Eight). Some report that incumbent female administrators often fail to help other women because they fear the added competition in a field with so few openings for women. Others describe female administrators as too wrapped up in their own careers or too concerned about having to excel in their own jobs to have the time or energy to help other female aspirants. Although aspirants in this study understand why some female managers react as they do, many of them expect to take a more active mentoring role should they attain positions of power in the public schools. Perhaps once they succeed, their perspective, too, will change. But at this point, they envision themselves as strong supporters of other female aspirants, as this coordinator explains:

> I think older women did not ask for help and when they made it, they did not know how to give it to others. It's a two-way street. I worked for a female principal, but she was so involved in running an excellent school that she wasn't interested in promoting others. I have two or three young women that I see potential in, and I point out to them when it's time to move on in their careers. But I missed out on that encouragement myself.
>
> (Western suburb)

*Successful Mentoring*

Once a mentoring relationship is established, women describe many ways a sponsor can be helpful beyond just pointing a female aspirant in the direction of administration. Because only twenty percent of the women in this study sought formal career counselling, informal advice offered by mentors often compensated. In some instances, this may simply mean taking the time to describe the details of administrative work. Now an assistant principal (western metro), one woman remembers her principal making her a quasi-administrator: "She would always tell me the things I should be doing if I were an assistant principal." Another assistant principal (northwestern city) recalls how her principal set explicit goals for her to achieve: "He wants me to get specific experiences in different areas; he takes me step-by-step through things." Some mentors share their inner thoughts with aspirants, as one student recollects:

If ever I looked for a mentor, my principal is it. He said, "I am going to bring you into my inner sanctum and let you know my other self. I am going to let you hear how I think about making my decisions".

(Northeastern city)

In a similar way, an administrative intern describes how her principal keeps her involved:

My principal gives me input on all the things she has to deal with. Often she'll call me in and say, "This is just so you are aware of what I'm doing now." I'm not in a position to observe teachers, for example, so she talks me through the whole observing process.

(Western suburb)

In addition to verbal instruction, mentors can also supply a wide range of practical administrative experiences that aid aspirants in gaining proficiency and familiarity with the everyday tasks of school management. As not all administrators have the time or inclination to arrange practical experiences for aspirants, women particularly appreciate working in districts where individuals support such activities. Women delineate the importance of this kind of mentoring relationship:

Our principal has delegated every responsibility to get us ready for a principalship. He has held nothing back, and not all principals are like that. Some principals won't delegate certain responsibilities because it would be threatening to them. Our principal is secure enough on his own to teach you what he knows. Had he not done that, I would not have felt as prepared as I do right now. He had been a very supportive role model that way.

(Assistant Principal, Southeastern town)

My principal has been encouraging by appointing me to various committees, asking me to do things that widen my professional horizons, letting me go to conferences for personal development and giving me tips. He sees the assistant principalship as a stepping stone to other positions. He made it very clear when he was hiring for this position that he only wanted someone who had the potential to go on in administration.

(Assistant Principal, Northeastern metro)

My female principal has been very supportive. She told me in the beginning that she didn't think all women should try to be administrators, but she would help me if I felt like I liked it and could do a good job. She's given me opportunities to go to seminars and workshops, and sometimes she even passes on her consulting jobs from around the nation to me. She is definitely a mentor for me.

(Counselor, Midwestern suburb)

Aspirants especially appreciate mentors who arrange practical experiences in areas where they lack skill. A teacher (western suburb) recalls an assistant principal giving her "a variety of responsibilities in the discipline area which gave me the opportunity to prove myself." Not only does such training bolster the confidence of the aspirant, but these experiences allow women to answer affirmatively to the question of whether they have administrative experience. Since many of the aspirants spend a large part of their educational careers in the classroom, they generally lack exposure to the whole spectrum of administrative work. For a mentor, offering comprehensive administrative involvement is a major undertaking, yet women often report finding willing sponsors:

My principal gives me duties that expose me to just about everything in administration: budgeting, discipline, evaluation and so forth. Whatever he does, I do. I'm like an assistant principal, although my title doesn't indicate that.

(Lead Teacher, Southern suburb)

My principal has given me a wide variety of experiences. I've done curriculum, budgeting, discipline, attendance and end-of-the-year reports. I've had the run of the store several times; he just leaves it in my hands.

(Assistant Principal, Southern suburb)

All aspirants—but especially those outside formally established networks—need knowledge about job openings. Yet, half of the women studied disclose difficulties in hearing about administrative openings.

Mentors who provide access to employment networks furnish significant assistance to female aspirants—particularly for those who are in the classroom all day. In a western suburb, a specialist reports that her male principal told her about the two jobs for which she has applied. By circulating formal position announcements or by sharing their informal knowledge about employment opportunities gained through conversation with other colleagues, administrators can supply important information that many aspirants would not otherwise hear.

> My principal has done more to help me find jobs than anyone in the system. He sends me notices that I would never have heard of but for him. He has taken me under his wing, and I really appreciate that.
>
> (Teacher, Southern rural)

> I have a principal who provides a training ground for his assistant principals by giving them a lot of experience and encouragement. If he receives a new job announcement, for example, he comes in and talks it over with me. If you have such an open-minded principal, it's pretty easy to hear about openings.
>
> (Assistant Principal, Southern metro)

Because not all districts across the nation openly disseminate job information, the informal way mentors provide this knowledge offsets the bias many women contend exists in school districts. For women who receive job offers, mentors can further supply aspirants with "inside" information about the position and the district before they accept the job. Many aspirants find their mentors' advice helpful when they have concerns about a particular position, as one newly hired assistant principal notes:

> My superintendent is the one who got me started. In fact, I called him about a job offer I got recently. He said, "Take the job." When I hesitated, he said, "Take the job, I keep telling you." I can touch base with him on my perceptions whenever I need to. If you can find yourself a friend—a mentor—who is knowledgeable about the district, you can get a perspective on whether you want to make the move or not.
>
> (Northwestern town)

Another assistant principal concurs:

> Our superintendent is very supportive and encouraging. He knows I am actively pursuing educational administration, so he keeps his ear to the ground to pick up any available information. If I get to the point of making a decision about a job, I will go to him to get good, candid advice.
>
> (Northeastern town)

*Summary*

Whether it is encouragement to seek administrative careers, feedback on job performance, added training in weak areas, information about job openings or advice about whether to accept a position, mentors unmistakably furnish female aspirants with valuable support. No one knows this more than women who do not have such help. Female aspirants without mentors feel adrift, separated from sources of support and encouragement frequently afforded to promising male colleagues. An assistant principal (southern metro) expresses bewilderment over who could possibly be her mentor, as her principal has little influence within the district. "I don't have a mentor, and I don't know who could be one for me," she confesses. A supervisor adds:

> I've never gone around and asked anyone to be my—what is the word?—mentor. Maybe that's been wrong. In such a small community, I've always thought people knew that I went back to school for my credentials so that I could apply for all these jobs. I guess I really haven't taken that necessary next step of finding a mentor.
>
> (Northwestern town)

Among female aspirants seeking mentors, classroom teachers encounter special problems. Many report their reluctance to approach potential mentors for fear of jeopardizing their rapport with other teachers. "I haven't sought out a mentor as much as I need to," a teacher (northeastern town) notes, "because I have been straddling the fence between teachers' and administrators' viewpoints." Such conflicts can be immense for beginning female aspirants, as they have much more to lose than men by aligning themselves with management. Teachers and administrators, alike, expect and encourage men to move up the career ladder; therefore, men undergo little risk of censure in their quest to move out of the teaching ranks.[9] On the other hand, with less opportunity and encouragement, women are more hesitant to isolate themselves from their teaching colleagues by seeking leadership roles. This ambivalence is, perhaps, the foremost reason that women lacking mentors waiver in their search for sponsorship.

Despite the difficulties and conflicts that some aspirants experience when seeking a mentor, they realize that they—more than men—must have sponsorship to advance. If having a mentor is as critical as it appears to be, then the old adage—"it's not what you know, but *who* you know" may, indeed, be true for women seeking executive positions in public schools.

# *Part Two* ──────────

# Reflections

# 7    Marriage and Families

I think it's important for young women to realize they have a potential for contributing in addition to being wives and mothers. I would never minimize that potential. Sometimes I think back on what I've done as a mother and wife, and I ask myself: "Why am I going to school *now*? I don't have to be studying for exams at my age!" But I *do* have to—for myself. There is just this unrest, a feeling that I can do more. It's a wonderful feeling, but it is also a curse. I don't know if I'll succeed in becoming an administrator, but I know it's something I have to try.

(Teacher, Midwestern metro)

I don't have a family, so I'm spoiled. I've never experienced the conflict of responsibilities that some women have. If I have to be on the job until 10:00 p.m., I can be here. I see how I'd feel guilty if I had young children though. My first commitment would be to them, and I'd put off pursuing administration until I was older or until the children were in school. Around this district, a lot of older women whose children are now grown are just starting to make a push into administration. They are finally feeling free. Younger women today, however, marry and have families later, making it possible to go back to graduate school and pursue administrative positions earlier in their careers.

(Specialist, Midwestern suburb)

FEW DECISIONS SIGNIFICANTLY SHAPE women's work careers as those of whether or not to marry and have children. In American society today, Pleck argues, a career means "full-time, continuous work from the end of one's education to retirement...and the subordination of other roles to [it]."[1] Given this definition, he recognizes that working women with family responsibilities seldom fit the career model. White presents an alternative description of women's careers: "They have a full-time commitment, but do not always plan to work on a full-time basis ... [A]n alternative mode might be represented schematically by an ascending spiral movement, indicating career choices which are upward in direction but slowly paced, with long horizontal stopovers."[2] Although men also face difficult decisions about careers and families, the strain for wives to manage both work and home continues to be greater in this culture than for husbands. Much has been written recently about "househusbands" and greater participation by fathers in child reading; however, wives continue to handle the majority of home responsibilities. Pleck concludes that, except in rare instances, "husbands contribute about the same time to family tasks whether or not their wives are employed."[3]

In her research on female administrators, Paddock finds that "the divided role of professional and homemaker is one of the biggest barriers to women's career development."[4] Female aspirants in this study also feel that marriage plays a large part in their lives; however, they assess its impact differently. Unlike Paddock's female administrators (largely older women with children over eighteen), female aspirants in this study range in age from twenty-three to fifty-eight, and of the half who have children, the majority are of school age (six to seventeen years old). In addition, sixty-six percent of the aspirants are married, one percent widowed, and twenty percent divorced. Only fourteen percent of the women are single, but only one believed she would remain so (and she has since married). Thus, most aspirants are directly or indirectly involved with issues surrounding marriage and families; however, unlike Paddock's respondents, only twenty-seven percent of the aspirants consider family responsibilities a barrier to their career plans.

What accounts for the difference of opinion between Paddock's incumbent female administrators and female aspirants in this study? Equal opportunity legislation of the 1970s provides a possible clue. Whatever the shortcomings of Title IX and affirmative action programs (see Chapter Ten), women in this study report having a more expanded sense of their own possibilities because of this legislation. Papanek argues that now "women have become motivated to achieve and perform in the same spheres and with the same skills as men."[5] Whether they will gain access to their chosen fields remains to be seen; nevertheless, women now push both society's external limits, as well as their own internal, individual limits of what is possible in the work world. Today's female administrative aspirants, like the women in scientific professions studied by White, do not "see their maternal role as bringing their professional life to an end."[6]

Although they seldom perceive marriage and family as a barrier to their careers, aspirants continually reflect on the subject. Even for those unmarried or childless respondents, the married professional woman with family responsibilities remains the focus of their attention and the measure of their lives. Sheehy describes the difficulties that professional women face: "The life cycle of a career-minded woman must still be carefully, almost exquisitely, calibrated if she is to integrate her professional aspirations with a personal life worth living."[7] These aspirants carefully balance—day by day—their many complex roles and responsibilities in an effort to advance, not derail, their careers. The following sections detail their reflections and insights on how they seek that equilibrium.

### Supportive Husbands

One of the first things most married women mention is the support they receive from their husbands. Indeed, many credit their spouses for being among the first to encourage them to pursue administrative careers. In Pavan's study, female administrators in Pennsylvania mention their husbands (after principals and professors) as being their most significant mentors.[8] Similarly, women in this study praise their husbands for showing support and concern, as this director confirms:

> My husband is the one who really encouraged me. He knew I would not be satisfied sitting at home, even though he is traditional himself and would have preferred his wife not to work. Instead, he encouraged me to look further.
>
> (Northeastern town)

A coordinator (northwestern city) concurs: "My husband is the one who has been pushing me and encouraging me all along." In fact, some find that their spouse is the *only* one urging them to enter school management.

> The only person encouraging me is my husband. He says, "If you want to be an administrator, you can do it." Part of my problem is not getting any support from colleagues at work. In this county, we have only had women in administrative positions the last three years, so there has been little incentive for the rest of us to go on.
>
> (Department Chair, Southern metro)

For women with few role models and little support at the district level, their husbands' backing takes on added weight. In some cases, husbands first notice their wives' growing discontent in the classroom and suggest they try something new, as an administrative intern (western suburb) relates: "My husband supported my career change because he said I wasn't coming home from work excited anymore." A student (southern city) remarks that her husband is always the first to encourage her higher aspirations. She adds, "He probably pushed harder than anybody else when he saw me getting tired and disgruntled as a teacher." A specialist (northwestern rural) credits her husband with encouraging her when no one else in the district would, "because he sees the problems I've had as a classroom teacher."

After deciding that a change is needed, the first step many women take is to return to graduate school. In this study, forty-five percent of the women are full or part-time students, as well as educators and home-makers. As women go back to universities, husbands and families can lend critical backing to a woman's change in career direction. "I made a conscious decision to return for my Master's, and my husband and kids were very supportive of this choice," declares a coordinator (western metro). A student (southeastern city) labels her husband her "big pusher." When she was debating whether to go back to school, he said: "Just go, because there are more important things to consider than just your lost salary."

Going back, however is not always easy. These women understand that returning to school will bring more demands to a life already full of commitments. A department chair describes her situation:

> My husband was a big help. He encouraged me to apply for this program for minorities and, when I was accepted, he kept encouraging me. We knew we would have to be apart while I went to school, but he was one-hundred percent for it. If he hadn't been so willing for me to go, I wouldn't have done it.
>
> (Southern rural)

An assistant principal relates a similar experience:

> My second husband is his own good, strong person. As an established teacher himself, he wonders why I even want to be an administrator! But he's never seen me as one who would stay home and take care of the house. When I go off to school for the summer, he says he'll miss me. But he is all for it, because it's what *I* want to do.
>
> (Northwestern town)

Despite personal risk, lost income, less time for marriage relationships, and the possible commutes or living away from home that are associated with returning to graduate school, many husbands actively support their wives' career aspirations. While admitting that returning to school is not easy, most aspirants contend it is not only necessary for a career advance-ment, but important for their own personal fulfillment, as this newly selected principal explains:

> You divide yourself between your job and being a student, wife and mother. The school work is not *that* bad; it can be done. Sometimes

you just have to toe the line, because you thrive on doing something you really enjoy.

(Southeastern town)

Husbands who also understand the barriers women face when moving into a male field, lend unique support to their wives' goals. A new principal comments on her husband's awareness of gender issues in educational administration:

The only thing my husband was hesitant about was the fact that there were no other female assistant principals in the district—absolutely none. We knew there would be hassles with male administrative colleagues, but I knew I could hold my own. My husband, however, was afraid I would have a hard time being accepted by the other males.

(Southeastern town)

Some husbands personally understand the barriers their wives face because they are educators themselves. Of the spouses in this study, fourteen percent work in public schools as teachers or administrators. Those husbands who are successful educational leaders often serve as role models, prompting their wives' initial interest in administration.

My husband is also an administrator and supports what I am doing. When I get home at a quarter to one in the morning and tell him I've been at the high school dance, he knows that's where I've been. Some men would probably be threatened, but he knows what's expected of an administrator.

(Assistant Principal, Northeastern city)

My husband is achievement oriented, like me. Although he jokes that I must be crazy to go into administration because he knows the hassles of being an administrator, he encourages my aspirations. In fact, he pushed me into doing my Master's program, when initially all I wanted to do was take one course.

(New Principal, Northwestern suburb)

My husband is one-hundred percent supportive. He is an excellent administrator himself, and I've learned a lot from him. If I have a role model, it would have to be him.

(Head Teacher, Southern suburb)

*Traditional Career Paths*

Although a husband's support is critical for married female aspirants, a woman's personal expectations about family and career—often coupled with her age—plays a major role in how she will pursue her goals. The women in this study appear to follow two different paths in their search for leadership positions. The first is the more traditional or expected route for female educators: they begin teaching, then have children, and later pursue administration. The second or emergent route often involves early identification of administrative aspirations and a subsequent delay in having a family. Turning first to those women who already have families, many do not feel free to pursue administrative careers until their children are in school or, in some cases, out of school and on their own. Older women in this study tend to follow this pattern. Several explain their thinking:

> I didn't aspire to administration earlier in my career because I was married and the children came first. My husband was an aspiring administrator then, and I am a firm believer in the husband being in charge of the household. Since that's his responsibility, I pushed him to arrive at his potential first. I thought of myself as a secondary wage-earner and a mother, and with those priorities, I missed a lot of job opportunities. But I felt I needed to be home when the kids were home, and classroom teaching allowed for that. Also, administration is a twelve-month job, and I felt I owed it to my children to be home with them during the summers at least. Only after the children were grown did I start looking at administrative positions. Now I am actively aspiring.
>
> (Assistant Principal, Southern metro)

> I came into education as an older woman with kids in grades four to twelve. In my first year of teaching, my principal encouraged me to go into administration. But I wasn't ready to assume that kind of position then. Instead, I stored the idea away for the future.
>
> (New Principal, Northwestern metro)

> Although I felt dissatisfied just being at home, the fields open to women in the 1950s were limited to teaching and nursing. Because teaching enabled me to be home when the kids came home from school, I went that route. I did exactly what "they" always say women in the 1950's did; I am definitely a product of my times.
>
> (Supervisor, Northeastern town)

The issue is rarely one of whether they wanted to work or not; eighty percent of those studied are employed full-time and sixteen percent work part-time. The issue, instead, is one of priorities. For these women, raising a family came first, and administrative career aspirations were postponed until a later date. As one women who just obtained a principalship remarks:

People were pushing me to go on for a doctorate when I was doing my Master's. But I had a young son, and we planned to have another baby; they took priority. I could always do a doctorate later, but I couldn't have children later. I loved being at home then, using my training with my own kids.

(Northwestern suburb)

A teacher shares similar thoughts:

I got my degree back in the 1950s and then quit teaching to raise my family. When I got involved in Brownies, I decided if I was going to work I might as well get paid. So I went back to teaching. I wanted to go for a leadership position, but being a principal is very time demanding. I didn't want to sacrifice time with my kids at that point.

(Northwestern town)

When they reflect back on their choices, many of these older women reaffirm the importance of having their children before embarking on administrative careers. Although they wanted a career, they wanted to raise their families first. Today, they transmit a special kind of peace about those early decisions.

One of the things I feel excited about is that I did what I wanted to while my sons were growing up, and that was staying home. I didn't try to be an administrator *and* raise children at the same time. I see now that the time commitment in administration is great and allows me little control over my evenings. As a teacher, I could raise my family. At times, I was afraid I was giving up the possibility of ever being an administrator by having to wait. But now I feel grateful that I got to do both.

(Assistant Principal, Western suburb)

I always had the goal of doing more than teaching. It is a fine field, but I feel I am capable and qualified to do more. Now that my children are older, I have more time to devote to myself and to my career.

(Assistant Principal, Southern metro)

Despite believing their former choices were correct, a few of the women express concern about picking up the threads of their careers. They openly share fears about how their past decisions may affect their futures in administration.

I have tried to do some honest and thorough soul searching about whether I really have the ability and temperament to go into administration. I have some limitations as an older [forty-six] female aspirant. In my age group, we developed passive women. I have lived most of my life as a wife and mother in that mode.

(Teacher, Midwestern metro)

I did the typical thing for the 1950s: I got my degree, got married and had three children. I was a person who liked approval, so I did what was expected of me. I've had to mature quite a bit to get out of that. I was afraid to start teaching, so I used the excuse of waiting until my kids were older. Then one day my principal asked me to be a counselor, and I began to feel so good.

(Assistant Principal, Northwestern town)

I was never unhappy as a housewife, but then I wasn't happy with bridge and shopping either. I decided to go back to school because it was unfinished business for me. I was afraid, but I wanted to get over that fear.

(Assistant Principal, Midwestern suburb)

I was hoping to get a school of my own next year, but I've been hesitant because I have a son in high school and a sick mother at home. I'm afraid being a principal might take away from the time I'm supposed to be giving at home. But maybe that's just an excuse. I *do* feel ready for my own building.

(Assistant Principal, Southern city)

Although many express hesitation, they also speak of feeling compelled to move on in their careers. With family duties largely completed, they experience a new sense of excitement and freedom to pursue postponed career goals.

My husband never said he wanted me to go into administration, but he never stood in my way either. Poor fellow, he just wanted a wife to stay home and take care of the children. (In retrospect, maybe he picked the wrong woman). Although I had few other options when I graduated from college, now I am driven to see if I can do something besides mothering. I realize I can enjoy aspiring now, largely because I *did* take time to be with my family earlier. I don't carry the guilt I see in a lot of our younger women who try to divide themselves up so many ways.

(New Principal, Midwestern suburb)

Some of the younger women who choose to have families before pursuing careers seem less content with their decisions than the older women. Of course, they are in the midst of the struggle, while many of the older women are reflecting back on their lives. Although they clearly choose to have their families first, they seem less comfortable with the consequences of that decision than do their older counterparts. The conflicts they share suggest tremendous tension:

> I'm extremely anxious to be an assistant principal. If I didn't have family responsibilities, I feel confident that I'd be one right now. But as a working mother, I feel tremendous guilt pangs when my career demands extend beyond four-thirty in the afternoon. With each additional responsibility I take on, I must reassess my needs at home versus those of career development. It's a never ending juggling act, and I know my ambitions are hard on the family. In the end, however, my personal obligations to my family come first.
>
> (Teacher, Western metro)

> My job hunting has been limited because I have young children at home. I don't have time to consider the next job I ought to be going for, so I just let people know that I'm still interested in administration and try to do a good job where I am now.
>
> (Coordinator, Northwestern city)

> I have thought about becoming a principal, but I would have to see if I could manage it with my family. So far, I haven't done anything professionally without thinking of my family and how it would affect them. I know a principalship in this district would take too much time. If I can't leave work when my kids are sick, I wouldn't want the job. That's the way I am.
>
> (Specialist, Midwestern metro)

To reduce this conflict, younger aspirants often choose a career path that delays their administrative aspirations. They have the full-time commitment to work that White mentioned earlier, but by postponing their career plans, they are able to avoid some of the problems inherent in trying to raise a family while simultaneously pursuing leadership positions. Because they make active, conscious choices, younger aspirants do not feel defeated or powerless. Rather, they select job opportunities that show upward movement, but with the "long horizontal stopovers" that White describes. An assistant principal (southern city), content with her current position because she has two boys to raise, admits: "I like not having the full responsibility of the building right now, as I want the boys to get through school before I jump in all the way." An administrative assistant makes a similar observation:

> I would like to be a principal someday, but not in the near future. A principalship has far too many duties and responsibilities for me right now. As an administrative assistant, I can still operate well with a six

and two year old. I'm home so little as it is, and I feel grateful that I
have my holidays and summers free. I went to graduate school when
my children were tiny, but as they get older my responsibilities of
work, graduate school and home become more complicated. The children want to do things with me now, and I'm conscientious about that.
(Southern metro)

No matter what their age, women who place family before career
aspirations share one thing in common: their involvement as mothers
precedes any personal desire for professional advancement. On the other
hand, they continue to maintain their interest in administrative careers.
Although professional goals may lie dormant for a period of time while
raising children, many of these women keep their aspirations alive by
undertaking university courses or on-the-job training. Whether or not they
eventually attain their goals following the traditional career path, these
women seem satisfied with their choices. Interestingly, women who choose
to delay their careers seldom entertain the possibility that their husbands
might consider deferring their careers instead. In short, they accept
traditional role expectations: while husbands advance, wives should care
for the family.

### Emergent Career Paths

The second group of women in this study challenge traditional role
expectations and follow a different career path towards leadership
positions. Younger, and often with less school experience than their
traditional counterparts, these women seek to blend the responsibilities of
career and family. Although no less committed to their families than the
traditional women described above, these women hold different beliefs
about the proper roles for men and women in this society. Possibly
influenced by the women's movement or the equal opportunity legislation
of the last two decades, they share an assumption that women "can do it
all." For some, this means delaying having children while they pursue their
careers. Although a few of the women in this study choose not to have
children because of their careers, most want children *and* satisfying work
lives. A lead teacher highlights the difference between these women and
those who choose traditional career paths:

I am unique, because the other women administrators in the district
are older and have had their families. I am just now considering having
a family, and it's going to be interesting to see how the district views me
and how I will fit back in—because I don't intend to quit. A teacher
would be allowed to continue working, but they are unsure about how
to treat an administrator with children. I held off having a baby until now,

but at thirty-two, I don't feel like I can wait another three or four years.

(Midwestern metro)

Although looking forward to parenting, she admits to wondering about the added demands children will bring. Unlike the women in the first group who know these pressures first hand, aspirants following the emergent career path are just beginning to deal with the conflicts involved in blending their professional lives with family responsibilities. These latter women assume they can and will do both in their lives, and they have no way of knowing what the personal and professional costs will be. As the lead teacher quoted above concludes:

> One woman administrator said to me: "Why in the world are you considering having a baby at this point in your career? You're right on route to being one of the first female principals!" Being first isn't my priority, however. My intention is to not give up children or a career, but to blend the two. Maybe I'll be the first woman in the district to have a baby *and* a principalship!

(Midwestern metro)

An experienced mother might consider this sentiment naive, but many younger aspirants manifest a resolve to succeed "no matter what." A department chair, awaiting word about a baby she and her husband wanted to adopt, expresses her determination to combine work and parenting:

> I want to be a mother, but not a home mother. I plan to take a week or two off when the adoption goes through, but I want to continue ahead with my own career at the same time. I've seen other women do it, and I don't know why I can't.

(Southern rural)

Unlike most aspirants, this department chair personally knows other women who are blending work and families. But even in situations where there are no role models, these women persist in the belief that they can somehow manage both, as a teacher explains:

> I hope to have children in the next couple of years, and to stay active in education while parenting. I don't think it's impossible to do both and do them well. In the past, women administrators seemed forced to make a choice: either they had no children or they waited until their children were grown before pursuing leadership positions. I think that's unfortunate.

(Northeastern metro)

Whether they wait to have children or have them simultaneously while pursuing their careers, many of these younger aspirants appear to thrive on high levels of activity. One aspirant (midwestern suburb), not only holds a full-time job as a director, but in addition she pursues her doctoral degree and raises two children under the age of four. In the only indication of the pressures she endures, she confides: "There are times when I really get tired out, but for the most part it isn't a problem."

Although many women admit that the arrival of children further complicates their already busy lives, they tend to view the added responsibilities not as burdens, but rather as challenges. For women who thrive on high levels of activity, the birth of a baby, can provide an opportunity to return to graduate school. One student, feeling she would "go crazy" if she just stayed home, states:

> I saw a needlepoint kit once that said, "A clean house shows a life misspent." I'm going to get that, because I enjoy doing a variety of things in life. I stayed home after the baby came, but it was not with the idea that I'd be involved with soap operas and chocolates. My husband and I both knew I'd need more, so I went back to graduate school.
> (Southern city)

Some women following emergent career paths never consider staying home full-time after the birth of their children. Others, however, reduce their work commitments to insure spending some time with their infants. An administrative intern explains her plans:

> Now that I am expecting, I plan to cut back to a half-time position. That would give me time with the child the first year, as well as allowing me to finish my Master's. With the physical weariness of pregnancy I look forward to a little time of my own, but I don't want to let go of my career. I also think now that we've decided to have a baby, we should raise the child and not take it to a sitter all the time. Never having been a mother, I may find my six-month leave too long. Maybe I won't even want to go back, but I doubt it. I've worked for ten years, and I can't imagine staying home full-time.
> (Western suburb)

Unlike the aspirants following traditional career paths, aspirants pursuing the emergent route agree that their careers are an integral part of their lives. They cannot imagine themselves apart from their professional roles. Whether they articulate this understanding before or only after their babies arrive, their aspirations to blend career and family remain strong. By returning to school, reducing their work loads or continuing to work full-time, these women assume success is possible in more than one role. On the other hand, Patterson and Engelberg note, "As long as women are primarily responsible for running the household and rearing the children, they will have to work at managing their careers in order simply to maintain them, much less make it to the top."[9] Despite the possibility they may only "maintain" their careers while parenting, veterans of such fast-paced living persist in believing they can succeed and go to extraordinary lengths to do so. An assistant principal describes how she handles her complex life:

> While I taught, helped the principal and worked on my doctorate, I still found time to be a den mother and a camp fire sponsor. I also drove the neighborhood bus shuttle for orchestra practice. We always find time for the kids. You get very tired, on three or four hours of sleep a night, but then once a month you just sleep a whole Sunday away and wonder where it went! When I rest a whole day, my family understands why.
>
> (Southern metro)

Valuing work and motherhood equally, aspirants who follow the emergent career path expect to enjoy a professional life that includes parenting. If their chosen route allows for more options than those available to individuals choosing a traditional career path, it also creates more stress and conflict. Without hindsight to guide them, however, these younger women remain convinced that their struggles are worth the costs.

When women blend both career and family, they struggle not only against the personal demands on their time but also against the stereotypes that women should care for the family and that administration is a male profession. By failing to conform to these expectations, women who work and care for their families experience an added strain on their lives, as the following women attest:

> It was a difficult year after my child was born. The birth was over, but then the hard part set in. I fussed with her in the evenings until eight, and then worked on school stuff until eleven. My principal knew it was difficult, but he didn't do anything to help. I thought of staying home, but we couldn't afford it.
>
> (Administrative Intern, Midwestern suburb)

> My aspiring has been a strain on our marriage. With two busy career people in our house, no one was nurturing our relationship. We were growing apart, but we caught it in time. We got into therapy, and we are OK now.
>
> (Director, Northeastern town)

> It's been a strain on my children, because they're involved in lots of things. We go in all sorts of directions. Sunday is the only time the

family sits down for breakfast and dinner together.

(New Principal, Southeastern town)

Because these women are still viewed by others (and often themselves) as primarily responsible for the family's well being, they are continually pulled in various directions. In describing the dilemma, a supervisor recounts:

> Part of the stress I experience concerns my family. For example, there was a conference I was supposed to attend across the state, but I went to my daughter's recital instead. Our curriculum director later told me my family would have to come second from now on. I told him I recalled him missing an important meeting once because of a pro-football game he attended. I said, "If family comes second, so should football games." He replied, "Well, you got me on that one; now we're even." But he's been very cold to me ever since. I understand that your family should not come between you and your job. But they make it seem like the exceptions only happen to women, and that feels like added pressure to me. The whole incident only verified for me that women do have a harder time.
>
> (Southern rural)

As this last woman indicates, colleagues at work often exacerbate the tensions women experience when combining work and family. Bourne and Wikler argue: "The pressure not to appear weak, to ask special favors, or to make demands on others, and even to define the problem as a structural one rather than a personal one, is what sometimes forces women to choose between family roles and professional commitments."[10] The pressures work twice as hard on women in a field with mostly male leaders—leaders who do not, for the most part, contend with the same complex problems female aspirants do. According to Bourne and Wikler, "Men know that they could not do their work as they currently do it if they lacked a wife to keep their private lives in order."[11] Consequently, they reason, men know indirectly the difficulties of trying to do two jobs at once. Most of the female aspirants in this study, however, feel that their male bosses are unaware of the problems they face. Yet some male administrators are sensitive to the complexities of women's lives and willingly assist female aspirants to cope with the various demands. An assistant principal describes how two male administrators make her life considerably easier:

> After nearly twenty years of marriage, I became pregnant and was assigned an interim principalship about the same time. I thought, "Boy, if I go through this experience and don't come out sour on administration, it will really be something!" My assistant superintendent was very concerned with my being pregnant: he wanted to work

with me, so it wouldn't be too stressful. He was so great. And now that the baby is here, I sometimes take her with me to night games. My principal says if I don't feel ill at ease, he has no problem with the arrangement either.

(Southeastern city)

Children can also assist in releasing some of the built-in pressures of working and parenting by taking pride in their mother's work, as these cases illustrate:

Combining work and a family is balancing out well for me, because my particular family *makes* it balance. My boys are dependable, and they have never known a time when I haven't worked. If ever a problem came up, they knew I was only thirty minutes away. But they've never called me, and I've never missed a day of school because of them. I think that's unusual. If I had had to choose whether to stay home with a sick child or go to work, I would have stayed with my child. But then, that is the typical dilemma for women in a dual role.

(Assistant Principal, Southeastern city)

My daughter is proud of the work I do now. When she was little, she sometimes wished I was like other moms who stayed home. She would come home and tell me so and so's mother makes chocolate chip cookies. And one time she told a neighbor she was going to make a pie with me. No way was I going to bake a pie! I'm just not the type to do all those domestic things. I spaced my kids so I could raise one at a time. That way, I felt I could do a good job as a mother and continue working as well—not as a housekeeper, mind you, but as a mom. Now my daughter understands that a lot of the traditional moms are unhappy, and she is proud that I work.

(Supervisor, Northwestern city)

Whether the understanding comes from the home or from the job, such support enables women following an emergent career path to mesh their family responsibilities with their professional obligations.

*Careers or Children?*

In addition to women who choose the traditional path of raising their families before pursuing careers or those who follow the emergent route of blending family and career, some women in this study decide not to have children at all. "I'm a career girl," states one assistant principal (northwestern city), "and we made the decision some time ago that I was going to have a career rather than children." Another assistant principal (southeastern city) expresses contentment being a "surrogate mother to 900

kids," rather than having children of her own. Although these women are
only in entry-level management positions, they know the myriad demands
administrators must face and wonder how women with children cope.

> I don't see how people with children can do it—work, go to school and
> raise a family. They are super human. I mean, my husband is
> fantastically cooperative and cooks and everything. I don't see how
> we'd do it with children as well. Kids take time; I just don't see how
> people do it all.
>
> (Department Chair, Southern metro)

In deciding not to have children, these women report feeling unencum-
bered in their pursuit of leadership experiences and free of the guilt they
might otherwise sustain as mothers.

> I've been going to school for twenty years, so my husband is used to my
> not being home at night. He is very understanding and has other things
> he likes to do. I do not have children, so there is no problem seeking
> administrative work.
>
> (Acting Assistant Principal, Southern metro)

> We have no children. If we did, I probably wouldn't even try for
> administration because it would take time away from them. But as it is,
> my husband has his own hobbies and he views administration as mine.
> We each do what we like.
>
> (Teacher, Southeastern rural)

### Maintaining Households

For those who combine careers with parenting, the problems of household
maintenance can loom large. Women with supportive husbands report
they seldom feel forced to choose between their work and their children.
Indeed, some couples have always shared the "home work."

> I work days and nights, and my husband is very helpful. There are the
> meals and housework to split, and sometimes I must study all
> weekend. He is supportive throughout.
>
> (Supervisor, Northwestern town)

> My husband is super. He goes to the laundromat, cooks most dinners
> and does whatever is needed. He wouldn't even hesitate to pick up a
> vacuum if that was needed. He's always been that way.
>
> (Coordinator, Western metro)

My husband has been a strong supporter, counselor, everything. He shares the responsibilities at home, because he realizes I have a full-time job, too. I feel very luck.

(Assistant Principal, Southern city)

Some maintain their homes with simple, informal arrangements, as an assistant principal (southern metro) notes: "We always determine the cook by who enters the kitchen first." But whether a couple resolves the division of labor in an informal manner or whether they develop a detailed plan, aspirants agree that the need to share these responsibilities is critical.

The division of home labor described by these women, however, does not always come in the initial stages of marriage. Frequently, changes in household responsibilities occur only when time demands related to a woman's career increase. During these transition periods, some husbands and wives move away from more traditionally accepted roles toward shared home management. Although both men and women may find it difficult to change long-established patterns, some women find it especially hard to surrender the family responsibilities over which they once had sole control. Nevertheless, because a reorganization of work at home makes such a difference to aspirants' careers, some wish they had relinquished those tasks earlier. Several women give detailed accounts of the transition in their own homes:

> For five years I was the happy little first grade teacher who supported her husband's career goals. Then I went to a summer institute about women and educational administration which proved to be a catalyst for getting me to view myself as important, too. At first, I went through a rebellious me-centered stage, but now we have a more shared experience in terms of the home. I no longer worry that if the house isn't clean, it's my fault. And I no longer make fancy schedules about who does what, because we work a lot more casually now. Sometimes I say: "I have three papers and nineteen report cards to do tonight. You make dinner, because I can't deal with it now."
>
> (Teacher, Northeastern city)

> When we first had our child, there was no sharing of the tasks at home whatsoever. But when I went back to work, I told him I couldn't do everything any longer: either we shared, or we wouldn't make it. It was as simple as that. He has been very helpful ever since. I often think I was a fool the first six or seven years of our marriage, because I could have had a lot more help if I had just asked.
>
> (Administrative Assistant, Southern suburb)

> We've worked on sharing things, with both of us accepting responsibilities at home. We have reached a point where I feel we are pretty much equals. For instance, I haven't cooked a meal in a year. When we first

married, it wasn't like this, of course. Now the only problem I have is thinking every once in a while: "This isn't right; he's cooking or doing dishes while I study." I have to tell myself it's OK.

(Student, Southeastern city)

Early on, my husband wasn't so encouraging about my career. He was involved in his own career and had more traditional expectations. My responsibility was the house and the children, the typical thing back then. But now he is more concerned that I do what fulfills me.

(Coordinator, Western suburb)

For several couples in this study, however, traditional expectations proved intractable: changes in family responsibilities, necessitated by the woman's expanding career goals, failed to materialize. Unable to accommodate a changing division of household labor, these marriages ended in divorce. For those who later remarry, a new set of expectations emerge:

This is my second marriage, so my new husband has never seen me as someone who stays home and takes care of things. We organize things at home equally, if they're organized at all.

(Assistant Principal, Northwestern town)

My second husband is a full partner in the house. In fact, he does all the cooking. After twenty-four years of cooking in my first marriage, I was burned out. I have cooked my last steak, and cookies went a long time ago! This is an entirely different set up from my first marriage, because we want the same things for ourselves and for each other. He is so supportive and understanding.

(Assistant Principal, Southern city)

Some couples, especially those with grown children, find it easy to establish routines for sharing the work at home. Other couples find it necessary to adjust their responsibilities daily, as the situation demands. Some husbands, especially those holding more traditional views of family roles, only allow for temporary shifts in responsibilities. For example, some husbands make conditional allowances when their wives return to school. "My husband is very supportive around the house when I am in school," explains a teacher (midwestern metro). He is willing to assist at such times, she believes, because "he knows what it's like to go to school." Other temporary shifts in responsibilities may occur with the birth of a child. On those occasions, some men seem willing to adjust their work schedules to accommodate changing family needs.

My husband and I have a very workable relationship. In order for me to be here now, he is at home with the sick baby and will take her to the doctor. I have never had any desire to stay home full-time, so I am fortunate that my husband helps with child care. He has flexible working hours that enabled us to plan in advance what we would do the whole first two years of the baby's life.

(Assistant Principal, Southeastern city)

My husband stayed home part of the first year of both of our kids' lives. He's just a better mother than I am.

(Supervisor, Northwestern city)

I was very fortunate, because my husband deliberately chose to work a different shift from me to help with child care. Throughout my career, I've only needed a sitter maybe a maximum of three hours a couple of times a week and for the occasional night meeting. But I have to admit that I have an unusual case. My husband made the sacrifice in his career, because we believe one of the parents should be with the kids rather than an outsider.

(Assistant Principal, Western suburb)

Whether greater sharing of household responsibilities is a firmly established part of the marriage or whether it is only conditionally granted on a temporary basis, female aspirants understand that a division of home labor is essential to their well-being and to their career success. Dual-career couples that report satisfaction with their lifestyles, divide household labor according to availability and efficiency, rather than upon traditional divisions between men's and women's work.

For some aspirants, child care issues far outweigh concerns over dividing household chores. Because many women continue to work while raising families, financing child care arrangements seldom proves insurmountable. On the other hand, personal considerations and spousal expectations frequently make decisions about the type of child care a source of anxiety. Women who can afford to hire someone to help in their homes with the children experience little conflict. A new principal (southeastern town) recalls using the services of a housekeeper when her children were young and admits: "We couldn't do without the extra help for a lot longer than I had anticipated." Similarly, an assistant principal relates:

Things at home work fine, because I have a live-in housekeeper. If you have the room, hiring help makes life simpler with young children at home. With both my husband and I having careers, it was obvious from the outset that somebody else had to do the child care. He didn't want to, and I didn't want to. Yet we both wanted someone consistently there, so we didn't have to drag a kid to a day care center where who knows what happens. And we wanted someone bilingual to maintain our language with our children. When you come right down to it, a housekeeper hasn't been more costly than employing outside babysitters.

(Western suburb)

Another assistant principal credits not only her supportive husband, but a "super mom" babysitter for making her home life run smoothly:

I have all the confidence in the world in my sitter. If I had to worry about the baby, I don't know if my working would be worth it. My sitter is very understanding if I have to work late. If I do, I just call her. In some ways, I resent the hours that eat into my role as homemaker. On the other hand, I know I get more done when I am busy and working.

(Northwestern city)

These families are fortunate in that they can afford to buy such care for their children. It is unclear, however, if the couples considered shifting the primary child care to the husbands or, if in fact, this was even an option. As Pleck notes: "Expansion of the scope of the male *family* role without accommodating changes in the male *work* role will lead to role strain in men similar to the strains now faced by working wives...If these goods and services are available, purchasing them may be less stressful than trying to increase men's family role" (emphasis added).[12] Indeed, where both the wife and the husband pursue careers, stress falls on both the mother and the father. The option of buying child care allows for a reduction of the pressures on both parents without drastically changing the expectations of either sex within the family. In short, these female aspirants are very much aware that their career aspirations depend, in part, upon the paid services of someone else—and that someone is usually another woman.

For other aspirants, however, hiring outside help to ease the strain between family and work responsibilities is either financially unrealistic or personally undesirable. In many cases, women's salaries cover the cost of full-time child care, but it is not financialy expedient to incur such expenses. Alternately, family financial needs may dictate that a woman's income is essential to basic household solvency and that child care expenses are simply beyond the budget. In other cases, some aspirants are not comfortable with leaving the care of their children to someone outside the family. In instances where women must or choose to shoulder the primary load at home while seeking to advance their careers, frustration and even resentment may result. The tensions that surface over the issue of child care—especially when there is little adjustment of traditional male and female role responsibilities—is evident in the lives of the following three women:

Although I know it's no excuse, it's very difficult to have a family and go to school at the same time. Sometimes I think I'll have dark circles under my eyes forever. I have a daughter in junior high, and the housework is all my domain to the point where I am absolutely bushed. When I get to that point, I finally get some help from my husband. But the support isn't readily given.

(Student, Midwestern city)

It's hard to work, take classes and raise a family. My family is very forgiving in a number of ways. On the other hand, I feel a lot of guilt, which is probably more my problem than theirs. I'm programmed more to my husband these days, now that the kids are getting older. And he expects his share of my time. My family also doesn't help with the housework, the dishes or the washing. I still have all the responsibility for that.

(Teacher, Northwestern town)

My husband has been helpful driving the kids here and there, because he can arrange his hours. But he draws the line there. He does one meal a week: the same snack every Sunday evening. And then he gets in a rage about how much he helps! My God, one meal! He does no other cooking, no laundry and no dishes. He's older than me, so I'll never get him to believe in this "equal stuff." The home is a woman's domain to him. I knew it was going to be a battle when we married, but I haven't really accepted his inability to change yet. He'll share with the kid's care, but all that other stuff is mine.

(New Principal, Southeastern town)

These three aspirants depict the strain that many working women experience today. Whether willingly or unwillingly, women who accept more traditional roles almost inevitably experience some marital stress, and some report having difficulty coping with all of the responsibilities.

*Marital Tensions*

Many of the women in this study state that their career aspirations, along with the attendant demands on their time, result in growing marital friction. Often outwardly supportive of their wives' aspirations, some husbands dislike having to readjust their lives, while others feel threatened by their wives' new roles.

My husband is very proud of my achievements, but not totally accepting of the time commitments involved with administrative work. He finds it difficult to handle being home alone when I am not there. Even though he works a lot of evenings himself, he would like *my* time to be more flexible.

(Assistant Principal, Western suburb)

My husband is both supportive and apprehensive. When we first got married, I was a teacher. He felt teaching was an acceptable profession for a woman, and he wasn't intimidated by my job. But now, my enthusiasm for my work and my growing independence is a little threatening to him. Once we were business partners, but now I want to go out on my own. We've had some discussions about the time I want to spend doing other things and being with other people. I still don't know if I can have an administrative career that is compatible with my demands as his wife.

(Assistant Principal, Northwestern suburb)

I think I underestimated how threatened my husband would be by the idea of my being an administrator. He is a business manager himself, and my being an educational specialist was OK with him. But now, being an administrator makes me more like him. I get all kinds of little indirect digs about how the house is managed and planned now that I am taking management and planning courses. We've talked about it directly, but he denies it's a problem.

(Student, Midwestern city)

Many of these women think their husbands feel intimidated by their expanding career aspirations and fear that their marriages might suffer as a result. One newly hired principal, concerned about her marriage, reports:

This is the first time I'll be making more money than my husband. I think it's nice, because we'll be able to put our kids through school with this extra money. But I've sensed it also creates a problem for us. It's not so much what he says, but the look on his face. He's grouchy now, too. After thirty years of marriage, you know when something's wrong. When we talk about it, he *says* he's proud of me, but I think he feels a little jealous. He has worked hard as an educator himself, and he feels discouraged in his own job when he sees how I am doing.

(Northwestern suburb)

Her premonition proved correct. Shortly after our initial interview, she was divorced.

Another potential area of stress for two-career families occurs when both husband and wife work in the same field or in similar jobs. In this study, fourteen percent of the partners are either teachers or administrators, six percent are businessmen, and another twenty-three percent are professionals in other fields. Although many aspirants become interested in educational administration because they see their husbands managing schools, working in the same profession may precipitate an uncomfortable competitiveness. The potential for conflict exists in these often overlapping work worlds, and female aspirants occasionally find themselves in awkward situations, as these two women describe:

> My husband and I are both aspiring administrators. We've even applied for some of the same jobs! We're in different areas of education, but we've still had some problems.
>
> (Supervisor, Southern rural)

> I got hired as an assistant principal at the school where my husband teaches! It's the reverse of the usual problem where the man is the principal and his wife is one of the teachers. The superintendent wanted to know if it would be a problem for us, but we just keep the personal part separate from school.
>
> (Assistant Principal, Southern city)

Issues concerning job mobility create other problems for couples with dual careers. When both partners desire to advance their careers, difficulties arise in deciding whether or not the family should relocate for a single job opportunity. Unlike the past, when women seldom questioned the need to move for their husbands' careers, women today carefully examine other options. While many women continue to move with their husbands, they now actively evaluate the impact each move will have on their own careers. An assistant principal describes how she dealt with her husband's transfer to a new city:

> When we moved, I knew I could not go back to just being at home. I wrote ahead to the district office to inform them that I was interested in administration—but that I'd teach or do counselling just to get a job. Eventually they told me they wanted me to come and "hang loose" until they figured out what openings there would be.
>
> (Midwestern metro)

She adds that the security of her husband's job in the new area enabled her to wait until the district found her a position as well. Another female student describes how she made the best of a move when her husband returned to school:

> When my husband finishes his schooling, we'll be returning to my old district where I previously had five years of administrative experience. Since I've been here, I've only added a department chair to my resumé. But I also worked on my doctorate while my husband studied, so I

have something to show for the lost time in my own career when I go back.

(Southeastern city)

Although some wives in the past undoubtedly sought career opportunities when their husbands accepted new jobs, many others simply followed. Today's aspirants—both young and old—report assuming a greater commitment to finding rewarding work for both partners when a move becomes necessary. When both partners work in the same field, job opportunities may be limited—especially if the couple chooses to move as a team. One director (midwestern suburb) tells potential districts, "If you want me, you will have to find something for my husband." She admits this approach narrows their options, but enjoys the spirit of cooperation they have developed. After an interview for a position that either of them could have applied for, she reports her husband saying, "I don't think they are interested in me, but I think they would *love* you. Why don't you apply?"

Two-career couples must reexamine traditional role expectations and explore different options. Some couples choose to alternate career moves; others reverse their former patterns and now move only for the wife's job; and still others consider living apart from each other and commuting between job locations. Three women provide examples of these options:

This is the second move we've made for my career. My husband will move anywhere I go. He is willing to substitute if he can't find a job. When I interviewed with the superintendent, he wanted to know if my husband would move with me. I said, "You don't have to worry about those things; that's all worked out."

(New Principal, Northwestern town)

My husband brought up our future plans, and we agreed that since we moved for his job during the first thirteen years of our marriage, the next thirteen years we would move for mine. While I am finishing my schooling, he will look for a job around here. If he simply couldn't find a job and had to move away, we'd maintain two homes. But we don't think it will come to that. The important thing is we have agreed I will get the next job, and then that's where we will settle.

(Student, Midwestern city)

My husband has been fantastic. I could not be married and do the administrative work I do, if I had not chosen this particular man. I think we could even work away from each other if need be—living apart some of the time and commuting.

(Lead Teacher, Midwestern metro)

Of course, not all the stories are so positive. One supervisor believes her career needs are too closely tied to her husband's:

> I'd like to work on a Ph.D., but I don't think my husband would support the idea for me alone. I think I could convince him if we both did it. We've had two offers to do our degrees together, but he couldn't pull away from his family here. I felt a big let down in *my* career that we didn't take one of those offers.
>
> (Southern rural)

A teacher shares another frustration:

> I fought tooth and nail against coming to this small town. Even though my husband had a job, I knew my chances of finding an administrative position would be very slim. We said we would give it two years, but this is our third. Maybe I should have fought harder.
>
> (Southern rural)

Whatever solutions couples find to solve the job mobility problems of two-career families, it is clear they no longer assume that only the male's career plans are significant. When discussing job-related moves, couples weigh the advantages and disadvantages for both partners and explore options that may be mutually beneficial to their careers. Nevertheless, couples are aware that alternating career moves or living apart may ultimately prove costly and unsatisfactory.

In addition to problems of job mobility, many women experience difficulty establishing a professional work identity separate from their husbands' and independent from their role as mothers. A teacher explains:

> Through my work in the teachers' association, I've made an effort to build a distinct identity for myself within the district. I want to be viewed as more than so and so's wife. We both teach, but I don't think people tie us together as having only one career now. But that's always a problem.
>
> (Northeastern city)

Building a separate work identity is more problematic for women with husbands who are prominent in the community. Three women describe how their husbands' reputations affect their own aspirations:

> I think one stumbling block I have is that my husband's name is well known in the district. I may have been held back in administration because of who he is and the fact that his job is not popular right now. I've never been thwarted in anything I've ever wanted to do in life, and I've never felt any barriers because I am female. But just now, I am

beginning to feel some pressure because my husband's job reflects on me and my goals.

(Teacher, Northwestern town)

My husband is very visible in the community, and I know there were some scowls when I came back into teaching. People probably thought: "She doesn't need to teach; why is she here?" I don't capitalize on his position or tell people about him, but they know. As I go into administration, I may have to leave the district to get out of his shadow.

(New Principal, Northwestern suburb)

My husband is highly visible and has a lot of power and influence. But he doesn't like to play the political game. When I applied for this position, he wanted me to get it on my own merits. So he didn't talk to anyone about it, although he could have. People still said they saw the situation as two strong people trying to move in on a position, even though I was the only one going for the job.

(Director, Northeastern town)

One newly hired principal underscores the need to keep active and not be overshadowed by one's husband:

Sometimes I get lazy. I think when we marry, we have a tendency to be a bit more easy on ourselves, to think of our work as only providing a second income. Or, we settle for living through a spouse when we need to continue achieving ourselves.

(Northwestern suburb)

When husbands are sensitive to how their reputations may negatively affect their wives' careers and are unthreatened by the possibilities of their wives' success, women experience fewer conflicts. An assistant principal (southern metro) credits her husband for not having "the ego problems that some males do. If I made twice the salary he did, for example, it would be fine with him." Indeed, some couples in this study report that having two careers contributes positively to their marriages. A counselor (midwestern suburb) states: "My husband is busy himself, so he has been very encouraging of anything I like to do." A coordinator concurs:

My husband and I are both professionals with goals we worked out a long time ago. He has his career, and I have mine. Throughout our long marriage, we've found our work good for us. It keeps our marriage from stagnating as well.

(Western metro)

Yet, for women with husbands who are unfamiliar with the demands placed on school administrators or who simply wish their wives would not work at all, tensions inevitably arise.

> My husband does not want me to work. He thinks it's ridiculous, since he makes everything available to me. Before we had kids, it was OK for me to work. But now he wishes I was just a plain person at home. When my youngest started to school, I just couldn't stand not working. I was home two weeks, the house was clean and I had to have something to do. He now says I am an assistant principal because "she had to have something to do now that the kids are leaving home. Otherwise, she'd have nothing to do but bitch and complain." At least he is finally that far.
>
> (Assistant Principal, Midwestern suburb)

> Sometimes it's painful to go home to a husband who doesn't ask about my work. We just don't know how to share it. It takes real commitment to continue in a profession and to maintain a feeling of competence without this understanding.
>
> (New Principal, Northwestern suburb)

### Single Aspirants

Although single female aspirants do not experience the same problems facing women in two-career families, they do suffer from the same stereotypes as other women in the field: they are viewed as potential wives and mothers and as such, caretakers of children—not managers of adults. Single women also encounter other limitations to their aspirations. For example, many contend that being unmarried is a barrier in school administration, as this student explains:

> I think my being single and aspiring in administration is a problem. On one hand, people hiring are attracted to me because I am free to move anywhere. On the other hand, the image of an administrator in this state is of a married person. I don't have a husband to go to the club with or to attend church meetings. This is a state with traditional values, and administrators have an image to keep up which is more easily done if you're married.
>
> (Southeastern city)

This woman is concerned about her social life as well as her professional life. She worries that without social contacts, she will end up working most of the time and concludes: "I don't see myself as the perpetual old maid

who works ninety-nine percent of her life." Another unmarried woman
worries about moving:

> As a single person, my main concern in moving to a new job is leaving
> my friends. When you're single, all of a sudden you find yourself in the
> middle of a whole new environment—alone. How do you make friends
> in a small town, especially if administrators are not expected to
> fraternize with the staff?
>
> (New Assistant Principal, Northwestern town)

Lacking the familial support system of married women, single
aspirants often feel quite alone when seeking and moving into new
leadership roles. Many single women rely on their parents and friends for
the support they might otherwise expect from husbands. One assistant
principal tells of her mother's recent encouragement:

> My mother once discouraged me from going to law school because she
> thought I would scare away any man who might marry me. Now she
> supports my administrative desires, because she realizes she, too, was a
> victim of never being encouraged as a young girl. She could have been
> a business person like her brothers, but she was never trained. Yet she
> supported her brothers' training. I think she now sees women's
> aspirations in a different light.
>
> (Northeastern suburb)

Ultimately, single women aspiring in school management do so without
the same built-in support systems available to married women and men in
the field.

When questioned how marrying in the future might affect their goals,
single women are understandably hesitant. One teacher (northwestern
metro) admits she has "a lot of questions about integrating marriage with
being an administrator." But she concludes, "That will have to be one more
obstacle to take in stride, and hopefully my husband would be right there
for me." Although these women face their own set of difficulties as single
administrators, many married women will tell them that they will only
exchange one set of problems for another should they decide to marry.

Divorced women, too, meet unique problems when seeking management positions. For some, a divorce opens up new vistas. A supervisor tells
of new challenges that followed her divorce:

> I think if I had not gotten divorced, I probably wouldn't be where I am
> now. I didn't have an encouraging husband and if I hadn't divorced
> him, I would be living a very humdrum life now.
>
> (Southern rural)

Because of divorce, many women critically review not only their professional aspirations, but their past roles as wives.

> When I got my divorce, I did some major rethinking. I realized I had sublimated *my* career and profession to *his* professional needs and moves. I mainly ran the family. I always kept a job, but I never took my career seriously. I was really riding on my husband's coattails, even though I always did a good job in my positions. Most of the jobs I got, I got because I was his wife. I was a beneficiary of the old boys' network: I was hired because I was the wife of a super administrator, and we were a package deal. At forty-six, I decided I wanted to give myself what he had taken care to give himself: some additional education that would enable me to do something professionally.
>
> (Assistant Principal, Southern city)

> We really are what happens to us, I believe. Although my divorce was very negative and nearly destroyed me, in another way, it also made me. Because of my divorce, my career is going to be far greater than it would have been. I never would have allowed myself—within my marriage—to do some of the things I've allowed myself to do outside of it.
>
> (Specialist, Western suburb)

> I thought I was always going to be supported by a husband, have children, and maybe I'd work or maybe I wouldn't. I tried the home "number," but it drove me straight up the wall. I was a compulsive house cleaner, because I wanted something to show at the end of the day. I was programmed to believe every woman needed to stay home and breast-feed her children, or otherwise they'd be screwed up for life. I began teaching after my second child reached a year old, and then my husband and I separated.
>
> (Assistant Principal, Southern city)

None of these women thought about administrative careers prior to their divorces. Now they have new career goals, as well as new self-images. An assistant principal recalls:

> When I went into education, I basically went in thinking of a husband and family—with no career aspirations. Things went from bad to worse in my marriage, and I was losing all esteem for myself. I chose administration because of monetary needs; I knew I couldn't live on just a teacher's salary after I divorced. I also needed an ego boost, because my divorce nearly destroyed me. I was as low as you could possibly get at the time.
>
> (Southern suburb)

After setting administrative goals, a divorced woman finds the same lack of support any single woman faces: no partner to support her aspirations.

> Although my former husband wasn't willing to move for my career, he always encouraged me to get my doctorate and to become a principal. I am not sure how the loss of that personal support will affect me. I am going to have to develop some other supportive people, because I don't have them now.
>
> (Specialist, Northwestern suburb)

Sometimes children validate their mother's aspirations, filling the gap left by divorce. "My children are very proud of me," notes an assistant principal (southern suburb), "and I discuss my career decisions with them." A new principal describes her situation:

> My children have been very supportive. I think it would be hard to go it alone. I had to move away from them to take this job, so now I have tremendous phone bills to keep in touch with them.
>
> (Northwestern town)

The pride children display in their mother's work is a strong motivating force for divorced women. An acting assistant principal (southern metro) claims her children "love" her administrative goals and are encouraging her to earn a doctorate in the field. "My three sons think I am the smartest mother in the world," she reports.

On the other hand, children create unavoidable problems for divorced aspirants. For those solely responsible for parenting—often in addition to working and studying—there are tremendous time demands. One student describes her complex life following divorce:

> It's intense on a daily basis: working, going to school and then parenting, too. In terms of my schooling, I've gone from Plan A, to Plan B, to Plan C. And I'm about to develop Plan D. There are just times when I have to make choices. When those choices involve my young son, there really isn't any choice as far as time and what I will do. I guess if I had someone sharing the parenting responsibilities, I would have finished my degree as planned. However, it would have been difficult then, too. Everyday I feel pulled from all sides and think I won't make it. I go from one office to another, then back to the first, and finally home again. I've managed, but I'll be glad when it's all behind me and I can put all my energy into being an administrator.
>
> (Midwestern city)

Although some single mothers find that their divorce merely slows their career progress, others feel sidetracked altogether. They feel isolated from the field and wonder whether they will ever be able to reestablish themselves as active administrative candidates. Because of work and parenting responsibilities (and the lack of a spouse to relieve them), these divorced aspirants cannot take advantage of the informal social mixing so important to maintaining the informational networks in administration. Not only do they receive less information about job openings, they also become less visible to those who do the hiring. As a result, their career aspirations may not be widely known, and they may feel completely unsupported in their desire to become administrators. A teacher explains her dilemma:

> I saw a lot of people getting ahead, and I thought, "I knew them when . . . . " I wondered why there was never anything passed on to me; apparently, I wasn't traveling in the right circles. But as a single parent, I put my all into work and then had to go home. I couldn't really mix with my colleagues other than at the Christmas party, so I didn't know what was going on.
>
> (Northeastern metro)

While some divorced mothers must curtail their careers to accommodate their children's needs, others accelerate their efforts because higher administrative salaries might alleviate their financial problems. One assistant principal acknowledges the importance of her additional salary and finds her status as a single parent helpful in her career aspirations:

> Now I can say to the men: "Well, you know I am the breadwinner in my family now just like you. I have house payments to make, too." They hush up after that. Being divorced gives me an advantage, because now the men understand money has a lot to do with my aspirations. They can identify with that.
>
> (Southern suburb)

She realizes, however, that their empathy encompasses only common financial needs; it does not extend to any deeper understanding or acceptance of her as a woman who also wants to manage schools.

### Summary

In various ways, marriage and family influence female aspirants' career goals. Regardless of their marital status, and their involvement or lack of involvement with children, all female aspirants are affected by the stereotypes of women as wives and mothers and men as husbands and executives. Laboring under such limitations, women in this study seek to balance their personal lives with their professional aspirations. Although fifty-eight percent of the respondents grew up in homes where mothers were traditional homemakers, these women believe that they must actively explore other options. The current image in the media—that women *can* take on multiple roles and succeed—puts great pressure on these women. Each of these women's ability to balance work, family and (in many cases) graduate school will dictate their patterns of career progress. Although it is unclear what costs are involved in their choices, they are steadfast in their goals: Whether delaying careers temporarily while parenting or combining these responsibilities, the desire to attain management positions in education remains paramount. The family responsibilities, so often referred to in the past as insurmountable barriers for female aspirants, are now simply givens. In one sense, these women see no viable options: they *do* believe they can "have it all."

# 8    Women in Administration

I think there are precious few opportunities for women in educational administration. On the surface, the field looks as if it is opening up a lot, but it's not. It's only opening up a little. In the systems I know of, they are putting women with twenty years of teaching experience in as assistant principals or principals in elementary schools, and they think *that* is making great progress!

(Student, Southeastern city)

ALTHOUGH WOMEN IN THIS STUDY share a common resolve to succeed in public school leadership, they express myriad opinions and hopes about female administrators in the field. While all of the informants support the hiring of qualified women for administrative positions, they express a wide range of beliefs and attitudes about how receptive the field is to female aspirants. They also disagree in their assessment of incumbent female administrators. Some informants share great enthusiasm for current female administrators and believe women are making tremendous strides in school management; others are subdued and cautious in their evaluations and are pessimistic about the future of women in the field. Examination of these diverse perceptions reveals a number of misapprehensions about the status of women in educational administration and serves to broaden our understanding of the complexities women face when aspiring to school leadership positions.

## Hiring Trends

Many women report feeling strongly that "the time is right for women in administration." These women express great optimism—based on their perceptions or, perhaps more accurately, their hopes—that school districts are, in fact, now seriously considering female administrative candidates.

115

Such beliefs are understandable for women who have entered the first
levels of administration or who belong to districts that internally promote
female aspirants. One assistant principal (southern suburb) enthusiastic-
ally describes the time as "ripe for women" in administration. Another
assistant principal optimistically concurs:

> I think it's a new day for female educators. Our new assistant principal
> has a card saying: "The best man for the job is a woman." We all laugh
> about it, but in some instances the best-run schools *are* handled by
> women. I think if women are brave enough to go on, we can go to high
> places in school leadership. Everybody is accepting that now, and
> there's a lot of support for women.
>
> (Southern suburb)

In a northwestern town, a recently hired principal agrees that times have
changed. In her supportive community, constituents tell her: "Boy, are we
glad you're here! It's about time we had a woman administrator."
    The basis for this kind of enthusiasm comes from women who believe
districts are changing their evaluations of, and their attitudes toward,
female applicants. A specialist says districts now view women as a new
source of potential administrators because of the increased numbers of
women being interviewed:

> I think women are "in" right now, but I am sure we are going to have to
> prove ourselves. I know the feeling the last time around was that the
> male candidates for jobs in this district were far inferior to the females
> who applied. And then there are a lot more women out there applying
> who never tried before. We may be tapping a whole new source of
> applicants we didn't even know was there.
>
> (Western suburb)

Whether women are truly "in" or not, many people believe that administration is now open to women. They think women receive more
encouragement to aspire and that today, more women actually apply for
administrative positions. "I was told by a guy going into administration
himself," notes a student (northwestern city), "that I should go in as well,
because there were openings for women now." Likewise, a specialist
(midwestern suburb) feels encouraged because "things are getting to the
point where they will change drastically—they're interviewing more
women now."
    A number of women point to demographic evidence to support their
view that "the times are changing." One head teacher presents her
argument:

> Our district is small and independent, but we provide a good example

of promoting and hiring women. There are four out of twenty principals at the elementary level and a couple of assistant principals at the secondary level. The numbers aren't high, but the latest openings have all gone to women. A lot of the men have been here a long, long time and are beginning to retire. I've heard somewhere that eighty percent of the principals in the U.S. are fifty-five years old. For someone my age, that's an encouraging statistic to think about.

(Western suburb)

Several other women speak of similar changes occurring in their districts. "Because women are now visible, I think people are beginning to see that women have far more potential than they have ever been given the chance to show," argues an administrative intern (southern suburb). An assistant principal believes that all communities need to do is to get used to women as managers and then the transition will be complete:

People—teachers, administrators at the central office and parents— are used to the old school of thought and have to get used to women in administration. They are just not accustomed to us. It reminds me of high school student body elections years ago: you could have ninety-five girls and one boy running, and whether he's competent or not, the boy will be elected president. Student elections are finally changing and girls, as well as female educators, are now being viewed as leaders.

(Southern metro)

Still others feel that female administrators have earned the respect of their communities and have thus helped to create a more favorable climate for female aspirants.

I think the time has long since come when women should be administrators. In the past, they were often forced into areas such as counselling because other options weren't open to them. But now, as a result of those experiences, they have many more skills to bring to administration. They are committed to working with kids and with people, rather than going for the money and the title like some men.

(Specialist, Midwestern suburb)

Many of the women on my staff cheered for me when I got this principalship. So many of the men come fresh from the football field or the basketball court and are pushed right through administrative courses into leadership roles. Sometimes they get schools for an age group they've never even worked with, and I think this is wrong. Hopefully, there will be more and more women coming into administration because they earned the right to be there: they teach in the area and know the kids.

(New Principal, Northwestern suburb)

Although sharing a general optimism about changes in hiring practices, women debate whether new opportunities exist equally at the elementary and secondary levels. Some believe that greater possibilities occur only in elementary schools and temper their optimism accordingly:

> I think the field is now open for women, and our board is very fair in trying to select women and blacks for administrative positions. I should clarify that I mean at the elementary level *only*. We've only had one assistant principal hired at the secondary level.
>
> (Assistant Principal, Southern metro)

A teacher (northeastern rural) agrees that the "chances of finding a principalship in the elementary schools somewhere would probably be good." For women interested in older students, however, increased opportunity for women at the elementary level creates ambivalence, as this part-time administrator describes:

> I could almost kick myself for not having any elementary experience. I have two friends who do, and they are already principals. It's easier for women to get in at that level. Even though I prefer secondary-age children, at least I could get some building experience at the elementary level.
>
> (Midwestern suburb)

Many hope that the women just beginning to infiltrate secondary administrative ranks will open the doors for other aspirants. In one large district, an assistant principal asserts:

> Years ago, you wouldn't find a woman at the secondary level—they were relegated to elementary schools. In the last seven years, however, there's been a change in the attitudes of the general public towards women in secondary positions. That change has been prompted by so many women getting certified in secondary education and by the leadership they offer in church and community activities. Even the community folks see that women can contribute, not only in the home and at church, but in other areas as well. Productive women can change the attitudes of those hiring school leaders.
>
> (Southern metro)

In a smaller district, a supervisor describes a similar shift in her community:

> Our district is just beginning to open up, and we now have a smattering of women at the secondary level. I thought we were doing worse than larger districts in the state. Then I attended a county meeting and saw

only three women out of 100 principals. I was surprised to see we had a better balance in our own district.

(Southeastern city)

Some districts that appear reluctant to hire women for secondary administrative positions indirectly motivate aspirants to persevere at the secondary level, as these two women relate:

Our state has approximately 240 female principals out of 2,200, and only ten are at the secondary level. They have plenty of women in the system who are certified and applying at the elementary level. Where they can't seem to get women to apply is at the secondary and higher levels. So I think the market will be good for me, because that's the level I'm interested in.

(Student, Southeastern city)

I decided I didn't want to coach all my life, and I didn't want to go into counselling—even though it's a field open to women. I like being first, and I know there weren't many females involved in administration. So I thought: Why not be the first female to get a high school principalship? Everyone laughed at me. They said they weren't going to hire a female principal—especially a black one! The more negative things that were said to me, the more incentive I felt. It was just the catalyst I needed to pursue administration.

(Supervisor, Southeastern city)

What are the sources of these heightened expectations? Is there any basis for these women's beliefs that districts are, in fact, changing and welcoming women now? In tracing the origins of such beliefs, many women explain that their optimism stems from the acceptance they now feel on university campuses across the nation. When they return to graduate school, some encounter highly receptive departments of educational administration. This new eagerness to support female administrative candidates, however, may stem more from the practical concern of declining university enrollments, than from any new-found concern for educational equity. Whatever the reasons, recruitment of women for university administrative programs is a new priority on many campuses. Several women around the country detail their experiences:

I went back to school because a local university offered stipends to teachers to get their Master's in educational administration. They said there was a critical shortage of minorities and women. I had thought of administration before, but I couldn't afford to return to school. When I saw this announcement, I realized I was doubly qualified—being female and black. So I went back to school.

(Acting Assistant Principal, Southern metro)

When I finished my Master's, I looked into administration. There weren't any women in the program then, and there was a lot of talk about that fact. Some people thought it was a good time to start an administrative program, so I did.

(Teacher, Northwestern suburb)

I got a flyer about a summer course on women and educational administration. I thought: Why not? Administration might be interesting.

(Student, Northeastern rural)

While encouragement of female administrative aspirants on college campuses gives many women reason to be optimistic about their futures, hiring statistics in public schools do not. In brief, women have made few, if any, inroads into the male world of administration. Many women lack the information necessary to compare their beliefs concerning the improved climate for women in administration with the realities about the numbers of women actually being hired in schools. As one supervisor (southeastern city) acknowledges: "It is sometimes hard to get a handle on what is really happening to women elsewhere; we don't have the information we need." As a result, many women express a confusion about why so few women hold administrative positions when the time is supposed to be "so right" for female candidates. Some aspirants believe the reason for the underrepresentation of women in administrative ranks is that few women are actively pursuing such a goal.

I believe we should have more female administrators. I see so many female teachers in the classroom, and yet, when I go to administrative meetings, I see so few women. It's troublesome to me. Maybe I'm wrong, but I think it's a case of women not actively pursuing administration, rather than not being accepted.

(Assistant Principal, Northeastern metro)

Maybe it's naiveté on my part, but I don't anticipate problems getting hired because I'm female. I think there are few women in secondary administration because of it is a heck of a job and so few women apply. Maybe that's why we are so few and far between.

(Student, Southeastern city)

Women, however, *are* aspiring and applying for administrative positions; they just aren't being hired in the numbers one might expect. In the school year 1981-82 (roughly at the onset of the study), females comprised only one-quarter of the school administrators in the country.[1] As this figure has only risen one percent in the last few years,[2] the outlook is not encouraging—even for women who find themselves in a district that *does* promote women in the field. Although most aspirants cling to the hope that they will prove these hiring statistics wrong, eighty-three percent admit that few women attain the management goals they seek.

When discussing hiring statistics for women in administration, some respondents initially felt that their own districts were making more advances than others around the country. On closer examination, however, they realize the figures are minimal. One administrative intern illustrates the surprise many experience:

> I think our district is very good about hiring women. We have three now. [pause] Three, gosh, let's see. [pause] Three out of fifteen elementary schools doesn't sound like much, does it? [pause] And our secondary level isn't even as open as that. We only have one assistant principal at the junior high level, and *no* female principals at all. Hmmm . . . .
>
> (Western suburb)

When challenged to examine closely their own district's records, many expressed similar dismay.

Other respondents never harbored any fantasies about how many women actually get hired in school administration. Openly critical of the scant numbers of female administrators, these women share a different perspective about future possibilities in their districts:

> It's very hard for women to get into administration at any level. We have one female administrator in our district, and we're the sixth largest district in the state! That one woman has eighteen years of experience and a doctorate in administration, and she is only a specialist in a small school. At the same time she was placed, two men were also hired. They only had Master's degrees, and one only had a year of administrative experience. A lot of women have the experience and qualifications, but they are not hired for administrative positions.
>
> (Resource Teacher, Northwestern town)

> In our area, we have twenty-one elementary schools and only five female principals. There are no women at the middle or high school level, except for four assistant principals out of the sixty.
>
> (Assistant Principal, Southern town)

> About five to seven years ago, we hired our first Anglo female principal at the secondary level. This year, we finally placed our second one!
>
> (Assistant Principal, Southern city)

Districts with relatively high numbers of female administrators might suggest that women have far more opportunities than these three informants believe. The appearance, however, may be misleading, as some districts may hire more women for reasons unrelated to extending opportunity. An administrative assistant explains:

> The reason we have so many female principals and assistants in elementary education is because of the pay scale: it's so low, and the men aren't interested. We have no women at the secondary level where the pay is somewhat better. We do have quite a few women at the central office, but they're all in the lower, poorly-paid positions.
>
> (Southern metro)

In rural areas, the absence of female managers is even more apparent. Two women describe their districts:

> In our state, there are women in administration in the larger towns. When you go to smaller towns, however, there are no women. In my district, there is not one. In fact, I was the first woman ever granted sabbatical leave!
>
> (Student, Western rural)

> There are no women administrators in this part of the state. The males have been here forever, and they're so conservative they'd never hire a woman. My principal is supportive, but the board or the community wouldn't go for it. All they give to women are the assistant principalships, and those are just titles with lots of work and no increase in salary.
>
> (Student, Northwestern rural)

A specialist (northwestern rural) sums up the small town experience for many women: "I know we had a female principal here once, because there's a school named after her. But she's the only one I've ever heard of around here."

Whether living in rural or urban areas, aspirants continually comment on the conspicuous absence of women in school leadership. A student (southern city) points out: "They say women have an advantage in getting hired as administrators, but I haven't noticed it." A state department of education employee (northeastern metro) agrees: "When I do presentations at principals' meetings, it's just a sea of balding heads!" Thus, although a great deal has been said about the time being ripe for female administrators, women have made few advances beyond gaining more interviews. Even in districts that have hired women for entry-level administrative positions, the climate for women continues to be less than favorable.

Although our district looks good on the surface with regards to female administrators, it's a cover-up. At the leadership meetings, the women are not really listened to, and there are a lot of dirty jokes passed around just to see what kind of reaction they'll get from women. The men describe women getting administrative jobs at the secondary level, for example, as a "disease" that seems to be spreading everywhere.

(Assistant Principal, Northeastern city)

In spite of their interest and drive to become successful managers, female aspirants realize they have set difficult goals for themselves. Indeed, only twenty-five percent of those interviewed believe women's chances of getting hired are "good."

### Elementary vs. Secondary

Elementary schools have traditionally offered greater opportunities for female administrative aspirants. Although in some regions more women advance in the elementary schools than at the secondary level, even that picture is changing.[3] An assistant principal describes a common situation throughout the country in the 1980s:

In the early 1950s, about eighty-five percent of all the elementary administrators in the city were women. But that changed quickly when the men came back from the war and went into education with the support of the GI Bill. Now maybe the ratio of men to women is fifty-fifty at the elementary level—at best.

(Western metro)

Those who hope to move on to the secondary level, but go through what appears to be a more open door at the elementary level, often find themselves trapped. An assistant principal (southern city) admits she went into elementary work "like most women," but hoped to move into secondary management. Now she feels she cannot "change horses in the middle of the stream." Even a job at the middle school level provides no guarantee that a woman can move on to her preferred choice of high school administration.

My friend has been an assistant principal at the junior high, but she has not been happy there. She really likes older students. She thought she'd get her foot in the door by taking an administrative position at a lower level, but she has been locked into that level.

(New Assistant Principal, Midwestern suburb)

Because of these difficulties, secondary female aspirants are particularly vocal about the frustrations they experience when pursuing their career goals:

There are no female principalships at the middle school level. I could apply at the elementary level, but I don't *want* that level!

(Assistant Principal, Southern metro)

I love junior high kids, but I don't ever see this city accepting a woman in the junior high world. I base that on looking around and seeing no women beyond the elementary level.

(Assistant Principal, Southeastern city)

My superintendent told me outright that women who aspire to leadership roles in this state should be in elementary education. "After all," he said, "women are very good with small children." But I have absolutely no interest in elementary education!

(Student, Southeastern city)

Some women obviously feel cornered. To get administrative experience, they apparently must apply at the elementary level; however, as noted earlier, elementary experience will not guarantee a later move into secondary administration. For this reason, some secondary female aspirants eschew opportunities at the elementary level.

Women have traditionally worked with little kids at the elementary level, but I have no interest in little children or in being an elementary principal.

(Lead Teacher, Southern metro)

There is an opening at the elementary level, but I have no intention of applying for it. I'm sure they'll hire a woman, and that's one reason I don't want it. I can't cope with them saying, "Well, that's why you got the job." The principalship at the high school may open, and I will apply. But I don't stand a chance. There isn't another woman at the secondary level in this district besides myself.

(Supervisor, Southern rural)

One secondary administrative aspirant admitted she would take an elementary position if it were offered, but only because she believes she has no other choice.

I would consider an elementary principalship, but it's not what I really want. My experience, interest and training are all at the secondary level, and I'm good with those kids. But the chances are slim for a woman in this county. The county is just not ready for us.

(Assistant Principal, Southeastern city)

Even male mentors who support women for elementary administration, show a bias against female candidates pursuing secondary positions.

> Citing the need for women in school leadership roles, my principal has always supported my aspirations. But even though he supposedly sees no problems with a woman being an administrator, he still asks me how I would see myself working with little kids at the elementary level! I have to remind him that I like working where I am—at the secondary level.
>
> (Teacher, Midwestern suburb)

Although some women gain administrative access at the elementary level, the unofficial criterion of maleness hampers the aspirations of female candidates at both the elementary and secondary levels. Female aspirants quickly learn just how much they have to overcome in changing peoples' images of what appropriate administrators can look and be like. They are acutely aware of the dissonance they cause in merely aspiring to such positions. Female administrative candidates are forced to examine themselves closely in ways male candidates not only do not do, but probably never *think* of doing. For example, issues of age, stature, physical attractiveness and femininity—hardly administrative job qualifications—arise regularly as they pursue management careers. Several women describe the negative impact that gender issues have on their career aspirations:

> Although no one says this out loud, I think people wonder about a female administrator. Is she a woman, or is she a woman who wants to be a man? Why would she want this job? I am a woman, and I don't try to be a man. I would have had a problem, though, if I had been profoundly ugly or dramatically beautiful. But luckily, I am just an ordinary person.
>
> (Assistant Principal, Midwestern suburb)

> One problem I have to overcome is being a young woman in this field. Older male aspirants consider me a child at twenty-seven. I know a lot of men are waiting to see me flop; they still think women can't handle the pressures of administration. Yet I see many men crack, so I think women should be given the chance to try.
>
> (Teacher, Northwestern metro)

> Being a female coach in the city counts for little in this district. In fact, I've heard derogatory comments said about women in athletics. You are considered more "masculine." And then people only see you in warm-ups and aren't very respectful of you. I don't think being a female coach will help me get into administration like it does the men.
>
> (Teacher, Northeastern metro)

I feel I need some more graduate hours in administration to gain more credibility. When you're 5' 3" like I am, you need as much extra going for you as possible to impress people. One assistant principal told me people underestimate me because I look like a "waif." But I can't help that. I dress professionally, and I stand up straight. Do I have to fool them somehow?

(Administrative Intern, Southern suburb)

*Sexual Harassment*

In settings where sexual harassment persists, female aspirants find it extremely difficult to gain professional acceptance. In these cases, sexual overtones or overtures have unique and upsetting repercussions for women in administration. Very few male candidates, for example, are ever accused of "sleeping with the boss" to attain a position. Women, however, frequently hear such comments from both men and women, as a teacher relates:

There are the typical rumors of women sleeping their way to the top. You hear them talking in the teachers' room about who has been seen around town with various people. For the men, it's OK to sleep around because that's part of proving yourself. I don't think there's much validity in the rumors about women doing such things, but they are discouraging just to hear. People are still stuck at that level, rather than saying someone was chosen for his or her competence.

(Northeastern town)

As in the case of sexist questions being asked in interviews, women vary in their responses to these rumors: some resort to humor, others respond with anger.

I got recruited for one position, and people began asking how I got the job. One woman finally said outright, "Who are you sleeping with?" I decided not to be so sensitive and said, "It's for me to know and you to find out."

(District Staff, Northeastern metro)

I applied for the assistant superintendent's position on the recommendation of my superintendent. I could write a book about the whole process in terms of the gossip and back biting that went on. Because both the superintendent and the assistant (who was resigning) were good friends of mine, everyone assumed I would get the job through our "friendships." I felt like I was fighting shadows: There were rumors about me and the guys, but I could never get a handle on what was specifically said. At first I thought it was funny, but then I began to feel like Mary Cunningham with the Bendix people. I got very angry when people would say, "Oh, she's in there with the superintendent."

(Director, Northeastern town)

Three women in the study related incidents of outright sexual harassment.[4] Because no direct questions were asked about sexual harassment in the study, there may have been others who experienced the problem but did not volunteer the information. O'Reilly contends this is not a new problem, but one that women are just beginning to discuss openly: "What women once saw as an individual, isolated problem—probably her own fault, she should never have left home—is now beginning to be seen as inexcusable and inappropriate behavior that should be subject to penalties."[5] One teacher spoke of several occurrences in her school:

Sexual harassment is typical here. My assistant principal told me once how great it must be for my husband "to wake up next to me in the morning" given my looks! Last year, our principal came up to me in the parking lot and said "I'd sure like to put 'something' up your--!" And another assistant principal is always asking me to meet him for drinks after school. After all, I dress like a professional person and in no way attempt to get someone hot for my body. I behave myself, I do not consciously make sexual innuendos to anyone. I do, however, talk honestly and directly to men—the way I'd expect a man to talk to me. Yet the way these men react to me is a "put down." Incidentally, I'm not the only one this has happened to. Other white females in the building have similar stories.

(Southern metro)

Two assistant principals give examples of men who are "supportive" of women—but not for professional reasons.

Some men have the reputation of giving a woman a job if she'll sleep with them. But *I* choose who I sleep with! One guy wanted a casual affair, so I told him I was only interested if he wanted to keep me in the style he keeps his wife. He said, "But I only meant a casual arrangement." I told him, "That's not the kind of arrangement I make." He never asked me again.

(Assistant Principal, Western metro)

Our superintendent started coming over to see how my classes were going. Everyone else was surprised, because he had never been in the department before then. I think he thought I would "fool around." He was interested in getting women into administration alright, but not because of their competencies!

(Assistant Principal, Midwestern suburb)

The experience of these women may be exceptions, but that does not lessen their dismay and displeasure at having to deal with sexual rumors or encounters on the job. Such experiences demean or even discount, they believe, the serious professional efforts made and gained by female school executives. Certainly, they contend, male educators do not have to put up with such occurrences in the workplace.

### The Impact of Gender

Whether young or old, attractive or not, female aspirants obviously cannot hide the fact of their femaleness. Yet, this one characteristic seems to be the most problematic for them in school management. A part-time administrator remembers one interview where they wanted a woman "to check the girls' johns." She tried to make a joke of it until she saw they were not joking:

> Later I heard they questioned whether I knew what the job entailed. Yet during the interview, I made it clear that I did. I hate to admit it, but I think I didn't get the job because I'm female. They just didn't think I could handle the job because I'm a woman. I never thought being female would make as much difference as it has. For example, if I get to a door first and open it, my male assistant principal comments about me giving into "women's lib." That just blows my mind. Why is he thinking of me as a woman right at that moment? Why does it make a difference to him? There have even been comments about the pitch of my voice over the intercom as compared to the men's. These little things bother me: I'm being treated as someone different, because I'm female. But I don't feel any different.
>
> (Midwestern suburb)

Ortiz and Covel found male mentors admit they scrutinize female candidates more closely than males.[6] They quote one male interviewer who stated: "When considering women, of course there's more rigor, not only because I believe it's harder for women to be successful, but because people in general expect problems from women administrators."[7] An assistant principal in this study describes some of her early problems with a male colleague:

> I had a coach who had a hard time taking directions from a woman. I finally just confronted him. He replied honestly that he just couldn't get used to working with a woman. But later in the year, he admitted that he had misjudged me. I was supportive of his teams and came to the games, and he had never had that support before.
>
> (Southern city)

Even if a female educator gets beyond the biases of her male—and sometimes her female—peers, she must face those of the community. Although many female aspirants find parents more accepting of them as educational leaders than males, forty-seven percent still believe parents prefer male administrators over females. Three assistant principals tell of their initial difficulties with parents:

A few families were surprised I was the new assistant principal. On the phone, some of the fathers seemed to think they could buffalo me. They'd say, "You're not the one. You must be the secretary. Let me talk to the principal." Some were belittling and rude, so I'd have them come in for a conference. By the time we finished, I had their support.

(Northwestern city)

I got a lot of interesting phone calls at first. People would want to talk to the assistant principal, and I'd say, "Yes, may I help you?" They'd say, "Yes, you can get him on the phone." I'd say, "But *I'm* the assistant principal." Then there would be a pause. It took some time to gain acceptance with the community. If they saw me first, they always assumed I was the secretary.

(Southeastern town)

When parents first called my office, they'd say, "Who's going to do the disciplining?" They'd add, "Little lady, I can't imagine you doing something like that!" Well, word travels fast: When I discipline, it's effective!

(Southern city)

The issue of discipline continues to be a major source of contention for female administrative aspirants, particularly at the secondary level. Discipline, respondents maintain, is most often given as the major reason for not hiring women in middle schools and high schools. They also argue, however, that the stereotype of a woman not being able to maintain discipline does not hold up under scrutiny:

I've had to work through the image of a woman being a soft touch. Parents and kids often feel double-crossed when I don't act like the sweet, supportive granny they were expecting. They seem to anticipate that kind of behavior from a woman. I think I am now recognized for what I *do,* rather than what I *look* like I might do.

(Assistant Principal, Northwestern town)

When I applied for the assistant principalship at the high school, people were amazed that I (and one other woman) even wanted the job. Traditionally, our assistant principals are responsible for school discipline and transportation. The very first thing people said was: "You don't want to have to get out there and drive a bus if a driver doesn't show up, do you?" I said, "I can drive a bus as well as anyone else." Driving buses wouldn't be the best part of the day, but it also wouldn't be insurmountable.

(Teacher, Southeastern rural)

So far this county doesn't think a woman can handle disciplining high school students. But I feel I do as well as the men. The county might not like to accept the fact that a female may be competent in that area, but it's true.

(Assistant Principal, Southern metro)

After overcoming the widespread belief that women cannot be effective disciplinarians, aspirants find further difficulty when they seek to establish their own styles of discipline.

Discipline is one area I find problematic. My assistant principal started talking about swats, and I was appalled. I can't imagine hitting children. My reasoning has nothing to do with my being female. I just don't believe in meeting violence with violence. It's simply not my way.

(Part-time Administrator, Midwestern suburb)

At first I didn't feel my personality was one that fit the administrative role. Administrators were supposed to be stern and forceful, and should give strong orders. But I have found, as an administrator, that you don't actually give orders, rather you communicate with students and staff in your own style. I feel good about the way *I* lead others.

(Assistant Principal, Southern city)

Rather than being a liability, some women in administrative positions find their gender aids them in managing disciplinary problems:

Being a woman, I can walk up to any student in the building and say, "May I help you?" The male administrators often seem threatening, particularly to the junior high child. Children know I'm not going to slug it out with anyone, so I can walk between two boys who are fighting and they immediately stop. I see being a female as a definite advantage: The boys are protective of me in a way they would never be with a male assistant.

(Assistant Principal, Southern metro)

I've had some individuals say, "My kids won't do anything for a female administrator," or "You're no bigger than my kid!" But I think people find out fairly quickly that their kids are better off responding to reason rather than to strength.

(Assistant Principal, Northwestern town)

Tibbetts argues that women must deal with the sexist nature of our society and its systematic labeling by gender, if they are to improve their own position in that society.[8] She concludes: "[Women] can become so certain of their own sex-identity that they know there is almost nothing they can do that can make them 'unfeminine,' for, in demonstrating characteristics and performing tasks now termed 'masculine,' they are not taking on a masculine role, but are expanding the feminine role."[9]

Some male educators are also beginning to reassess women's disciplinary abilities after seeing competent women in action. In such instances, men find they don't need to be protective of women, and they can, in fact, depend on female colleagues in the workplace. Larwood et al. argue: "By showing [the] men that women can be successful, the traditional images of the housewife and dependent female employee will be displaced in favor of the more realistic female co-breadwinner and colleague."[10] Three women offer examples of how some of these traditional images might be changing:

Originally the screening committee was concerned about my commuting, because the principal said it had been too fatiguing for him with all the other things he did. I don't think he realized that being a mother and an assistant principal, I had more stamina than he did.

(Assistant Principal, Midwestern suburb)

Our school is unique because we have two female assistants. I've heard people say, "Such and such is a bad school; they need a man out there." But although our principal said he could always release a coach if he needed help, we handle it all—paperwork *and* discipline.

(Assistant Principal, Southern metro)

Many people believe that it takes a strong man to discipline students. To my mind, discipline does not take physical force; in fact, sometimes thinking you need force is detrimental. Men on staff are always amazed that I can handle situations without being physical. But because I'm a woman, kids aren't threatened by me. If I ask students to break up a fight, they do. They save face because I'm female, and they don't have to bust me in the nose. That just wouldn't be cool.

(Teacher-Administrator, Midwestern town)

In other settings, however, educators still cling firmly to the old stereotypes. Seeing competent women in action not only surprises some of these people, but threatens them as well.

There are double messages circulating about being an administrator and a woman. On one hand, you're supposed to be competent; but competence in women is feared. The more accomplished women become, the more threatening they are to some people—both male and female.

(Student, Northeastern metro)

She goes on to add:

I think there may even be a backlash against competent women. They won't be recognized for their capabilities, because that's too threatening. Instead, they'll be called too aggressive, or will be criticized for not being team players. Women find it hard out there.

(Student, Northeastern metro)

In rural areas, female administrative aspirants face even greater hurdles because of community traditions. One student states:

There is a strong feeling in rural areas that women aren't supposed to do administrative work. Women are just not considered for positions of authority. The principals are all males and are usually hired from within. They are all older and have kids in college, and because they are so tightly ensconced, nothing is going to move *them* out.

(Northeastern town)

Another student explains why this condition continues to persist:

There are no women in administration because this is a conservative, farming community. The father is traditionally the dominant figure at home. They've never seen women in leadership positions, so they don't even think of women being administrators.

(Midwestern rural)

Nevertheless, this student's commitment to rural communities is strong. She admits: "I want to continue working here—hopefully as an administrator. But I don't think I will be permitted to do so. I'll be very surprised if I get hired."

Despite the lack of encouragement from those around them, this woman and many others continue to persist in their quest for administrative positions.

When I began talking to people about not wanting to be a counselor all my life and that I wanted to be even more than a principal, the response was: "Oh no, here we have another one who thinks she can do more than we really want her to do or more than she's capable of doing." Once I was explicitly told: "We wish teachers would tell us what their educational plans are, because a lot of times we do not see them in administrative roles and they are wasting their time. We would never hire them as managers in this district." I got the message right away that I would have to leave that district or be a counselor all my life.

(New Assistant Principal, Midwestern suburb)

Other aspirants report more subtle forms of discouragement:

During one interview, a superintendent said if the choice came down to a female or a male candidate—both with the same experience—he would hire the woman. The point is, few women *have* the same experience. Gaining that amount of experience one has to start early in a career, and few women get the chance for that. There are very few people encouraging women to enter administration early enough.

(Department Chair, Northwestern suburb)

A new assistant principal who left her district for an administrative position concludes:

I'm good at what I do, but I hate to wave my own flag. But *someone* has to wave the flag for women in administration! People are tired of hearing women themselves say they are competent. The people they work for should be promoting them.

(Midwestern suburb)

### Women vs. Women

Paradoxically, other female educators often fail to provide the encouragement and support that so many female administrative aspirants seek and need. Instead of forming alliances, many women in education often find themselves drawing up battle lines. Given the expectations in this society that women are nurturing, aspirants who are not supported by other women experience frustration. Caplan finds this a typical response: "It is not surprising to encounter this lack of a nurturant attitude in men, but women who seek nurturance from other women and are disappointed in their expectations may experience a kind of resentment."[11] A teacher explains the problem:

The only women who give you insight and information are the ones who feel confident that you don't want what they have. As long as my aspirations aren't the same as theirs, there is no problem. Men, however, always seem to pull together for one another.

(Northeastern metro)

Will argues that a "cold war" is going on between many women because of the perception that some women prefer to work for men.[12] Over fifty percent of the women in this study believe female teachers prefer to work for male administrators. A teacher (midwestern city) explains her beliefs: "The anti-female sentiment in this district comes from female teachers who are envious of other women's success." A supervisor concurs:

> In my experience, men are not the problem; it's the older female teacher who most threatens women aspirants. I don't know if they hate to see another woman achieve or whether they don't like the idea of a woman being the boss. Or maybe jealousy is the biggest factor. I have known women who have not shown the least bit of interest in administration, but once another woman is hired they try to get her removed or try to outshine her.
>
> (Southeastern city)

Women seeking administrative positions claim their problems with female teachers begin when they first let their aspirations be known.

> I was told by female teachers that I should give up administration and let men with families have the jobs. They think because I am married, I don't need the money.
>
> (Assistant Principal, Northeastern metro)

> Quite a few of the teachers think I'm going after a goal I'll never achieve. They say: "Why are you bothering to do all this extra work in graduate school? Why don't you just stay home and watch T.V., rather than commuting at night to school?" I usually ignore them, because if I said what I think, I'd make a lot of enemies. I think they are stagnated and are wasting their lives sitting around doing nothing. In one sense, my aspirations challenge their complacency, and that's threatening. They don't want a woman as principal because they're jealous. And when they criticize the few women administrators we have in the system, it bothers me.
>
> (Teacher, Southeastern rural)

Once an aspirant begins interviewing, the opposition of other females may intensify. In a district where they almost hired a female assistant superintendent of personnel, a specialist reports:

> The female teachers just went wild. They ripped that poor soul to shreds, and she did not get the job. Their comments had nothing to do with her skills. All their concerns were sex-linked: "How could she do this job and be married too?" "She ought to be home with her family." The men didn't say a word, and I know they would have accepted her if

she had been hired. It seems that every time a female becomes a candidate for a certain job, the uproar comes from the women.

(Specialist, Midwestern suburb)

Even when a woman is hired, she may continue to experience opposition from female colleagues, as an assistant principal recalls:

After I was introduced at the staff meeting, six to eight men came over to introduce themselves and to wish me luck, but not a single woman did so. One female department head was even aggressively challenging, as if to say: "Don't think you're such a hot shot just because you're an assistant principal!" It really bothers me that the women stereotyped me without even getting to know me.

(Midwestern suburb)

A specialist (Midwestern city) tells how female teachers in her district were outraged over a woman "who had the audacity to be pregnant and be a principal at the same time!" They thought she should be home with her family, and yet they did not see the contradiction in *their* working away from the home. This specialist also describes being personally challenged by the female teachers in her district:

I was told point blank that they liked me, but that they would work to eliminate my position. I was constantly being asked what kind of certification I had to be in such a position.

(Midwestern city)

What accounts for this hostility among female educators? Although simple jealousy is frequently mentioned, some women explain the negativism of their female colleagues in more complex ways:

Women teachers have had fewer experiences with women administrators. Many of them are unsure of themselves because they are docile, middle-of-the-road people. They view women in administration as a radical departure from the status quo. I have greater difficulty proving myself to them than I do to the men.

(Teacher-Administrator, Midwestern town)

The older women seem jealous because they never had the opportunity to go back to school and advance. There was simply no incentive or encouragement when they were young. I think they feel, and rightly so, that they could have been qualified for some of these jobs. But they lacked support, and they resent that. Also, they don't realize how many women are going back to school these days. It's no longer as unusual as it once was.

(Supervisor, Midwestern suburb)

Confusion and controversy concerning women's roles is not limited to the field of education. The women's movement and changing family and work patterns leave many women frustrated and unsure of what is appropriate or is expected of them as women. Perhaps the negative comments and actions toward women with higher aspirations is an understandable response to the general shift of social values. Kanter, describing the problem in terms of advantage and disadvantage in mobility opportunities, argues that workers tend "to protect themselves against their own lack of advancement prospects" through the use of negative comments and actions.[13] She continues: "People who 'escape' disadvantaged situations, [such as] women who rise from the ranks to prestigious positions ... have frequently been criticized for not acting as advocates for former peers, with little recognition of the mobility conflicts such people may face."[14] Kanter reasons that "low-mobility peer groups" must put aside their criticisms and support individuals who, once in positions of power, can pull others up with them. But with limited opportunities, these groups tend to criticize, rather than support, those individuals who might ascend. The vicious cycle comes full circle, Kanter concludes, when those who *do* attain success conveniently (and perhaps understandably) tend to forget those who made the going rough. Nevertheless, because women seem to worry more over interpersonal relationships on the job than men, upwardly mobile women are doubly mired.[15]

Nowhere is the conflict between women more graphic than in the phenomenon of the "Queen Bee Syndrome," in which a woman who makes it into management neglects to support the advancement of other women. Staines et al. describe "the true Queen Bee [as having] made it in the 'man's world' of work, while running a house and family with her left hand. 'If I can do it without a whole movement to help me,' runs her attitude, 'so can all those other women.' "[16] They further claim that these women fear competition for their jobs in the same way men do, and that they identify with their male colleagues rather than with the vague notion of women as a class. In their rare position as the lone or top woman in a work setting, these women are perhaps understandably concerned, notes Caplan, "when a second women enters ... [and] destroys the first woman's uniqueness and accustomed label: the first woman is no longer 'our woman here.' "[17] Staines et al. conclude: "The irony of it all is that the Queen Bee, because of her access to power and male favor, is in the best position to advance the cause of women, but is the least inclined to do so."[18]

Since the early 1970s, many have tried to understand the behavior of the "Queen Bee." Berry and Kushner defend her as a high achiever who actually needs little recognition from others (either male or female) to feel satisfied with her work; furthermore, she has little power to help other women because the system is controlled by men.[19] Huws would agree, arguing that because these women distance themselves from other women in their efforts to identify with male behavior, they fail to understand they are as much victims as the next woman.[20] Kanter, also, would be forgiving, if only because the "Queen Bee" got so little support from anyone as she fought her solitary way to the top. And finally, Harragan dismisses the importance of "Queen Bees": "[They are] of little help to the influx of new [women] because they have never penetrated far [enough] inland and have had too few conversations with the natives to learn the language. None of them was offered a map of the territory, so most believe that the interior is an uncharted jungle."[21] One woman in the study sympathizes with the dilemmas these pioneering women face:

> My female principal is a clone like every older female public school teacher in the city. She isn't encouraging of other women, but she grew up in a time when you couldn't be married and still teach. That rule, by the way, remained in force here through the mid-1950's. I believe that's why we have all these Queen Bee spinster types. Those women faced some hard decisions, and I can sympathize with some of them.
> (District Advisor, Northeastern metro)

Many older, established female administrators feel that younger women do not understand or appreciate the difficulties they faced during their careers. They achieved their positions of authority with little help from their male or female colleagues, and did so during times that were less supportive of female advancement. Frequently, they feel that younger aspirants conveniently forget this legacy.

For whatever reasons, female administrative aspirants must deal with the fact that some female teachers—and even some female administrators—will not actively support their career goals. Each aspirant responds to the negativism in her own way. One lead teacher (southern metro) confides that she "spent many hours of soul searching and a few sleepless nights" over the problem. She concludes, however, that "the women teachers have the problem, not me." Another aspirant (northwestern town) has learned to keep her career objectives under wraps: "Some women administrators are supportive, but some of the women teachers are envious. I try not to make a big issue of my plans or to force myself on anyone."

Not all women report negative treatment from their female colleagues. In fact, some respondents speak highly of the support they receive from other women. One aspirant (western town) tells of the "excitement" generated among female teachers in her building when she received an assistant principalship. Another teacher (southern rural) remembers the encouragement she got from a female resource teacher: "She told me to 'go for it' and said that 'the future is yours.' " She adds this was the *only* encouragement she ever received. These two anecdotes, however, are the only ones describing support from female teachers. Most women report that the main source of encouragement for aspirants comes from other female administrators, rather than teachers.

> I have never had any encouragement from male supervisors or bosses. All of my encouragement has come from other women in education, usually administrators in other buildings. They are very insightful and knowledgeable. I would never have made it if it were not for these women.
>
> (Assistant Principal, Southern city)

Women in leadership positions have a unique opportunity to help other women achieve their career ambitions.

> I got interested in administration because I was *asked* to consider it by my principal. She recognized my ability to work with her and with the teachers. I began by merely helping her and now, because of her encouragement, I am working in administration.
>
> (Administrative Assistant, Southern metro)

> I helped the principal do a lot of administrative tasks, and she was very encouraging. She kept saying, "Go ahead and get your credentials."
>
> (Student, Western metro)

> My previous principal said she'd recommend me for a position. I realized she saw me as upwardly mobile and as having the ability to do the job. That gave me confidence to move ahead.
>
> (Administrative Intern, Western suburb)

Women who sit on school boards also have the opportunity to influence policies and practices that aid female aspirants. Although nearly eighty percent of the women in the study contend that school boards still prefer to hire male administrators, they feel differently about boards that include female members.

> Now I'm encouraged about administration because I see a difference in our new school board. Before, they didn't think of women as potential administrators. The new board, however, has women on it who ask questions about the number of women in administration and why there is such a predominance of men at the assistant principal level.
>
> (Assistant Principal, Southern suburb)

Another assistant principal (southern suburb) notes a similar change in her district: "Our superintendent said he would push for women when he was interviewing for his job. But that was probably because of the three women we now have sitting on the school board."

Regardless of the source—teachers, administrators or school board members—positive encouragement from other females mitigate the negative stereotypes and practices that female aspirants encounter. Such support from other women can tip the balance and send a signal to aspirants to "keep on trying."

> Women need to be encouraged to pursue administration sooner. They need to hear other women say: "You can do what you want to do. Don't let cultural expectations shape your future."
>
> (Assistant Principal, Northwestern town)

> Women should know administration isn't easy, but it's not so hard that they should be scared off either. A lot of the scariness is all in the mind. Women need to be told they can do it.
>
> (New Assistant Principal, Northwestern town)

### Working under Pressure

Women already working in entry-level administrative positions realize that paving the way for other female aspirants is not easy work. These women know that they must continually prove themselves in the administrative arena and that gender issues often interfere with their work.

> Women still have to struggle with community acceptance. In my first year as an assistant principal, I constantly had to prove that I was capable of controlling students. Often high school students and parents cannot adjust to the fact that a woman is in charge. When parents come in for a suspension hearing, you can see the shock on their faces when they see a female assistant principal. If I were to go to a new school, I am certain I would have to prove myself all over again.
>
> (Assistant Principal, Northeastern metro)

> When I applied for this position, thirteen men were also candidates. After I was hired, a lot of negative things were said about the decision of filling the position with a woman. Now I constantly feel that I have to disprove those statements.
>
> (Supervisor, Southern rural)

> Along with another new female administrator, I was served with a discipline grievance. When the grievance went to the school board, one of the female board members asked the teachers' union rep: "Does the fact that this happens to be two new *female* administrators have anything to do with why this grievance is before us today?" This turkey

turns around and says, "Yes." The board member was floored; she couldn't believe he said that. But then, women are tested a lot around here.

(Assistant Principal, Northeastern metro)

Women have to prove themselves more than men. I have always had to do a little bit more than the next guy. Most men seem to feel a male's ideas are more valuable than a female's; therefore, women have to have well thought out reasoning, where a man's answer is just accepted. I think that bias is one of the hardest battles I fight.

(Lead Teacher, Southern suburb)

I think women administrators have to prove themselves by being even more competent than men. I know I was faced with some things a man would never face. I've been tested a lot, but I think people believe I am capable now.

(Assistant Principal, Northeastern metro)

Some admit they are troubled by this constant pressure, while others once again use humor to deflect the stress they experience. Regardless of their coping styles, female aspirants desire the same chances that are afforded to male administrators.

We share equally in everything here, including all the extra-curricular activities. I get out there like everyone else, and I wouldn't want it otherwise. I would resent them saying, "It's too cold for a lady to be out tonight." Unless you're sick in bed, you should do the job.

(Assistant Principal, Southeastern town)

Despite their desire to be treated equally, many women know from first hand experience that they must be prepared for unexpected situations where their gender may become an issue. One assistant principal recalls a particularly trying day when her principal left her in charge of the building:

A worker accidentally broke the glass on the fire alarm. I remember one man in the cafeteria saying, "Why would that dumb woman have a fire drill now?" I replied, "That dumb woman is not having a drill; it may be the real thing." I went on to write it up as my fire drill for the month, but that man has never looked me in the eye again.

(Southeastern town)

Not only must female administrators deal with added tensions because of their gender, they must also perform exceptionally well while under that pressure if they hope to advance in the field. First or lone women in school districts may experience even added pressure:

When I first came to this job, one man said flatly that he couldn't take orders from a woman. Whenever I say something, he still goes to the director to see what *he* says. That hits me hard. It's difficult being the first women in this position.

(Supervisor, Southern rural)

I'm nervous about being the first woman in this district. Already I notice eyebrows going up when I am introduced at meetings. I know people will be watching to see how I do, and I'm scared. I want to do a good job so it will be easier for other women to get into administration. I know it will be hard work, but I also know I can do it.

(New Assistant Principal, Northwestern town)

A minority female assistant principal expresses similar concerns about being so closely watched:

When I came into this district, I really felt they were testing me. As a black woman, I'm sure everyone was watching to see how I would fare. At a PTA meeting, the principal didn't even introduce me because he thought the community wasn't "ready" for me. But I believe that's their problem, not mine. You must have a positive self-concept to be in that kind of situation, or you won't last. I felt good about myself and my qualifications, so I didn't let the waiting bother me. I went along with my daily work as if they weren't watching, and I didn't trip up as they might have expected.

(Southern metro)

Another minority women comments on her experience:

When I got this position, people would come around to just look at me. The secretary and the female teachers had never worked with a woman before, and it made me nervous. With all that attention, you feel you're under the microscope. But eventually they learn you don't have two heads, and you can go about your business.

(Assistant Principal, Midwestern suburb)

Although one new assistant principal (northwestern town) senses "people watching me a bit," she believes that people seem to appreciate her as she is. Another assistant principal finds support from the people in the community—despite of the fact that women at the secondary level are still a rarity:

When I went out to open a new bank account, people said, "Aren't you the new lady principal?" I feel good when I meet the parents in this small community.

(Southeastern town)

Many women seem motivated by their ability to change people's
minds about the appropriateness of women managers. Although they
dislike being in the spotlight, especially when the scrutiny of others is not
related to job performance, these women feel they have much to
contribute.

> We have opened peoples' eyes here, because women are making good
> strides in administration. That's not to say we haven't been under close
> scrutiny, because we have. All females in administration are. We just
> know we have to perform better to change people's minds.
>
> (Assistant Principal, Southern metro)

But even when women are successful in administrative positions, there is a
fear that women's accomplishments will be played down.

> One female principal started to turn a very rough school around in our
> district with no support from the administrators or the community.
> She had to rely solely on her own expertise and that of her teachers.
> But only in closed circles is she ever given any credit for her
> achievements, and then people just say, "Yeah, she's OK."
>
> (Teacher, Northeastern metro)

If women fail to meet the expectations of others, however, the news travels
fast and is hard to put to rest. Given these circumstances, perhaps the
informants are correct in worrying how their own personal performances
may affect other women in the field. When a first or lone woman does a
poor job, the repercussions can be far-reaching, as a teacher notes:

> I desperately want the job as assistant principal at this school. Because
> I know the students, the teachers and the parents from when I was the
> acting assistant principal, I know the job would be great. But I've
> heard through the grapevine that they probably won't hire me, because
> they say the district isn't going to hire any more women. We only have
> two women out of fourteen administrators, but while one is doing an
> excellent job, the other is not. I really believe her poor performance is
> influencing everyone to say, "God, we don't need another woman."
>
> (Teacher, Midwestern town)

Because women believe that they must be so careful about what they
do on the job, many think they have to play games or be political in order
to advance in school management.

> When I make out an application, I purposely put down all my years as
> a coach even though it was years ago. That's what they want to hear

when they hire a male, so that's what I tell them. My husband laughs, but I play the game.

(Specialist, Northwestern rural)

Even once they attain administrative posts, some women still feel they need to continue the façade just to fit in—particularly with male colleagues. An older woman explains her strategy:

I can be brassy and pushy if I need to be, but with male administrators, I put on a different front. I know how to react to them, and I handle their egos *very* carefully. I think I was hired for this position because my principal thought I "knew my place," as most men would put it. For example, I always talked with him before I did anything out of the ordinary, and I never ran over anyone to get their job. After six months in this position, the three men I work with are finally at the point of being open with me. I had to hang around them at first, but now I am a part of them. I joke with them, and we get along. I still have to coddle them, but that's just a survival tactic we women learn from day one in administration. By handling them this way, I believe I will end up on the top when I finish my career.

(Assistant Principal, Southern metro)

Some resent this game playing on the part of other women and wonder how it might affect their own aspirations. An assistant principal shares her perspective:

Sometimes I look around at other female assistants, and I see they are still playing their female games. They play coy and don't seem to take themselves seriously. I wish they would just come out and be competent. They are falling into the trap of being females first, instead of being people.

(Western metro)

She also believes these women have little empathy or understanding of those who choose "to go by the book" or who are experiencing problems trying to advance in the field. But younger or more successful aspirants who use gaming techniques believe they are justified, given the hiring bias in school management. They assert such games will probably disappear when competence and qualifications—not gender—become the main criteria for selecting educational leaders. Until such time, however, the few who feel compelled to play the game believe they have little choice.

*Summary*

Given the history of hiring in administration, female aspirants remain at a disadvantage. The gains have been small and slow to accrue, and there is nothing in recent hiring statistics to indicate this trend will change in the near future. Although more women are in the workplace than in the past, the administrative ranks of most professions remain predominantly male. Furthermore, women who achieve administrative positions continue to have problems on the job, not only with their male colleagues, but with female peers as well. As Goodman writes: "Many of us calculated, or hoped, that when women formed a critical mass in the work force, things would finally change. We now have this megageneration. Many are trying to have it all by doing it all themselves. Others are struggling to keep their heads above water. Still others are burning out."[22] Although some doors in educational administration (assistant principalships, for example) are beginning to open, others (such as high school principalships and superintendencies) remain stubbornly closed. Despite what some aspirants may hope, the time is *not* necessarily "right for women in administration." The "massive change" Goodman and others envisioned has not occurred, and women must consider these realities before launching an administrative career. If they fail to do so, they risk suffering what Goodman refers to as "massive disappointment."

# 9    Men in Administration

Men have pushed me all the way, so I have
nothing but good things to say about them.
I've had black men and white men helping
me, and that's a plus. They were the ones
who got me where I am today.

(District Staff, Western metro)

When I started to think about going back to
school, I realized that I had subconsciously
been looking at all these incompetent male
administrators whom I had worked for. And
I thought to myself: Heck, if they can do it,
why can't I? I certainly believe I can do a
better job than they're doing.

(Teacher-Administrator,
Midwestern suburb)

AS NOTED EARLIER, female aspirants experience difficulty finding
role models and mentors in educational administration. With so few
women in the field, this important function typically falls to men, if to
anyone. In terms of their competence and their support for women, two
distinct views of current male administrators emerge. One group of
aspirants hold their male colleagues in high esteem and find their job
performance excellent. These women praise male administrators who are
willing and able to further women's careers. A second group of aspirants,
however, adamantly disagrees. These women criticize the abilities of male
administrators and find themselves motivated to enter the field because of
their perceived inadequacies. Because of their negative opinions about
male managers, women in this latter group often find themselves at a
disadvantage when they try to move up the administrative career ladder.

## Able Male Colleagues

Women in this study who have positive experiences with their nearly all-
male colleagues speak highly of the encouragement and support they
receive.

At the county and district level, I believe men are very open to working with women. Often I've worked with all male administrators or have been one of two women in a district. Nevertheless, I have felt an openness from those male administrators.

(New Assistant Principal, Northwestern city)

There are only 2,000 people in this town, but unlike other communities I hear about, I don't believe men have been a hindrance to women here. These people are open to women, at least at the elementary level where I am.

(Part-time Administrator, Midwestern rural)

Some women realize this more favorable climate towards female administrators is relatively new. In many cases, they attribute recent changes in male attitudes to the women's movement and to recent equity legislation.

Men in our district are now more sensitive to the needs of women in administrative positions. Some know deep down that administration is not just a man's job and that women can do equally well given the chance.

(Assistant Principal, Southeastern town)

My principal knows the issues women face when seeking management positions because his wife just completed her Ph.D. in administration. She says five years ago her husband wouldn't have hired me, because he thought administrators should be males. Last year, he decided he definitely wanted a female assistant principal.

(Assistant Principal, Southern metro)

Some men find it difficult to alter their long-held beliefs about female administrators; however, women appreciate the efforts of those men who earnestly try to change their perceptions about women's management abilities. One lead teacher (southern metro) appreciates her principal's attempts to change discriminatory hiring practices in the school: "I know deep down in his heart he is finding change hard, but he's really trying."

Because of the efforts of men like this, many aspirants sense a new openness towards women seeking school management positions. Although hiring statistics fail to document their optimism, many feel it is only a matter of time before genuine change will occur. Throughout the country, female aspirants admit they might never have considered administration except for the encouragement of those male colleagues who are changing their attitudes about women.

When I first began teaching, my principal said he wanted me to go into administration. I said, "Hold it a minute, sir! I haven't even taught a full year yet!" But he kept pushing and pushing. He's the one who started me thinking about school management.

(Assistant Principal, Western metro)

Because the director of the program was very interested in my leadership abilities and potential, he recommended me for a higher position. I didn't get the job, but he planted the seed in my mind that I could be part of something more.

(District Planner, Southern metro)

My principal said. "Our assistant principal is retiring. Have you ever thought of administration? I think you would do well in that position." I was very happy in the classroom. My husband laughed when I mentioned it, but only because he thought I wouldn't be happy unless I was teaching. When I got the assistant principalship, he stopped laughing.

(New Principal, Southeastern town)

They needed curriculum specialists in our district, and my assistant principal asked me if I was going to apply for one. I said, "No, I can't do that job." He said, "Who do you think is going to get those jobs? Teachers who can do what you can do!" After I landed the position, I went through a mental transformation from "Can I?" to "I Can!"

(District Advisor, Northeastern metro)

Male administrators who actively teach female aspirants about the everyday details of school administration provide invaluable assistance— the kind of help that goes beyond just giving verbal encouragement.

You know, that's not God sitting up there in the principal's office: He's just a good and fair man who allows me to try my wings even when he disagrees with me. He let's me *try*, and that really does help.

(Teacher, Southern suburb)

I worked with male administrators in the past who didn't mind teaching me their jobs. When work got hectic and they needed help, they said, "Come on!" I liked their attitude when they said things like: "We need you to help," "You better learn this," and "You never know when you might need to know this." As a result, I had experience in most of the things I do in this job.

(Assistant Principal, Southern metro)

Male administrators, who verbally encourage female aspirants but who are unwilling to let them take over the actual tasks of administration, limit aspirants' abilities to prepare for leadership roles. Recognizing the risks that male administrators take when delegating tasks to female aspirants, women give a great deal of credit to the men willing to do so. In this study, encouragement from other administrators (presumably mostly men, given how few women are in the field) was the fourth highest motivating factor for those considering administrative careers. Likewise, in a 1976 study of Philadelphia's practicing administrators, the forty-four women in that study ranked the encouragement received from other administrators as the key reason they became interested in educational administration.[1]

### Inadequate Male Colleagues

Not all women experience such positive and supportive encounters with their male managers. To this group of women, male administrators often appear to have insufficient professional background and are generally poor leaders. "I would say the incompetence I see has been entirely among the male administrators in the field," notes one assistant principal (northeastern suburb). A team leader in another district in the same region agrees: "The high schools have very ineffective administrators, and when you're talking about high schools in this city, you're *not* talking about females." The emotions women report about such male incompetence range from pity and embarrassment to anger:

> There are many stultifying people—mostly males—who go through the motions of getting administrative certification or even an Ed.D. They aren't even successful human beings, much less successful teachers. And they end up horrible administrators! Believe me, I have encountered too many of these principals in my years of experience.
> (Teacher, Southeastern city)

> I know some assistant principals who are just collecting their money and not doing their jobs. I'm embarrassed at the poor name they give to the rest of us. I encounter more incompetence in men than in women.
> (Acting Assistant Principal, Southern metro)

With opinions such as these, many women believe they can do a better job of administering schools than their male colleagues.

> Women have an interesting ability to balance responsiveness with organizational planning. I seldom find this quality in men; the climate in their buildings is entirely different from what you'd find in a school run by a woman. We have some very strong, even exceptional, women in this district—especially in comparison to their male counterparts.
> (Assistant Principal, Southern city)

> I believe women generally make better leaders than men. Men always

seem to set their sights on future positions, rather than concentrating on the job they have.

(District Advisor, Northeastern metro)

Women often *are* the best "men" for the job: they follow through, they are basically workaholics, and they don't tire on the job. Women bring more enthusiasm and energy to the job than do men. They'll go the second and third mile, while men consider administration a nine to five job, except when they attend evening athletic events. Basically, all the principals I have worked for—and they were all male—think that athletics is the most important part of schools.

(Assistant Principal, Southern suburb)

According to a number of women in this study, preoccupation with sports is one of the major failings of male administrators.

Most men who try to move into elementary and junior high administration have secondary coaching backgrounds. That just doesn't work because an altogether different approach is needed at these levels.

(New Principal, Midwestern suburb)

I burn up when I see a male coach two years younger than me moved through an elementary position to a secondary principalship. I'm not the hating kind, but I get angry knowing the struggle I'll face as a woman—even with my doctorate!

(Student, Southeastern city)

Halfway through one administrative interview, I realized I didn't have a chance of getting the job; the only one who had a chance was the man they hired. He was a PE teacher, and how many principals are former PE teachers? About ninety-nine percent of them!

(Teacher, Midwestern rural)

Female aspirants, among others, do not believe expertise in physical education sufficiently prepares someone for administration. Moreover, several women in the study with backgrounds in athletics find that this questionable qualification works differentially for them. An assistant principal (western metro) muses: "I worked summers on the playground and not many women have that background. Still, all the men I worked with on the playground were made principals, and I was bypassed."

Athletic experience aside, many aspirants contend that male administrators in their districts are less qualified for their positions than some women.

I've had to work for men that didn't have my qualifications or education. For example, you might mention someone's educational or administrative theory, and they've never heard of it. They could read and keep up like I do, but no, they're just automatically moved up because they're male. I don't mind working with someone qualified, but . . . .

(Counselor, Northwestern city)

Rural women, in particular, report being frustrated because disctricts continually alter job requirements to place male candidates. A student states:

No one in our district has administrative certification—not even the superintendent. None of the men are even close to getting certified. In rural areas, rules are bent, and districts hire who they want—males, of course.

(Northwestern rural)

Women's frustrations about the limited abilities and backgrounds of some male leaders increase when many of these weak principals must depend on the strong women in their buildings to manage the schools. One assistant principal (northeastern metro) remarks: "People in the schools joke about the fact that men have the positions, but women run the schools." Most women, nevertheless, willingly accept whatever administrative opportunities come their way—even if they end up managing someone else's school.

My principal is awkward in his job. He is so overwhelmed that he has given me many opportunities to do administrative tasks. Although he relied on me to keep the school going, I'm grateful for those experiences now that I am to get my own building.

(Newly Hired Principal, Northwestern metro)

Other women, however, resent having to do the work of their male superiors and feel exploited when forced to do so:

My principal had something wrong with his eyes, so I did his work *and* mine. He showed up when he felt like it, while I travelled between two schools getting only a teacher's salary. But at the time, I was a newly divorced mother of three and had a grandmother to look after as well. I needed the job, and I needed the experience. Because I knew how difficult things were for women without experience, I had no choice but to go on.

(Assistant Principal, Western metro)

I have no respect for the man I now work for, and I no longer want to put in the extra effort to make him look good. I don't like being the woman behind the throne, so to speak. I covered for him before he was promoted, but I won't do it again.

(Assistant Principal, Northeastern metro)

I worked for a principal who was absent much of the time. I decided I would be the one in charge because *somebody* had to run the school. So I ended up doing his work on top of mine—before, after and during school.

(Assistant Principal, Southern metro)

One new principal (western metro) sums up these feelings: "I didn't mind being second-in-command when I was an assistant principal, except when the leadership was lacking." But another district coordinator worries about the women who do the work of their male bosses:

I see a number of young, bright women getting pulled into the office to assist male principals. They can get stuck there for as long as ten years. I think they are being exploited, and they need to become aware of it.

(Western metro)

Women who accept added responsibilities to gain administrative experience feel betrayed when districts pass them over for new leadership positions.

When the administration found out I had good clerical skills, they asked me to work in the assistant principal's office a couple of hours a day. I was thorough and conscientious, and was willing to give up a lot of free time for the experience. When the head counselor went on leave, the district hired this old timer—a nice man—to fill in rather than asking me. And then they pulled *me* in to assist him! I always felt I was doing a good job, because they kept expanding my hours and responsibilities. But others around me were placed as assistant principals and principals, and I wasn't given a chance.

(Assistant Principal, Western suburb)

Women who assume the administrative responsibilities of their male colleagues frequently find the experience a catalyst for seeking management positions themselves:

The principal used to hide in the office: He didn't talk to parents, he didn't talk to teachers. I started thinking about the impact his behavior was having on students who would be running the country sometime. I knew there had to be a better way to run a school.

(Team Leader, Northeastern suburb)

I worked for a horrible, horrible principal, and that was the turning
point in my career. I had to do everything for him. In return, I got
patronizing encouragement, but only because he wanted me to take
over as much of his work as possible. That's when I decided to get my
degree and pursue administration.

(Student, Southeastern city)

We had a change in principals, and we got a very weak one. Through
all of our problems with him, I began to think about administration
myself. I thought if he could do it, I could do it.

(Assistant Principal, Midwestern suburb)

I'd like to work with a principal who could teach me. The one I worked
for taught me what *not* to do. If he taught me anything, it was that I
could do the job better than he could. I believe I know enough to be a
principal *right now*.

(Assistant Principal, Southern city)

Women who work for weak male administrators not only lack the
guidance and support that a mentor provides but often find their
aspirations undermined by the very men they have supported in the past.

One reason I didn't get the new job was because my principal was very
dependent on me. This fact was known throughout the system. He was
ineffective and inefficient; consequently, he appreciated everything I
did. Because of his dependency, he opposed my leaving and spoke with
the other principal who had invited me to apply.

(Assistant Principal, Northeastern town)

I was discouraged with my principal because he got a lot of acclaim for
something we teachers wrote for him. When the time came to rewrite
the work, he didn't like the questions I asked and told me to look for
work elsewhere.

(Teacher, Northwestern city)

Sometimes women feel undermined before they even begin their administrative duties, as this assistant principal relates:

I was transferred to an inner city school to work for a blatantly sexist
and racist principal. He greeted me with the words: "We don't want a
white woman in this school! Why don't you tell them down at central
office that you can't make it here?" Now there I was, a woman who
wants to be a principal and who is slowly and methodically building
towards that goal. I knew full well that my future advancement
depended on his recommendation, and I felt doomed. I underwent

constant harassment to quit, but I hung on for a year before I asked for a transfer. I didn't leave sooner because I didn't want to risk a notation on my record that would say: "Couldn't get along with the principal."
(Western suburb)

Some men, who verbally support women's aspirations, fail to provide the practical job experiences that women need to move forward in the field. Whether consciously or unconsciously, their failure jeopardizes the advancement of women as much as those men who are openly hostile to women's career goals. An assistant principal explains:

My principal is very supportive on one hand, but he will not delegate major things like budgeting and teacher evaluations—experiences I need to move on in administration. I've made several attempts to suggest sitting in on evaluations, for example, but I think he's afraid to give up that authority. Without experience with budgets and teachers, my career will be at a standstill.
(Southern metro)

Women who work for male administrators that fail to teach and support them frequently report feeling angry and disappointed.

The assistant principal I work with just laughs when I ask him to show me how to fix something mechanical. He says I'm better off not knowing because I can get someone else to do the job for me. But men do those things, and I might be expected to do the same sometime. I felt put down and angry at his response.
(Teacher-Administrator, Midwestern suburb)

My principal disappointed me when he didn't let me know about this opening. He pushed me toward management all the time, telling me I had the potential. And yet, the whole summer I was away in school, he never let me know there was a job available. I applied on the last day only because I came home a week early and, by chance, read about it in the paper. I still need to talk with him about my feelings.
(Supervisor, Southern rural)

Other women describe similar situations of "benign neglect." An assistant principal (southern metro) states: "My principal knows I want my own school, and I don't think he would do anything to stop me. But I haven't gotten any encouragement either." A student provides another example:

I've mentioned my interest in administration to my principal, and although he said I could do a good job, he hasn't done anything in particular to help me. When he is gone, he always gets the PE teacher

to fill in, despite knowing of my interest and desire to gain experience.
(Northwestern city)

As Adkison concludes: "Stereotypes held by male administrators may
affect their receptivity to the efforts of female aspirants to get their
attention and sponsorship."[2]

*Underlying Tensions*

Whether praising the competency and the support of male administrators,
or decrying their inadequacies and lack of encouragement, female
aspirants realize the complexities of male/female relationships in educational administration. Why, for example, do apparently supportive male
administrators sometimes forget to nominate female candidates for
leadership openings? Or, why do other male administrators show open
contempt for women aspiring in the field? One reason, aspirants suggest, is
that many males still feel that women cannot do administrative work and,
consequently, will not consider them as viable candidates for management
positions.

> My principal was not encouraging when I told him I wanted to be an
> administrator. He doesn't think a woman could do the job as well as a
> man. He said, "Go ahead, but I don't think your trying will do much
> good."
>
> (Department Chair, Southern rural)

> My current principal doesn't like women in administration, or in any
> positions of authority for that matter. When I was hired, he made it
> known that he was very disappointed that the district selected a
> woman counselor for his building. He still calls the other counselor (a
> male) before he'll call me. His bias gets to me.
>
> (Counselor, Midwestern suburb)

> My principal suggested I go back to school in English, but I told him I
> wanted to go back in administration. He told me he didn't approve of
> women in administration, but thought I could handle it better than
> any woman he knew. He then suggested curriculum and instruction to
> me, but I didn't want a degree in that "female" area. He said, "You
> can't be a principal because your mother and daddy didn't raise you to
> be like that." He was trying to do his best to help, but he is so
> conditioned by his own upbringing.
>
> (Teacher-Intern, Southern suburb)

Sometimes the lack of acceptance of females in leadership roles stems from
age bias, especially against younger women:

I never got any feedback from my principal. He did not work well with women. He only had one other woman on staff—a sixty-year-old grandmother who he turned to for advice. He didn't know how to deal with me because I was too young and aggressive.

(Teacher-Administrator, Midwestern suburb)

The bias against female administrators in this district comes largely from older males. They don't like the possibility that they may have a younger female boss telling them what to do. They would take orders from a man, but not from a woman.

(Teacher, Midwestern city)

In addition to feeling that females are unsuited for administration because of gender and possibly age, aspirants report that a second reason male administrators react as they do is because they feel threatened by women seeking leadership roles. Some acknowledge their feelings of vulnerability openly, others deal with their insecurities in a less direct fashion. Both approaches have the same result, as these two assistant principals describe:

I interviewed for one assistant principalship, but didn't get the job. The man said, "You should know why I didn't hire you. First, you aren't from our district, so it would be politically unwise. Second, you are more competent than I am, and you should be a principal not an assistant."

(Southern city)

In this case, the woman respected the man's honesty, even though she was not hired. The second assistant principal provides an example of a man who was not so open about his insecurities:

A male prinicipal presented this poem to intimidate me in front of the staff:

A gal at college named Ms. Breeze,
Was weighed down by MAs and Ph.D.s.
She collapsed from the strain,
Said her doctor, "It's plain,
You are killing yourself by degrees."

I was working on my doctorate, and he was uneasy about the fact that I was as smart or smarter than he. This is the kind of thing women have to go through.

(Western metro)

Although most women speak of making concerted efforts to assuage the fears of their male peers, some eventually leave a building to escape from having to deal with what they term "fragile male egos."

> In the spring, my principal admitted he tried to undermine my influence with teachers. He thought I had been given too much authority by the previous principal. At that point I began to think it was a good time for me to go back to school and to finish my degree.
>                                          (Teacher-Administrator, Midwestern suburb)

> More than anything else, my principal influenced my decision to go back to school for administrative credentials. He was an aggravating individual who kept challenging me by saying, "You don't really understand; you're not an administrator." I went for my credentials because I wanted to show him I *did* know. So many times the counselors would settle a problem and just let him *think* he had done something wonderful. He might have had administrative knowledge, but he couldn't handle staff and parents. During my practicum with him, I did three times the necessary work. I finally had enough of his nonsense and went to another district.
>                                                      (Specialist, Midwestern suburb)

After both of these women moved to different schools, they began receiving male administrative support for their career choices—suggesting that their former bosses do not represent the attitudes of all male administrators.

### The Male Legacy

Whether male administrators promote or discourage the aspirations of women, the respondents agree that school administration remains a solidly male domain. "Men have filled all the slots throughout administration," claims a supervisor (northwestern town). A lead teacher (southern metro) concurs: "The positions in administration are predominantly filled with men these days." Another lead teacher concludes:

> Women have to be head and shoulders above other candidates to get hired. When you look at the caliber of men who apply for jobs and get them, you sort of shake you head and say, "My God." There are four or five women—black or white—who could do a better job, but they will never be given the chance because it's a male-dominated field.
>                                                            (Northeastern suburb)

In a profession employing so many females, the preponderance of male administrators is remarkable.[3] Instead of hiring competent individuals of either sex, the main selection criteria appears to be masculinity. Carlson described the typical administrator in 1972 as a white, married, Protestant, Republican male.[4] A student (southeastern city) in this study gives her candid portrait: "I see today's public school administrator as an over-weight coach with an IQ of ninety-five, wearing a polyester suit and patent leather shoes, and with a slight tan from a lot of golf." Physical stereotypes aside, female aspirants recognize that men do advance more easily and rapidly in the field. An assistant principal (western metro) concludes: "Men make strides in the field more quickly than women. Practically all of the men I went to school with are now superintendents, and they weren't that bright."

Concomitant with their dominance in administration, men also exert the greatest influence over hiring practices. Because men persist to hire other men for administrative positions, female aspirants find few oppor-tunities to achieve their career goals.

> Basically men are always going to stick together, whatever their differences. When our superintendent moved, he left some recom-mendations for filling different positions. We felt he was thinking: "I have to take care of my buddies who are all males." If a minority person does get promoted, that person will be a male as well. The essential message is to stick with males.
>
> (Teacher, Northeastern metro)

Even with greater and greater numbers of women holding administrative certification, the pattern of men hiring men—the "old boys' network"—continues to flourish throughout the nation. An acting assistant principal explains hiring patterns in her district:

> Do you wonder how some of those principals got there? Well, we have a reputation for hiring football coaches—the good old boys' syndrome is alive and well here. When one gets in, all of his buddies come in, too.
>
> (Southern metro)

"Because very few women are practicing administrators or in a position to hire others," Stockard argues, "they are not part of . . . the informal web of contacts that practicing administrators use to recommend people for jobs and to promote themselves and their friends."[5] Some women admit they would not be as frustrated with this system if it didn't seem to reward incompetence so often. They realize administrative jobs go to people who are well-connected; they would just like to insure those well-connected individuals are also qualified and competent.

> A lot of the professionals here have gotten in like men always have: by the buddy system rather than by their qualifications. I'm not saying connections are bad. In fact, if I said I made it here on my own, I'd be

lying. People had faith in me, but I also had the skills.

(New Principal, Western metro)

When districts begin to stress "who you are" not "who you know," female aspirants believe the male legacy will cease to be as influential and women will become viable—even sought after—administrative candidates.

### Summary

Until the issue of gender in school administration becomes archaic, female aspirants will continue to face difficulty in achieving their goals. Although some women benefit from male encouragement and attempt to advance in the field through established male networks, others lack that sponsorship and must create their own compensating support systems. Whether accomplished or incompetent, male administrators continue to dominate school management, and because of this, they will continue to influence female aspirants in either positive or negative ways. When aspiring to positions of public school leadership, therefore, aspirants should carefully assess their own relationships with and perceptions of incumbent male administrators.

# Part Three _____

# Special Concerns

# 10    Affirmative Action

> I didn't go into administration because it's a man's or a woman's job. I'm a liberal and a strong believer in affirmative action, but I never went overboard about women's issues. I figured if a woman was going to succeed, she would do so despite the odds. The challenge is there in this field, and women *are* going to make it. But I am amazed how sex figures into the hiring process: I never thought my gender would make such a difference.
>
> (Teacher-Administrator,
> Midwestern suburb)

AFTER YEARS OF WOMEN'S RIGHTS movements and a flurry of equal opportunity legislation in the 1960's and 1970's,[1] the implementation of affirmative action programs promised women and minorities new opportunities to gain leadership positions in education. By requiring federally-funded programs to initiate affirmative action plans, the U.S. Department of Labor formally recognized in its regulations that "procedures without effort to make them work are meaningless; and effort, undirected by specific and meaningful procedures, is inadequate."[2] As a result, school districts had specific written guidelines to aid them in determining who was "underutilized" in their work force. Terms such as "affected class" and "corrective action" became part of the lexicon— whether willingly or not—of those responsible for hiring school personnel. The federal regulations exhorted school superintendents and others "to increase materially the utilization of minorities and women, at all levels and in all segments of [the] work force where deficiencies exist."[3] In education, affirmative action criteria pointed to the obvious: Women and minorities lacked access to top managerial positions in public schools. In such a promising context, many people throughout the nation expected affirmative action programs would permanently reverse discriminatory hiring practices and would insure equal opportunities for women and minorities in school administration.

161

Although few people would deny that Title IX brought about significant changes for female and minority students, the expected results for female administrative aspirants are far less apparent. The anticipated surge in numbers of female and minority administrators failed to materialize during the ten years since the last piece of consequential legislation was passed. Kanter notes that the promise of opportunity can be "seductive."[4] Would female educators in the 1970's and early 1980's fall prey to those promises, only to find them unfulfilled? According to the women in this study, the record of affirmative action remains mixed, and many unanswered questions remain.

When asked about *other* women's careers, seventy-four percent of the 142 respondents believe affirmative action will prove helpful; however, only forty-seven percent think the same programs will aid *their* careers. Conversely, nearly thirty percent believe that affirmative action will be of little or no help to them in furthering their administrative aspirations. When compared with women from other regions of the country, aspirants from the Northeast are most skeptical about the programs. For these women, the assurances of equity legislation contrast most sharply with the realities of the job market.

### Who Should Benefit?

In nearly every section of the country, respondents express confusion over the intended beneficiaries of affirmative action programs. Only in the Northwest, where fewer minorities reside, does the legislation clearly imply women. Informants in other areas, however, remain unsure whether such programs are designed for minority candidates—both male and female— or women alone. A student (southeastern city) notes, "Most affirmative action programs mean minorities here: The question is open about whether to include women in that category or not." Others report similar interpretations of the effects of the legislation:

> Affirmative action is definitely working for minorities—both male and female. For example, many Mexican-Americans have been promoted. But affirmative action is not helping white women.
> (New Assistant Principal, Southern metro)

> Minority women have done well in this district over the past few years. I believe affirmative action might be the reason.
> (District Staff, Western metro)

> A document came out yesterday pointing out that too many white people are being recommended for positions in this city. Here, affirmative action does not mean "women," it means "minorities."
> (Assistant Principal, Northeastern suburb)

Nonminority women are not the only ones confused about the intent of affirmative action. Several minority aspirants believe the legislation was expressly designed for females. Before receiving her principalship, one minority woman stated:

> If districts were real smart, they would fill a position with a qualified black woman and kill two birds with one stone. But that's not what's happened in my experience. Affirmative action means women here, not minorities.
>
> (Southeastern town)

In a reverse situation, a nonminority district planner describes her feelings about affirmative action:

> I was recommended for a position, but it went to a minority. If I had really pushed the district, I might have gotten the job. But I didn't question their choice and backed off. I didn't particularly like being on *that* end of affirmative action.
>
> (Southern metro)

Clearly, school districts interpret laws differently and adopt their own unique hiring practices to fit those interpretations. In a study of personnel hiring practices in Oregon, Schmuck and Wyant found that "despite an increase in formal laws and regulations affecting hiring, local school districts retain considerable discretion."[5] Although legislation and court rulings have altered the situation somewhat, they conclude, "it remains easy for school districts to avoid the letter and spirit of the law."[6]

### Districts under Fire

Although confusion exists in the minds of many women over who actually benefits from affirmative action in schools, most women in the study believe the *original* intent of the legislation was to aid female professionals in education. Without the force of law, many believe the field would never have begun to open up to female candidates. Some credit Title IX, while others point directly to affirmative action; however, all seem to agree that districts would not have changed on their own initiative. An intern (western metro) believes that Title IX is helping to change her district's implicit policy of "We don't hire women here." Likewise, an assistant principal (northwestern city) recalls how her district only had three female administrators out of thirty to thirty-five, and only one woman in sixteen buildings until affirmative action passed. "I know the district is feeling some pressure now," she states, "to at least seek some women in secondary administration." Another assistant principal (midwestern metro) agrees: "No one put the gun to their heads here, but I think they thought it might come soon. So why not go ahead and get with it?" Still others note that districts no longer feel free to rely so heavily on political connections when hiring school executives. "Because of affirmative action," a teacher (northeastern town) observes, "they have to be a little more attuned to equal opportunities."

Despite the desire to be recognized for their skills, many aspirants admit that equity legislation may be more important to their career success than their experience and ability.

> Women would never have moved so far in our district without the legislation; they probably wouldn't even have been considered. I grew up thinking that if I studied hard and prepared myself, someday my chance would come. But my career has not worked out that way. The main reason I am here is not because of the good jobs I've done, but because of Title IX. There's no doubt about it.
>
> (Lead Teacher, Southern metro)

A recently hired principal sums up recent results of equity legislation:

> Let's face it, affirmative action is a national policy. I'm certain that smart male administrators realized it was only a matter of time before the issue was pushed in administrative employment. So why wait? They finally *had* to be aware of the legal issues.
>
> (Southeastern city)

This belief—that districts would respond to legal pressure—contributes to the prevailing notion that the time is right for women to enter school management. Many women assume that districts now *must* let them into the field.

> Because of Title IX and affirmative action, I think there is a national trend to bring women into administration in *all* fields. That leads me to think it's a good time for women in educational administration.
>
> (New Assistant Principal, Northwestern city)

> After Title IX, people started talking to me about going into administration. They thought the field would open up for women.
>
> (Assistant Principal, Midwestern metro)

> I am one woman who obtained an assistant principalship because of affirmative action. The county felt they needed more women in administration, so I happened to fall into it at the right time.
>
> (Assistant Principal, Southern metro)

> Being a female in administration counts an awful lot in this county

right now. I would hate to get hired merely because of "the feds." I'd rather get the job because I'm a good administrator. But if the time is right, I'll take a position anyway I can get it.

(Teacher, Southern suburb)

A specialist sums up the optimism many women have about new opportunities in educational administration:

Well, let's face it. If you think you have a chance, you are much more apt to go for a position than when you feel it's a long shot. Affirmative action gives us that chance. It gives us the *feeling* that there is a good possibility our preparations will pay off. I think affirmative action made a big difference.

(Western suburb)

Most districts conduct their hiring processes differently since the advent of affirmative action. On paper at least, there is a new concern to include women and minorities in interviewing pools. As districts worry about federal intervention into areas once considered under the exclusive jurisdiction of school boards and administrators, the atmosphere around some districts becomes charged with feelings ranging from caution to fear.

Because of affirmative action, our superintendent is a little more cautious about getting women into administration. Our new personnel director seems to be hiring on the basis of job qualifications now, not just to get another male.

(Teacher, Northwestern town)

Our superintendent told my principal that we needed more women in administration, because the "civil rights people" will be looking in on the situation. We don't have any blacks or women in administration here.

(New Assistant Principal, Midwestern suburb)

There is some fear among the men in our district because of Title IX. I guess it takes some laws to break the ice and to begin talking about women having equal opportunities at the administrative level— especially in high schools.

(Counselor, Southern metro)

Although some women are pleased that districts must now "toe the line," many are frustrated at how individual districts manipulate the laws. Loosely written job descriptions, Schmuck and Wyant maintain, make it "difficult to monitor or prove discriminatory intent."[7] Other districts ignore the shortage of female administrators and merely focus on getting men into the elementary levels as teachers. Still other districts seem to think affirmative action just means interviewing women to fill quotas for "the feds." As a student (southeastern city) comments: "Affirmative action can get you an interview, but not necessarily a job. In other words, they know they must interview minorities, so they do." An assistant principal (western metro) observes: "They have the numbers of women on the lists, but the actual number hired remains low." In her extremely large district, for example, they only have four or five female principals at the *fifty-two* senior high schools.

For many women, the failure of affirmative action to increase their job opportunities results in frustration and anger. An assistant principal relates:

> From what I can determine unofficially, the hiring process we go through doesn't necessarily have any bearing on who is actually hired as an administrator. I keep getting feedback on how superior I am, but all the positions in the last four years were filled with men—white, black or younger. Some of them I had supervised, so I was upset.
>
> (Southern suburb)

Some aspirants resent being called for interviews, when they feel they are not being seriously considered for the job. A teacher expresses her dissatisfaction:

> Next time the affirmative action statement has to be filled out, I'm going to write "occasionally" where it says sex rather than "female." I've felt too often that districts just go through the motions of interviewing women to get a cross-section of candidates or a token woman. They already know who they want to hire. I don't like being just a woman to interview.
>
> (Northwestern city)

A specialist (western suburb) underscores the capricious manner in which affirmative action is administered in her district. "The drawbacks to the legislation," she claims, "are as numerous as the feelings of the people who are on the interviewing panel on any given day." A state department employee (northeastern suburb) concludes: "I don't think affirmative action hinders women, but I don't think it particularly helps them at the local level either."

Affirmative action programs frequently subject female administrators and aspirants to added pressures. A department chair notes:

> Because of affirmative action, there is now a perception that some women are hired who are not qualified for their jobs. When these particular women have any problems, they reflect badly on the rest of

us. People are left with a bad taste in their mouths about all women.
(Northwestern suburb)

An assistant principal (western metro) claims the idea that unqualified women are now being placed (whether it is true or not) puts undo pressure on other women in the field. Marshall argues: "Affirmative action implementation [in some instances] consists of simply shifting positions without regard to socialization, incentive, and support structures which prepare women for mobility in school administration."[8] Failing to aid women through this transition carefully, Marshall continues, defeats the intent of affirmative action and results in "discomfort and anxiety...so intense that they cannot succeed."[9] To reduce these added pressures, districts must implement affirmative action regulations by stressing competence, not quotas. An assistant principal states:

> I don't care if a person is male or female—black, white, pink or purple—they should be qualified. Although I don't think women have had the same opportunities that men have had, I think it's better to hire a qualified man than an unqualified woman. The latter just gives us a bad name.
>
> (Western metro)

In principle, many aspirants concur with this woman; however, they temper their agreement by pointing out how many qualified women get passed over in favor of unqualified men. With affirmative action now in effect, many hope that such hiring practices will cease.

*Legacies*

Aspirants differ in their assessments of the long-term effects of affirmative action. Although hiring statistics do not give rise to much optimism, some women continue to think positively.

> Ten years ago, I couldn't think of a single woman administrator. But now, legislation puts districts under the gun to search for women. We are still not bubbling over with women, but the prospects are good. In the past, we operated under the old boys' network. Today we are growing in size, and the district can't afford to work that way any longer. Our new deputy superintendent realizes this fact and is making changes to avoid a future law suit.
>
> (Student, Southern city)

We have more women in administration than five years ago. I guess affirmative action keeps people on their toes. They have to go through the motions of saying we have women and minorities, and that has an influence. Still, as a woman you have to be a superwoman to be considered, and that's unfortunate. I wonder how long it will take to get a woman into a regular high school principalship.

(Assistant Principal, Southeastern city)

The question of "how long?" is on many women's minds, and can be interpreted quite differently. One assistant principal (western metro) says, "Eventually, maybe younger women will reap some benefits from affirmative action." But as an older aspirant, she doesn't think she will. From a different perspective, a young student (northwestern city) queries: "The federal laws mandate women be given jobs today; but what about in five years when *I'm* ready?"

Aspirants express concern that what few gains have been made may be stripped away by subsequent legislation, or by a reordering of national priorities. Larwood and Lockheed, for example, maintain that affirmative action programs may "go the way of the dinosaur if they cannot be demonstrated to work successfully."[10] They note that government policy, economic pressure and public awareness—factors that initially stimulated equity legislation—can "vanish as rapidly as they developed." "The movement of women into nontraditional roles," they conclude, "can be reliably sustained only by the success of the women already in them."[11] Although McCarthy and Zent's recent study of forty-six school districts in six states reports some gains from affirmative action, they, too, recognize that declining enrollments and cut backs in federal funding could wipe out advances made in the previous decade.[12] Finally, aspirants in this study perceive the political and economic climate of the 1980s as unfavorable to affirmative action, and some believe that earlier gains are being reversed.

When districts realize they don't have to comply to get federal money, they won't. I think things will go back to the way they were: Women will have to be twice as good in order to get anything. It seems like they are doing away with affirmative action just at the time I am in a position to realize something from it.

(Teacher, Midwestern metro)

Because the government pushed equal opportunities, some of the people who didn't like the idea of women in administration are coming around to realizing the advantages of having women. The first battles have been fought, but now we're on a plateau because the country is on a more conservative swing. I doubt whether there will be any more movement for quite awhile.

(Lead Teacher, Southern metro)

Changes in the job market may significantly influence the final assessment of affirmative action programs. Some contend great potential for change exists, especially in districts where long-term administrators (typically males) will be retiring. Likewise, population growth among minorities may increase demands for minority administrators. At present, however, administrative opportunities in many regions of the country are limited for all aspirants—no matter what race or sex the candidate may be. A student observes:

> Finding jobs is tough all over—for men as well as for women. With all the equal rights talk, I think what jobs are available will be as available to women as they are to men. But a shrinking job market limits the advances of both sexes.
>
> (Southern town)

Even if times were better, a number of problems still exist in the administration of affirmative action plans. Schmuck and Wyant believe the program lacks specificity about redressing past inequities.[13] Harragan questions whether the programs were realistic in the first place: "An honest-to-God affirmative action program (which is daydreaming of the highest order) would have to leapfrog many female employees several supervisory levels before they reached an equal plane with men wherein the next promotion is a learning experience."[14] Finally, Adkison wonders if the legislation can overcome traditional hiring practices: "Despite charges in law and policy, educational organizations maintain . . . recruitment and hiring practices that exclude candidates outside their administrators' informal networks. Even when women's organizations made concerted efforts to identify openings and notify qualified women, traditional strategies favored men."[15] Only the passing of time will tell what the legacy of the equity legislation and regulations of the 1960s and the 1970s will be.

### Summary

Affirmative action heightened the expectations of women and minorities, and many believed that a new climate of opportunity would enhance their career aspirations. Perhaps these expectations explain, in part, why so many female aspirants believe that affirmative action is helping some women, if not themselves. On the other hand, as Adkison argues, "Federal, state, and local equal employment opportunity legislation and affirmative action policies may have had a greater impact on women's aspirations than on institutions."[16] To complicate matters, the existing equity legislation itself is fraught with many unresolved issues about fairness and justice. The long battle—begun with the drive for women's right to vote—is far from over. Although the laws mandating equal opportunity provided an impetus for change, Hennig and Jardim believe we are now in a second phase where "consolidation and disintegration of what has so far been achieved are both potential outcomes—and disintegration carries by far the higher costs."[17] They caution "laws alone will not ensure that women who aspire to careers in management—and who have the potential to be effective managers—will necessarily succeed," and that clearly much more needs to be done.[18] Noting that the current situation is far from ideal, an assistant principal concludes:

> As long as affirmative action is in the hands of those used to making all the decisions, they may hire more women, but their attitudes about women won't necessarily change. For example, some of the brightest women aren't the ones making it the fastest; they are too threatening to the powers that be. I don't know how you can significantly change these people.
>
> (Western suburb)

Perhaps the final test of affirmative action will be whether "these people" truly change their attitudes.

# 11   Minority Issues

You have to do special things to get hired as a minority candidate. I think that's unfair, but that's how it is. I felt some pressure after I interviewed for this job, because they didn't decide on the successful candidate right after the interviews were completed. Part of me wanted to say the hell with it! I didn't want to get the job because *they* decided I could do it or because I'm a minority. I don't want an assistant principal's position for any other reason than that I am the best candidate. But that's naive. You get the job for whatever the reasons are.

(Assistant Principal, Midwestern suburb)

## PART ONE: WHAT MINORITY WOMEN SAY

Apart from an occasional study, minority women in educational administration are rarely the focus of research.[1] Their small numbers may preclude thorough investigation for, in 1982, no category of minority women held larger than a two percent representation in any one school administrative position.[2] Despite their underrepresentation, minority females do aspire to administrative positions and the special concerns they face remain significant. If gender makes entry into educational administration problematic for all women, do minority women encounter unique problems when pursuing administrative careers? Jones and Montenegro contend that "whatever ground the white male group [in administration] does not claim is in large part obtained by white females."[3] Given these hiring priorities, do minority women believe they are in double jeopardy—being both females *and* minorities?

The national focus of this study made possible the inclusion of some minority aspirants; however, finding a large number proved difficult, especially in certain geographical areas such as the Northwest. Thirty-six minority women (twenty-seven blacks, seven Hispanics, one Asian and one American Indian) participated in the study, constituting roughly one

171

quarter of the total number of respondents. Small numbers and uneven distribution by group militated against any comparative analysis between different minority experiences. Clearly, such research is needed, but until more minority female aspirants are identified, such an undertaking is impossible. The views of these thirty-six informants, therefore, offer only a beginning picture of what it is like for minority women to aspire in educational administration.

To begin with, many women note that in the past race has had a negative effect on their career aspirations. In recent years, however, race appears to be less a barrier than it was earlier. "I'd say things are opening up for minority people," one minority assistant principal (southern metro) concludes. She hastens to add, "I wouldn't say wide open, but there is an opening now that was not there before." Like many other female aspirants in this study, would-be minority administrators sense the time is ripe and that leadership opportunities are increasing. Some aspirants report a new climate of encouragement from their administrative bosses:

> My superintendent was highly motivating and told me that I ought to consider something in administration given the skills I have. "Not only that," he said, "but there are not many Asian people applying for these positions. You really should think about school management."
>
> (New Principal, Western metro)

For many, this is the first time in their careers that race or ethnicity appears to work in their favor. They report improvements in both the quality of interviews and in the numbers of job offers they receive:

> Being a minority helped me get this job, I'm sure of that. It was a definite plus because they were involved in some busing and voluntary desegregation. I'm the only woman and the only black at the high school level in our district.
>
> (Assistant Principal, Midwestern suburb)

> Being a Mexican-American is helpful to me *now*—at least in getting me a job. Although no one ever said so, I know I got this position because of the large Mexican-American student population in the school.
>
> (Assistant Principal, Southern city)

> Once I was recruited for an assistant principalship by a man who said he wanted me at his school. He gave me support in a way I had never gotten before: recruiting me, asking my opinions, telling me he was glad I was there. I asked him if he was making a special effort to get black administrators at his school, and he said yes. That was OK with me.
>
> (District Staff, Northeastern metro)

*Affirmative Action*

Ongoing debates among minority researchers question the value of affirmative action programs. Contreras contends, for example, that recent recruitment of minorities is in part a direct consequence, not of legislative efforts, but of community pressure for racial and ethnic representation in schools largely comprised of minority students.[4] Ortiz, however, argues that the influx of minority administrators can be attributed to school districts that are concerned with controlling their diverse populations and, ultimately, with organizational welfare. She concludes: "The tendency has been to infer a connection between the community and the organization as long as minorities are hired by school districts . . . [based on the perception] that minorities must be visible in their minority group, control them, and thereby improve the organization's conditions."[5] Regardless of these explanations, those interviewed in this study believe that affirmative action, not community pressures or organizational welfare, largely accounts for the shift towards preferential treatment of minorities. Because of legislated mandates, minorities now report districts must consider race and ethnicity when hiring new administrators—a practice unheard of before affirmative action.

To be certain, these aspirants do not totally discount the explanations advanced by Contreras and Ortiz. In fact, several informants offer examples of the kind of community and organizational influences they report. One assistant principal (midwestern metro) believes she was hired because the school had a large Hispanic population and she had a Spanish surname (she is only half Hispanic, and speaks no Spanish). In a midwestern suburb, a black counselor believes her promotion to assistant principal was the direct result of a requirement to bus minority students to her school. Finally, when a district staff member (western metro) received an assistant principalship, she attributed her promotion to a "move to bring administrators into the district who could identify ethnically with the community." In the final analysis, however, most women believe their promotions were primarily governed by affirmative action—not by community and organizational concerns.

According to the respondents, some districts appear to take new federal regulations in stride, and move easily toward choosing minority candidates. "I think there's been a lot of consideration of race in the past years, but then our schools are eighty percent minority," explains one teacher (midwestern metro). The staff in her district is now fifty percent minority. An assistant principal relates a similar story:

I'm seeing a lot more blacks at the assistant positions in our county. They keep a racial balance with the population. Our school, however, is an exception. The student body is seventy-five percent white and twenty-five percent black, but we have a black principal. We have a super superintendent who believes in doing what is best for a school. When the previous principal died, he wanted to provide some continuity for the school. So he promoted internally, and the black man got the job.

(Southeastern city)

Ortiz would say this last example is definitely an exception and that most minorities are placed in schools with predominantly minority student populations.[6] Such assignments are self-serving management strategies, she alleges, and are not necessarily rewards for a minority's competence and prior accomplishments.[7]

Whatever the motivation for complying with affirmative action requirements, not all districts make a smooth transition. Some districts seem to comply only under the threat of losing their federal funding. One assistant principal (southern metro) notes that her board is open to anyone qualified, "especially now that they're under court order." Others describe similar problems in their districts:

Our district suddenly started getting some women in secondary administration because they were being investigated for alleged failure to follow federal guidelines as far as hiring Hispanics. They hired lots of blacks, but no Hispanics, and we hardly had any women. (They had female assistants to the principals, but that only means administrative responsibilities with a teacher's salary. You definitely don't gain seniority that way.) So they hired nine minority women at the beginning of the following year. Just "Poof!" From no women to nine!

(Assistant Principal, Midwestern metro)

My mentor said I probably qualified for an assistant principalship. Like other school districts, ours had been lily white for a long time, and they needed to integrate. I realized they needed me because I was black, as well as because of my qualifications. But that was OK, because I needed the job.

(District Staff, Northeastern metro)

## Double Bonus or Double Bind?

For whatever reasons, many women are ready and willing to move into districts now receptive to minority executives. They make no apologies for taking advantage of their new-found edge in hiring.

For so many years, my color worked against me. Now, my being black might be working in my favor. And I, for one, am not going to lose any sleep over the fact.

(Teacher, Northwestern metro)

An assistant principal (southern metro) contends minority women may even be benefiting from a double dose of preferential treatment—not a double bind—under affirmative action programs. Others in her region tend to agree:

> Some jobs were offered to me because I was a minority—both a female and a black. In other words, they could kill two birds with one stone. Our district is integrating all of the schools, and they need minorities at the assistant principal's level.
>
> (Assistant Principal, Southern metro)

> For awhile, the district was under a racial court order to bring in black administrators. So when I came in as an assistant principal, they got a triple minority: I'm over forty, black and female!
>
> (Assistant Principal, Southern metro)

Stockard postulates that hiring minority women "allows administrators to fill two affirmative action mandates [race and sex] at one time,"[8] and such a theory is borne out in the experiences of the women just quoted. Some minorities, however, resent obtaining positions merely on a racial or an ethnic basis. A district office member (western metro) claims, "When I was offered this position, the first thing they said was they needed me 'ethnically'; that was the *wrong* thing to say to me." Other minority aspirants also resent the implications of such statements:

> I *do* feel the pressure when people say, "Oh, you made it because you're Hispanic." I heard a lot of that when I became an assistant principal, and I really resented it. My ethnicity obviously hasn't helped me get a principalship!
>
> (Assistant Principal, Western suburb)

As these examples show, minority aspirants express different opinions about quotas and tokenism. Even though they know their minority status is useful in securing administrative employment, some believe—that once hired—their competencies will win over those who doubted their worth. In a southern town, a supervisor admits calling attention to *both* her minority statuses (female and Hispanic) to get into a position. "I have no qualms about getting in as a token, as long as they let me in to do what needs to be done." A teacher emphatically agrees:

> They may use me as a token, but once I'm a practicing administrator, they'll see I'm nobody's walking-around dummy. I know what I want, and I know how to do it. I want to tell the district: "Now just let me do it!"
>
> (Northwestern metro)

Likewise, another teacher states:

> With affirmative action operating, it might be a plus being female and
> black. But I hope they hire me for my qualifications, not for filling two
> quotas. But if that happens, it happens. You can't say, "I don't want
> the job if you are using me as a token."
>
> (Midwestern suburb)

These individuals believe their abilities will outweigh criticism about their
hiring. They believe if they fail to perform, they will not be promoted
further. "In all fairness," an assistant principal (southern metro) states,
"color helped me get this job, but further promotions will depend on my
record." Epstein finds similar sentiments in her study of black professional
women, who believe they deserve whatever benefits they can derive from
the recent emphasis on having women and blacks in hospitals, corpora-
tions and schools. "Some recognized they were useful because an employer
could kill two birds with one stone. One said pithily: 'I'm a show woman
and a show nigger, all for one salary.' "[9]
    Some women, however, remain uncomfortable with the trade offs, as
an assistant principal explains:

> Many times I was offered jobs because I could fill the bill in two
> areas—it was not because of my expertise. Because of my color, I was
> suddenly a prize catch. I'm very reluctant to take a job where I know I
> am just going to be a show piece and be introduced as "our resident
> female and black." Frankly, I don't seriously consider those offers. I
> need the extra money of an administrator, but money isn't everything.
>
> (Southern metro)

Another assistant principal (southern metro) states: "I feel strongly that no
woman or black ought to be put in a position simply because of gender or
race." She believes, "they ought to be qualified and certified." Ortiz argues
that minority women are right to be cautious, because many of these
positions have a temporary feel about them. Those who gain their jobs
under such circumstances, she argues, "may not seem as indispensable
after the difficulty has been settled."[10] Although Ortiz refers to schools in
trouble, the same caution may also apply to schools fully complying with
federal mandates.
    While some minority aspirants have the opportunity to debate
whether they would accept a position where race or ethnicity is a major
consideration, others face situations where being a minority is still a
liability. "Everyone says minority women have an edge," declares one
assistant principal (western suburb), "but I personally haven't felt it."
More in line with Doughty's argument that minority women suffer, rather
than benefit from their minority status,[11] these aspirants do not find

affirmative action helpful. A district staff member relates:

> I was talking to a black friend the other day who felt her sex and race
> were two things going *against* her. I thought that was interesting, since
> you hear so much about having the two work for you. When you are
> black and female, you are very aware of the problems. You carry the
> weight of everybody on your shoulders.
>
> (Northeastern metro)

In a similar manner, a teacher concludes that affirmative action legislation
has been of little help to her career aspirations:

> My being black and female isn't a plus. I am the only black female
> doing quasi-administrative work in the district, and it's not because
> there aren't others qualified. I'm just their token. The few black
> women I know of in middle management have a rough time. Many of
> them have had to buy into the system in order to survive. There is little
> or no support for these women once they're hired.
>
> (Northeastern metro)

In her study of black female administrators, Doughty notes the popular
belief that black women have a corner on the job market because they
satisfy two criterion at once. But if minority women are so much in
demand, she queries, why are so few visible? She contends black women
are segregated in "assistant to" positions, elementary principalships or
supervisory positions, and are not found in top administrative jobs.
"Perhaps an important consideration for the black women administrative
aspirant or practitioner," she concludes, "is to understand the double-
negative status and to realize the effect of such status, both negative and
positive."[12] Many minority women in this study concur with her
perceptions. Respondents question whether affirmative action or their
own administrative expertise will get them beyond the "assistant to" level
of executive leadership. As a result, many have a "wait and see" attitude
about the ultimate impact of equity legislation. A new district staff
member muses:

> When I was hired as an assistant principal, some people with seniority
> were upset. They look at people like me and wonder about our
> "connections." I try to ignore those comments, hoping that I am
> getting the position because of what I can do, not who I am. The fact
> that I'm Hispanic should help, given the fact that the district is so
> heavily Hispanic and we are underrepresented in our administrative
> ranks. But I don't know if equity legislation will be of any specific help
> to me. Time will tell.
>
> (Western metro)

*Persistent Discrimination*

Minority women remain dubious about the long range impact of affirmative action primarily because they believe that discrimination continues to limit their careers. One assistant principal (southeastern city) states, "Being black and a woman doesn't help; that's just two prejudices to worry about in this profession." Many allege that discrimination follows them throughout their educational careers, beginning with their teaching years.

> I was once the only minority teacher in the district—the only one they'd ever had. They didn't expect me to pass the qualifying competency exams; they assumed a nonwhite couldn't pass. Then when I not only passed, but "taught well" (taught as they would), they considered my performance "excellent." I got congratulations all the time! I began to realize how subtle racism is, and I learned fast in a number of ways. The painful part, however, was being the only black there and feeling alone.
>
> (District Office Member, Northeastern metro)

A counselor describes her early encounters with racism in these terms:

> I spent ten years trying to get hired as a minority teacher in this district. But I had determination. I kept applying and finally I got a position.
>
> (Northwestern city)

She believes the initial barriers she faced as a teacher continue to hinder her pursuit of administration:

> A few years ago, this district kept saying no qualified blacks applied for administration. And yet I was living right here and applying every year. I think the school board and principals wanted me to be invisible, even with a doctorate. But I'm not. I just want them to accept that fact.
>
> (Northwestern city)

Others agree that many districts are still unreceptive to minority candidates, despite affirmative action legislation.

> I knew it would be impossible to become an administrator in my former district. The schools were distinct and separate: Hispanics went to Hispanic schools and blacks to black schools. Under that kind of system, there were only three possible principalships open to me as a minority person. You had to wait until someone died or took a maternity leave. So I left the state and came here.
>
> (Assistant Principal, Western metro)

Black women in education are not traditionally held in high esteem here. I only know of one successful black woman in the district, and she's in the central office. I don't even think my doctorate will get me anything in this city.

(Teacher, Northeastern metro)

An assistant principal (southern metro) contends that the discrimination in her region is now more subtle as a result of affirmative action: "There is some kind of covert, built-in discrimination in the district." But others argue the opposite, saying bias is blatant in their regions:

We have many minority candidates with tremendous experience, but they never rank high in the district ratings. Many get all of the experience and degrees required, only to see other people with fewer degrees and less experience promoted. I think a lot of the problem is racism. I'm sorry to say that, but I want it to go down on record.

(Central Office Member, Western metro)

There are zero minorities in administration here, and they say it's because they lack of experience. Well, how can you get the experience if they're not willing to give you an opportunity? You just hear the same song and dance all over the place.

(Teacher, Northwestern metro)

The last black principal they hired here was my husband, and that was some twelve years ago. So I realize my chances are probably zilch. Look at the length of time the district took to hire white women as administrators!

(Teacher, Midwestern city)

Clearly, many minority women suffer from some of the same problems women in general have in the field. Like all women, Valverde maintains minority women "soon learn that being compatible has more priority than demonstrated skill."[13] In much the same way Epstein wrote about women's place in 1970,[14] Ortiz contends "minorities either must restrict aspirations in accordance with ascribed roles, or suffer the uncertainties of attempting to overcome the majority concept of their proper place in society."[15] She further claims that minority administrative aspirants may be misunderstood by their fellow minority members and may be viewed as deserters—ones contemptuous of their own kind—a phenomenon similar to the ways in which some female teachers view female administrative aspirants.[16] Valverde notes that minority candidates, like their nonminority counterparts, also experience trouble with sponsorship. In the same way that women do not fit the typical administrative model, he contends mentors may be unwilling to risk helping someone who, because of race or ethnicity, does not fit the accepted pattern. These mentors frequently counsel minority aspirants out of the field rather than risking identification with a candidate who may not "fit in."[17] Finally, while some women culturally rebel against becoming masculine to advance in the field, minority aspirants hold out culturally from identifying with nonminority sponsors. Because mentoring relationships demand faith and trust in the sponsor's counsel, Valverde argues, "ethnic minorities who have experienced discrimination [may] find it difficult to place themselves in such a dependent role."[18] Certainly minority aspirants might question whether nonminority mentors would be (or could be) sensitive to the cultural issues involved, much like other women who question whether male mentors can understand their situations.

"A case can be made that ethnic minority groups and women are better prepared to function as administrators," Valverde argues, "since most are unsponsored and hence forced to prove themselves by working more and performing better."[19] Performance aside, minority women in this study believe their specific career problems are more complicated than those of most female candidates in general. On one hand, they believe racism significantly impacts their careers. A team leader (northeastern suburb) states racism is so blatant, "that there is no way in the world this city would accept a black superintendent!" (Yet, superintendencies are the career goal of many minorities—far more so than for nonminority aspirants in the study.) On the other hand, some minority women insist that gender and race work in their favor. They believe they fare better in today's job market than nonminority women, especially if the alternative is hiring a minority male. Epstein supports this contention, believing that by focusing on the negatively valued status of being female, the negative effect of race is canceled.[20] Stockard agrees, speculating that "hiring black women over either white women or black men may be the least threatening approach to affirmative action for the men who make hiring decision."[21] She postulates that hiring white women challenges the supremacy of men over women, while hiring black men challenges the whole structure of white dominance in the workplace. "When pressured to hire someone other than a white male," she concludes, "the hiring of a black woman may provide the least direct challenge to a sexist and racist system."[22] Paddock's study of female administrators corroborates this idea: she found race a serious career obstacle for minority males, but not as much so for minority females.[23]

Although there is no way to prove conclusively whether white male administrators feel threatened by white females or minority males, Epstein maintains the notion alone "may act to discourage black men from seeking entry into white domains and encourage the black woman because she *thinks* she has more of a chance" (emphasis added).[24] Several women in this study reflect this sense of optimism. A counselor states:

I think white women will have more difficulty advancing into administrative positions than I will. The men who are threatened are white, and they already see a few black women in some areas of leadership. Therefore, white women face more discrimination, and minority women have a better chance.

(Southern metro)

Similarly, an assistant principal notes: "People who have the best chance for promotion are probably young white men and older minority women, such as myself, who are past the 'giddy' stage." With regard to Hispanic women, a supervisor (southern town) reports: "There are very few white women who have their administrative certification or who have any intention of pursuing management positions, but we have quite a few Mexican-American women in administration." Again, she believes that these Hispanic women pose less of a threat, and that is why they are encouraged and promoted in ways nonminority women are not.

Others in the study, however, disagree with the theories of Epstein and Stockard, as well as with the female administrators in Paddock's study. These minority aspirants still believe the greatest barrier they face in their careers is racism and, as a result, they do not feel optimistic about achieving their goals. They contend if any women get preferential treatment in school administration, it is nonminority women.

I've seen very few women in administration, and the ones who move up seem to be white. I don't see any minorities. Our district hasn't been ready for them for many years, and they refuse to *get* ready. They refuse to change their attitudes about and their behavior toward minorities, but white women are given the chance to move on.

(Counselor, Northwestern city)

As a black woman, I feel a great deal of competition for administrative positions now that we are classified as minorities. Many of the positions that might go to a minority now go to a white woman being *considered* a minority. That's going to make it more difficult for me to be placed as an administrator. I have to compete with both male and female whites. In many cases, they do not have the qualifications that I do. But the white women will be considered for a position before I will.

(State Department Coordinator, Northeastern metro)

### Infighting

It is debatable whether minority or nonminority women have the edge in today's administrative job market; however, many informants agree that conflicts frequently occur between the two groups of women. Lerner argues there is a history of "confrontation, competition and conflict" between the two groups: "Although they have their womanhood in common, black and white women could not escape the confines and limitations of a society in which a person's status and power are defined not only by sex but—more importantly—by race."[25] She further states that analogies between blacks and women in general only work when discussing the "psychological effect of inferior status," and that "a similarity of interests [between the two groups does] not always express itself in cooperation."[26] Lerner employs adjectives such as "complicated," "ambivalent" and even "hostile" to describe relationships between the two groups. A few women in this study use similar descriptors. A teacher (northeastern metro) believes that many minority aspirants feel isolated from their nonminority peers: "You don't even get support from white women," she claims, "because there is too much competition for openings between us." Epstein notes that while minority professional women *prefer* other women as colleagues, "*few* white women professionals favored other women professionals" (emphasis added).[27] A district staff member underscores this lack of support among women aspirants and fears the competition that exists in its place:

> I think there is going to be a big confrontation in the urban areas between majority women and minority women. Women don't promote other women candidates, but nobody talks about that.
>
> (Western metro)

Given the bias in favor of hiring males, she concludes, the lack of support among women has far-reaching consequences for all female aspirants.

Perhaps this woman's comments point to a complicating factor: No matter what women believe, the issue is not whether minority women or nonminority women have the edge—*men* have the edge. Black female administrators interviewed by Payne and Jackson seem well aware of this fact, and the authors conclude that "sexual discrimination or sexist behavior was encountered more frequently than racial obstacles."[28] One woman interviewed for that study noted: "If we eliminated all racial discrimination this very day, I would [still] have to go through the sex discrimination."[29] Hence, based on her 1978 study of female administrators, Paddock anticipated an increase in the numbers of minority males hired as school executives.[30] Informants in this study confirm this prediction:

> The old boys' school thrives around here. They would rather have a man, no matter what color. If they can't have a black man, they might hire a black woman, but only if she is head and shoulders above everyone else.
>
> (Team Leader, Northeastern suburb)

A supervisor (southeastern city) concurs: "If there is a push to have a minority, then we will have a minority man not a woman." Respondents report that the preference for men is particularly noticeable at the secondary level. A teacher (southern metro) states: "Black women do better than men at the lower levels, but no woman—black or white—becomes a high school principal or head coach in this district." A counselor (northwestern city) agrees: "Time after time, I've seen white males with less experience and less education than me move up and gain the necessary administrative experience for advancement."

To complicate matters further, those interviewed assert that minority groups often battle against each other for the few managerial openings available. As Ortiz claims, "advancement for minorities means advancement within their own structures," resulting in minorities competing among themselves for limited positions within school administration.[31] Nonminority educators, informants claim, consciously or unconsciously fuel this infighting. A staff member admonishes:

> Don't forget, they play minorities against minorities. For example, they believe in some myth that Hispanic women should not have authority over Hispanic men. That's an assumption on the part of nonminority educators.
>
> (Western metro)

In some instances, nonminority administrators assume minorities prefer to be together. One district office member recalls an example from her past:

> One time there was a substitute at our school who was nonwhite. The principal went out of the way to bring us together, and then didn't understand why we were cold to each other. We both realized why we, of all the teachers, were being introduced to each other, and we resented it.
>
> (Northeastern metro)

She admits this one incident caused her to draw away from nonminorities for a time, and prompted her defensive posture of talking about *them* as if "they all looked alike."

### Gaining Acceptance

Complex issues of race, ethnicity and gender shape, in large part, the administrative aspirations and careers of minority women. Many informants believe that interviewing is particularly difficult because employers must deal with entrenched attitudes toward race and gender.

When I interviewed, I knew there weren't any black people in the office. Some men said I had to understand the community was all-white, and that they had had enough trouble getting used to black kids in the school. But the fact that I was a woman overshadowed almost everything else. I am certain I was the only woman to apply, so I was pretty nervous.

(Assistant Principal, Midwestern suburb)

I interviewed for one assistant principalship which previously belonged to a black woman. I believe the principal already knew who he was going to hire and that he was just going through a routine with me. Later he admitted to me that he still had negative feelings about the first black woman.

(Assistant Principal, Southeastern town)

Instead of being considered for their own individual merits and experiences, minority aspirants complain they are lumped into categories of "other women" or "other minorities."

If a minority woman does get hired, her problems do not cease with the signing of an administrative contract. Many informants believe the hardships they face on the job are probably similar to those any woman faces when dealing with traditional, stereotypical thinking.

As a black, teachers and parents have a harder time accepting me than children do. Whenever I change schools or towns, I have to prove myself at each juncture. If you are a white male, you do not have to do that. *All* women in administration have to prove themselves in ways men do not have to do.

(Assistant Principal, Southeastern city)

There is pressure, I imagine, on any woman administrator. People want to turn around and say, "I told you women can't handle the pressure."

(Teacher, Northwestern metro)

Given this pressure and some of the difficult assignments they receive, many minority aspirants believe their chances of succeeding are minimal at best. In describing a minority woman who received a middle school principalship, a team leader (northeastern suburb) claims that the woman was hired only because "literally, no one else wanted the school." She goes on to add: "The school used to be a zoo, but she's turned it around. Only no one is giving *her* the credit." Difficult building assignments appear common for minority women, as an assistant principal details:

In assigning me a mainly Hispanic school, the district automatically assumed I was going to do a lot for community relations. But the community was angry and volatile, full of hardworking, salt-of-the-earth people who haven't gotten very far in this world. And here comes this spiffy little female who "knows it all." Although I try not to come across that way, I'm sure they *think* I think that. They don't know how hard I've worked to get here. But then maybe a fellow who works all day on the railroad or in the butcher shop and has eight kids—including a pregnant, fifteen-year-old daughter and a thirteen-year-old son picked up by the cops—doesn't really have to know how hard I've worked. My responsibility is to work with the community, and it's not necessarily their's to relate to me.

(Midwestern metro)

Ortiz calls these minority administrators "warriors," ones who work in schools where district officials have relinquished all responsibility. Frequently, the only reward these minority women receive for doing a good job, Ortiz states, is to get yet another tough assignment.[32]

Lack of appreciation for minority accomplishments and absence of support from school districts and personnel offices frustrates minority administrators. Nevertheless, most of the informants claim they do the best job they can under taxing circumstances:

Many Anglo staff members don't like minorities getting hired as school leaders. Maybe I shouldn't be that blunt, but the feeling is there, even if it's not openly expressed. *Some* people are just not used to having a minority direct them, even if that minority is qualified. You just have to go on, do your best, and not be bothered by that. We shouldn't have to prove ourselves, but we do.

(Assistant Principal, Southern city)

Color doesn't make much difference to me. I think people will eventually accept me, because I live in a way they can respect. For those who don't, I just bless them and go on about my business.

(Assistant Principal, Southern metro)

Other women take a harder line, stating that districts need to "grow up." A teacher (northwestern metro) recalls working in an area where she was the only black: "I didn't have time to sit around wondering if I was going to be accepted, we all had to adjust." Likewise, an assistant principal (southern metro) states: "As a black person, I've never cared if people liked me or not. I knew what I could do, and I didn't give a damn if they liked me."

Clearly, minority aspirants believe competence, not color, should be the criteria used in administrative hiring.

My principal said he asked my peers if it was OK with them if he hired a black woman. If I'm qualified, what difference does my color make?

Color is a dumb reason for choosing or not choosing a person.
(Counselor, Northwestern city)

If a minority woman goes into a new school with determination to do
well and to help children, then she should do all right. If you have the
skills and produce, the color of your skin doesn't matter.
(Assistant Principal, Southern metro)

Despite claims about the success of affirmative action, many informants
believe that their competence is responsible for their current achievement:

Well, I can say this: I don't care how black I am, they would not have
hired me if I had not had more experience than the other candidates.
Because I am a woman and a black, I am highly visible. They had to
rely on my strong background when they hired me, because if anything
went badly it would reflect even worse on them for putting me there.
So they wanted me to succeed as much as I wanted to succeed.
(Assistant Principal, Midwestern suburb)

The racial factor is obviously not the only one considered, for neither
the principal nor I would be here if it was. But there just aren't many
qualified minority administrators statewide like us.
(Assistant Principal, Southeastern city)

In the beginning, I felt I got this job because I'm Hispanic. The district
had their blacks and their whites, but they had no Hispanics. They
were between a rock and a hard place. But since then, I've decided I got
the job more through my professional relationships and by doing well
in the interview than because of my ethnic background.
(Assistant Principal, Midwestern metro)

One Asian assistant principal concludes:

I don't really sit and think about ethnicity, but I do think about
people—both males and females. I just hope people promoted in
schools are competent. The only way schools are going to change is
when the people in leadership roles assume responsibilities and take
risks to improve the lot of children.
(Western metro)

One assistant principal (southeastern metro) concurs when she speaks of
commitment, not color. "When we see kids," she emphasizes, "we see
kids—not colors."
By hiring more minority administrators, these women trust that both
nonminority staff *and* students will benefit. Many informants believe that

they can provide positive examples to nonminority children and adults—examples that will serve to dispel certain negative sterotypes that continue to shape attitudes and behaviors towards minorities.

> I know for a lot of my students I was the first black they had ever met in person. For the most part, these kids only saw blacks on TV—killing someone or pimping on the street.
>
> (Teacher, Northwestern metro)

> The white kids here do not see blacks in professional positions, and that puts them at a disadvantage. How can you get to know someone of a different race or culture if you never see or talk to them?
>
> (Counselor, Northwestern city)

> I've always felt that white school administrators lacked an awareness about minority cultures. I made a conscientious effort to become an administrator, so I could change some of the policies affecting that awareness.
>
> (State Department Coordinator, Northeastern metro)

She goes on to say:

> Since I've been here, the minority staff in the district has more than doubled. I believe I've raised people's cultural awareness about minorities. I talk to them about the reasons minorities should be hired, and what they can contribute to the school system and to the kids.
>
> (Northeastern metro)

Despite problems of gaining acceptance in school leadership, minority women remain strong in their commitment to education and in their pursuit of administrative positions. One assistant principal (southeastern town) declares: "Being a black, middle-aged woman makes me militant. I might give out, but I won't give up!" Although minority women report having fewer mentors (sixty-one percent to seventy-one percent for nonminorities), they consider themselves as strongly committed to school administration as their nonminority colleagues. In fact, many believe their minority heritage strengthens their resolve and equips them to face the barriers they encounter.

> All during my upbringing, my parents put ideas in my head about being special because I'm a minority. I think that helped me to have the kind of confidence in my achievements that I now have.
>
> (New Principal, Western metro)

These confident minority aspirants fit the description Epstein draws of female black professionals. By growing up in a society that narrowed their choices, they make themselves more visible and unique. "For these few," Epstein argues, "the effects of living in a world otherwise beset with limits fed their determination and made them feel the only road to survival lay in occupational success."[33] Perhaps this explains the higher professional goals of minority aspirants. Eighty-six percent say they aim for superintendencies to only twenty-four percent for nonminorities, and fifty-five percent of the minorities aspire to assistant superintendencies compared to ten percent for nonminorities. Also, minorities report a greater willingness to relocate to achieve those ends: forty-seven percent would move out of state for a job as compared with thirty-seven percent of nonminorities. Although many speak about the barriers they face, somewhat fewer minority aspirants claim they are hindered in their pursuit of school leadership positions (fifty-three percent to fifty-nine percent for nonminorities). For the most part, the picture of minority aspirations is one of commitment and determination. As one minority assistant principal summarizes:

> Things are opening up some for minority women, but it's still a hard road for us. I imagine many times that we don't know how far we can push the limits. But maybe the younger, more aggressive women will test those boundaries.
>
> (Southern metro)

## PART TWO: WHAT NONMINORITY WOMEN SAY

What do nonminority respondents reveal about the issues confronting minority aspirants in school administration? Like minority aspirants, nonminority women acknowledge the heightened importance of race in administrative hiring since the advent of affirmative action. A teacher (southeastern city) recognizes that now both race and gender are "thrown into the hiring hopper." While seventy-two percent of minorities believe affirmative action has been helpful to minority aspirants, eighty-three percent of nonminority women contend the legislation has aided minority candidates. Both groups, however, think the legislation has been less helpful to women in general. Nonminority women recognize that few minorities reach the top echelons of school leadership, but they react differently to the drive by some school districts to give minorities preference in hiring. Many nonminority women are supportive, aware that minority women—like themselves—are systematically excluded from school leadership. A lead teacher (southern metro) declares: "They desperately need minorities down at our central office." Another teacher (southeastern rural) expresses disappointment that more minorities are not placed where she lives: "In my opinion, we have so many capable black teachers who ought to be going into administration."

Other nonminority aspirants, however, are less sanguine about the preference shown to minority candidates. A district planner explains:

> More and more schools in this city are dominated by minorities, and a couple of school board members are pushing for a higher ratio of minority administrators. Even though an Anglo woman falls into the minority category, she is at the bottom of the totem pole. I think that will be a problem for me, wherever I go.
>
> (Southern metro)

A student notes that although nonminority women may be interviewed, districts often choose to fill those openings with minority women in order to fill two affirmative action mandates with one person.

> In the last positions they filled, the district only interviewed women and minorities. Minority women got the jobs because they could kill two birds with one stone right there. If the qualifications between me and a minority are the same, I think I will come in second to the minority woman unless I have some special contacts.
>
> (Southern city)

A teacher-administrator notes a similar trend in her district:

> One of the principals hired at the elementary level last year is named Garcia. Many people commented about how serious the board was getting, hiring a woman and one with a Spanish surname as well.
>
> (Midwestern suburb)

In some leadership programs, districts reportedly favor minorities candidates to the detriment of nonminority aspirants. In one school system (southern metro) where all administrators go through an in-district training program, a district planner reports: "Because I am an Anglo, my chances of getting into the program are slim; they constantly recruit a heavily minority class." A coordinator summarizes the equity dilemma for nonminority women:

> Those I see moving up in school management now tend to be minority women. There's nothing wrong with that, and we are lucky to have capable minority women. But favoring them over capable white women is a cop-out when you consider equity for *women* in administration. Some excellent women my age never got the opportunity to move up the ladder.
>
> (Western metro)

*Unanticipated Consequences*

Many nonminority women recall losing positions to minority candidates because of affirmative action mandates. Some of those interviewed accept the loss more easily than others.

> I was very upset when I didn't get the administrative promotion—especially when I heard how high I was on the placement list. But the district office told me they had to hire a certain number of Mexican-Americans. I told them I could accept that, although I didn't agree with them showing preferential treatment to minority candidates.
> (Teacher, Southern metro)

> I recently applied for an assistant principalship. But with 500 applicants for the position, I know my chances are very slim. Some administrators tell me outright, given my extensive administrative background, that I would certainly be promoted if my surname was Spanish or if I were black or Indian. I believe being female helps in this district, but not for white females. If I were a minority woman, I'd be in.
> (Teacher, Western metro)

> I received a promotion, but then the district rescinded the decision and placed a black man in the job. I naively thought I would get the job, based on my merits. But black educators in town put pressure on the district, and they were stronger than me.
> (Assistant Principal, Northeastern metro)

Because of affirmative action, nonminority and minority aspirants find themselves competing against one another as they try to enter school management. An acting assistant principal details the results of this competition in her district:

> My friend and I placed first and second on the promotion list, so we felt confident we'd be placed. Eleven of the top nineteen people on the list were females and six of those eleven were white. But not one white female got promoted! They picked other women—blacks and Mexican-Americans—even though our scores were higher. One of the administrators said, "Let's face it: We have certain affirmative action rulings, and the state needs a percentage of minority administrators." To make us feel better, the district made some of us intern assistant principals with no extra pay. When we heard that, all the white women just looked at each other. There was no doubt in our minds that the district was just going to use us as cheap labor.
> (Southern metro)

For many, outcomes such as these are unexpected consequences of affirmative action. Those nonminority women who earlier achieved entry-level positions in administration, now find themselves blocked from further advancement.

> One of the women I trained with recently made the promotion list. She has only been an assistant principal two years compared to my ten, but she is on the list and I am not. Since I know I am a better administrator than she is, you can understand how I feel. But then, she is a black woman and I'm not.
>
> (Assistant Principal, Western suburb)

A lead teacher, though similarly stymied, is somewhat more understanding:

> In this district, you don't have a chance of getting promoted in administration if you are white. I have no proof, but I think a black female assistant superintendent blocked my advancement in the field for two years. But I really don't blame her, given the experience most blacks have had in this part of the country. But I do find it ironic that a black woman blocked me, because a black principal was the one who first encouraged me to go into administration!
>
> (Southern metro)

### Male Competition

Whatever problems exist between the two groups of female aspirants, nonminority women agree with minority women that their main competition lies with males of any color, not with each other.

> My principal was pressured to hire a minority assistant principal, and in this district, women aren't considered minorities. You have to be black or brown. But as I looked around at a district meeting the other day, the participants were predominantly male. Given the choice, districts will still choose a male, even if the woman candidate is more qualified.
>
> (Assistant Principal, Southern city)

Another assistant principal underscores this continuing favoritism toward males:

> In this city, a combination of things affect women in management. First, our system is simply not capable of envisioning women in leadership positions. Second, there is strong pressure to place black males in leadership roles. Politically, the time has not come for women

here. Perhaps hiring practices are different in the suburbs, but that's how promotions take place in the city.

(Northeastern metro)

Even under difficult circumstances, some nonminority women defend the validity of hiring a minority—even a minority male.

We all compared scores after the placement exam, and mine was very high. So I was upset when I wasn't placed. I compared my scores with a very enterprising, energetic minority male. Even though he had lower scores, he got hired that year and I did not. But I decided to wait another year to try again, because we need minorities in the district.

(Acting Assistant Principal, Southern metro)

Similarly, a student (southeastern city) commends her university for reaching out to black students, many of whom "have similar problems that women students have." When it comes to the larger issue of who gets hired in administration, however, she quotes Shirley Chisholm: "The greatest problem is still being female, not black."

*Overcoming Stereotypes*

For the few nonminority women who advance in spite of preferences shown for minority candidates, racial tensions remain high. Nonminority aspirants report facing a range of stereotypes about being white.

When I was hired, the minority people in the program were suspicious of me. They expected a "honky," not someone who accepted them. They told me blatantly that they weren't used to "folks like me" and that I was a rarity. Some people in the program kept their distance from me.

(Assistant Principal, Southern city)

When I got this position, I got the sense that women didn't go into administration—especially in secondary schools. Women weren't supposed to be able to handle discipline problems, unless you happened to be a black female and in a black school. The message was that you cannot be white and survive in an inner city school. When they hired me, they wanted a token white woman in that particular setting, and luckily I survived. Without the support of a male administrator, however, I would probably have been just another statistic.

(Lead Teacher, Midwestern metro)

When I applied for a principalship, my ability to discipline students—

particularly black students—came into question. The male candidate was supposedly better at discipline because he was a father and had sons. That was ridiculous, because I have a reputation for being an effective disciplinarian. Although many of the black staff supported my candidacy, I didn't get the position.

(Assistant Principal, Northeastern metro)

*Summary*

Minority and nonminority aspirants, alike, agree that race and gender significantly affect their career aspirations, albeit in different ways. Despite laws to the contrary, Coursen and Mazzarella argue that minority women continue to be limited by ingrained assumptions that the races should be kept separate. "There are jobs for black administrators," they conclude, "but few of these jobs include supervising white teachers and students."[34] Likewise, some of the nonminority aspirants in this study report that they were not expected to discipline minority students because they were white. On the other hand, all the women believe that their administrative aspirations are circumscribed by the predominant vision of women as mothers. Both men and women frequently fail to see leadership potential in female educators because of the belief that authority roles "might conflict with the primary commitment of all women—bearing and raising children."[35]

Along with the problems of stereotypes, women in this study acknowledge the competition that exists between minority and nonminority aspirants. Many express surprise about the apparent outcomes of affirmative action mandates, and some remain perplexed about who, if any one, benefits from equity efforts in education. But stereotypes and competition aside, both groups agree their continuing problems in administration stem not only from each other, but from their male peers as well. Until the field of administration welcomes all female candidates—no matter what their color—minority issues will continue to complicate the lives of minority and nonminority women alike.

# 12  Discrimination

I couldn't believe a district this large would
so blatantly discriminate against women in
administration! I'm young enough that I
only vaguely remember all the fighting and
commotion for equality in the 1960s. But I
definitely thought something would have
changed because of it all. Instead, the discrimination—whether sexual or racial—is
still so aggressive.

(Student Intern, Western metro)

MANY WOMEN AROUND THE COUNTRY find it difficult to accept
the fact that discrimination in hiring remains widespread in school districts
across the nation. While all but three women in this study firmly agree that
educational administration is male-dominated, a quarter of those interviewed do not believe that women today face discrimination in securing
positions in public schools. Research about the diminishing numbers of
the once prevalent female elementary school principal, however, documents persistent patterns of discrimination.[1] Likewise, studies show that
female principals tend to be older and more experienced than their male
peers, indicating "women are apparently forced to undergo longer
apprenticeships in order to establish their ability."[2] "Consciously or
otherwise," Timpano contends, "someone has practiced sex discrimination in selecting educational leaders for the country's school districts . . . and
somebody *continues* to practice discrimination . . . . "[3] Although equity
legislation promotes female candidates, Thomas concludes: "As we look
around us, we see that the spoken and written word is far from reality."[4]
Despite dissemination efforts, many women in this study are unaware of
these and other findings about discrimination in administrative hiring.
Two women provide examples:

I thought I had a good shot at four different jobs. But the school
boards and superintendents are still very reluctant to hang their hats
on a woman. Apparently, women are fine in the classroom, as
cheerleading sponsors or as cookie bakers for fund raisers, but they

shouldn't have too much power. I really had my eyes opened as to how tough it is out there for women! I mean, it doesn't matter how qualified you are or what your letters of recommendation say. They skeptically ask, "Can *she* do the job?"

(New Assistant Principal, Midwestern suburb)

When I applied for this job, different people were saying that they were not ready for a woman. The superintendent told me what some of the people said and remarked, "I thought they were your friends." I replied, "At this level, I guess I have no friends!"

(Curriculum Director, Northeastern town)

While some informants willingly admit discrimination exists, only fifty-two percent claim difficulties in their own careers. Frieze et al. contend that "women have largely avoided such awareness [because] it is far more comfortable to see oneself as part of a privileged class than an underprivileged one."[5] Perhaps this explains why women in this study tend to separate discrimination against themselves from general barriers women face in the field. Sometimes the first discrimination they encounter does not occur until they begin interviewing for executive positions. Once such interviewing commences, several women began to see a pattern of discrimination taking shape. A resource teacher shares this account:

In one district that had no female administrators, they hired another new assistant principal who was male. I asked one principal, "Weren't there any qualified women who interviewed this time?" Maybe he's threatened by women, or maybe he just doesn't think. Even when he recommended me later for a position (which I didn't get), he forgot and commented: "Gee, there just weren't any women who applied." I had to remind him that *I* had applied! I thought the position was perfect for me, and the district could have put in at least a token woman. But they wouldn't even hire a token. In this district, if they place a female counselor, they think they are "letting women in." I hate to admit discrimination exists, but in this state it does.

(Northeastern metro)

Many of those questioned come to similar conclusions about continuing discrimination in the field.

There definitely is a barrier against women in school management. I have never experienced anything like it! The whole state has a history of being very negative and closed toward women. In the past, I've always managed to do what I want when I want. Now just because I am female, I'm not allowed to do what I know I can do as an administrator. I'm frustrated, and at times I get very angry.

(Teacher, Midwestern town)

A district staff member (western metro) summarizes: "Being female was and still is a big obstacle for women getting into some administrative positions."

### A Long-Standing Problem

According to informants, problems of gender bias in administrative hiring are not limited to the history of one or even a few states. They contend that bias in the administrative selection process—whether conscious or not—is both systematic and long-term. One new assistant principal notes:

> When I was first teaching and getting my Master's, I thought about becoming a principal. But those were not the right times for women to become principals. In the 1960s, only men were being considered for elementary principalships. Of course, the choice was mine, but I could see women were not getting hired as school managers.
>
> (Northwestern city)

The question remains: How many other women altered their dreams (or possibly negated their dreams) to fit the prevailing options afforded female educators? How many futures were irrevocably changed? Throughout the country, women still report that districts persist in equating management with men, thereby limiting women's careers. A teacher (midwestern metro) states she knows several "well-qualified women who have applied for positions but never got them." She assumes districts pass over women because "someone else has been pre-selected and that someone is usually a man." A director reports the same pattern happening in her district:

> I know the barriers exist, particularly when we apply for middle school principalships. I am aware that the secondary level is seen as a man's domain. That's a real barrier to break through if you're female.
>
> (Northeastern metro)

Most women believe that persistent stereotypes account for the discrimination they experience. Men are still seen as the disciplinarians, the athletic directors, and the ones with supportive wives who allow them to work the extra hours required of school executives. Several informants speak of these stereotypes:

> While I was getting the junior high school experience I was told I needed, the district hired a man for the secondary assistant principalship instead of me. He came directly out of the classroom, while I had

four years of administrative experience as an assistant principal. In so many words, my area superintendent told me he thought a man could handle discipline better than a woman—even though I have never had any problems with discipline.

(Assistant Principal, Western suburb)

The secondary principal's job requires day and night work. And maybe that's why the district is subtly keeping women out. Our principal is married and is out five nights a week all year long. The district apparently believes that you need a "wife" to manage a school.

(Lead Teacher, Southern metro)

There *are* administrative jobs in the district, but you have to be an assistant principal first to get hired. And in order to be an assistant, you have to have experience as an athletic director. There just aren't any women with that kind of experience.

(Specialist, Midwestern suburb)

Many times respondents see men getting the benefit of the doubt in terms of experience, while women do not.

I took over the responsibility for two principals in a row who fell ill. When the next opening in the school came up, the parents were very upset when I didn't get promoted to the position. At the time I wasn't certified, so I didn't get upset. But the parents pointed out that if I had been a man, the district would have *gotten* me prepared and would have helped in whatever way possible.

(Assistant Principal, Southeastern city)

*Interviewing*

Special attention, the respondents maintain, is something males in the field receive all the time. Although grooming may be subtle during the early stages of administrative preparation, informants believe that male favoritism becomes blatant in the interview process. Women argue that getting an interview is small victory, indeed, if they have little chance of getting beyond that point.

I always tell people there will be three finalists: the black, the woman and the man. Everyone knows from the beginning that he will get the job. So I expect to be a finalist, but I don't expect to get a principalship.

(Assistant Principal, Northeastern suburb)

Many districts still have the "male-as-principal" image. They will include women in the interviews, but when they come down to seriously considering who they'll hire, they weed out the women. These older men who do the hiring tend to see women as sisters and wives, not as potential hirees for these positions.

(Assistant Principal, Midwestern suburb)

School systems around here don't hire women. They might put a woman in the final screening, but then they say nobody qualified applied. I *know* there are some qualified women for assistant principalships. I just don't see how some districts continue to get federal funding, given the discrimination that goes on.

(Resource Teacher, Northeastern town)

During the actual interviews, women contend that they are frequently asked questions that would not be addressed to male candidates.

I've applied for other positions, but males were always hired. The interviewers would ask: "How can you be a mother and a principal too?" I wonder if they ask a man how he can be a father and have that position as well.

(Director, Midwestern suburb)

The issue of parenting invariably comes up if a woman is visibly pregnant. One State Department employee now believes her pregnancy became the critical factor when she was applying for building positions:

At first when I was interviewing, I was reluctant to believe my pregnancy was an issue. I've always resisted looking for rationales when I don't get selected for a job. But once they knew I was pregnant, they thought I couldn't do the job. One administrator who knows me well was amazed when I didn't get the job. I know now I won't ever interview again while I'm "showing."

(Northeastern suburb)

These are not stories from the distant past, for women continue to report examples of discrimination when interviewing for jobs. A recently hired principal sums up the problem:

I feel strongly that there is discrimination in job hiring. For example, I once interviewed for eight hours while the male candidates only stayed half the day. That tells me women still have a harder time than men.

(Northwestern metro)

*After Selection*

Unequal treatment of male and female adminstrative aspirants frequently continues when women obtain managerial positions. One of the major areas of discrimination involves administrative salaries. Some school districts in the country hire women knowing full well they can get away with paying them lower salaries, as the following example illustrates:

> For as far back as I can remember, our district has been inconsistent with female administrators. For example, years ago a woman was called a dean and given $200 extra a year; but a man was called an assistant principal and paid $6000 more a year.
>
> (Assistant Principal, Southern metro)

Another teacher (midwestern town) recalls, "I remember when all the elementary principals were women—but then the pay wasn't that good!" Some districts still operate in this manner. In a district with a large number of female assistant principals and principals, a district staff member (southern metro) explains: "The pay is so low, the men don't *want* the jobs!" In other districts, women note that they do the same work as males but receive lower salaries. Some women accept these pay inequities in order to gain management experience; but in doing so, they recognize that such practices are financially unfair.

> I feel if a man had this position, the salary would be upgraded. I don't worry about the difference most of the time, because I'm gaining some good experience. But at times, the salary issue bothers me.
>
> (District Staff, Western metro)

Respondents claim that differential salaries for male and female administrators presents a clear message to everyone: Women are not valued as highly as men in administration. One assistant principal shares her frustration:

> Administrators negotiate their own contracts, and when I asked to be within twenty percent of the highest paid teacher I was evaluating, they refused my request. I thought it was ridiculous to be in charge of those people and yet not get the added salary. The word came back to me that they just didn't believe that a woman was worth the extra money.
>
> (Northeastern town)

Women who attain administrative positions also face discrimination in promotion. Respondents believe that when districts *do* promote women, they only promote those that fit the acceptable image of what a female administrator should be—the "ladies." Women who deviate from the norm, regardless of their qualifications and experience, seldom receive promotions.

The girls' assistant principalships repeatedly went to women with no office experience. Even though I had the necessary background, I was passed over. I think the principal encouraged his favorites: the ones who met his image of being a hostess for the school, the charming ladies who brought out the refreshments. If you fit your superior's image, you can make it without any experience at all.

(Assistant Principal, Western suburb)

For a long time, there was only one woman in administration in this district. She was the only one in living history to get a department chair. She was a "lady" in the true sense of the word: an unmarried woman caring for her elderly father. The men even stood up when she entered the room.

(Assistant Principal, Northeastern suburb)

The portrait of an unmarried female administrator is strong in many aspirants' memories. In a western suburb, an assistant principal recalls: "Assistant principals used to be unmarried PE majors. There was a bias for such women, because they fit the image of a disciplinarian." Although this ideal is now considered old fashioned, some aspirants believe the questions they are asked in interviews about combining marriage and careers stem from such traditional stereotypes.

Women administrators suffer another form of discrimination when districts limit the numbers of women they will hire. In some cases where districts are reluctant to admit any women into the managerial ranks, they compromise by only accepting one or two. Safilios-Rothschild labels this "subtle occupation discrimination." "Men resent that their all-male atmosphere is being disrupted and they tend to isolate the woman...to prevent [her] bona fide integration into the group, regardless of her characteristics and her efforts to break the barriers."[6] Women in the study note that they never hear complaints about having too many men in school leadership, but the reverse criticism is common.

In our district, the screening committee recommended a woman, but she was rejected in favor of the second choice—a male. She was rejected primarily because there was already another female in the building. As a result, the district didn't give the job to the most capable and qualified person. The issue of sex should not decide the question of who gets the job.

(Assistant Principal, Northeastern suburb)

She goes on to say that as her district cuts back on administrative positions, lone female administrators are the first to go, "just because they are women." Another assistant principal describes the discrimination that takes place in her district:

On top of the poor economy and the infrequent job openings, we still have alot of chauvinists around—people who would rather have men in certain positions. Despite the great strides that women have made, these diehards say: "I've had my quota of women, and that's all I need."
(Midwestern metro)

The issue of quotas troubles women in this study. Thomas argues: "It is not enough to satisfy equality by having a woman in a welding class or a woman in a central office position . . . . Tokenism in any form is sophisticated bigotry."[7] Female aspirants in this study prefer to be hired for their capabilities, not for filling quotas. Some are initially willing to take a position based on filling a quota, but hope eventually to display their competence for the job. At least one woman, however, says she would decline a job offer if she thought she was only filling a quota for women:

I'm confident that our district seeks to hire the best people. I would never want to be selected because I was a woman. In fact, if I knew that was the reason I was offered the job, I'd be likely to say that I didn't want it.
(Teacher, Midwestern city)

### Dissenting Voices

As mentioned earlier, there are few women who do *not* believe their districts discriminate against female aspirants and administrators. These respondents believe that each aspirant must make her own way, and they do not believe that discrimination limits their opportunity for administrative employment.

Compared with the whole nation, we have a lot of women in elementary education. We only have one female assistant principal at the secondary level, but I don't feel that it's due to discrimination. I think this system is fair to women, or anyone else, most of the time. If you really want to proceed, I think it's up to the individual.
(Assistant Principal, Southern metro)

I'm not a "women's libber," and I don't think women are discriminated against in administration. That may be naiveté on my part, but I haven't experienced bias in this district. I have yet to hear of any prepared women who were unable to get into school management. In this district, becoming an administrator depends on politics, not gender. If you're qualified and have good contacts, then you find a position. And women don't have more problems making those contacts than men do.
(Student, Southern city)

I could be wrong, but I believe our school district faithfully follows the
written policy. There's a process, and that's the way the hiring is done.
I would be very hurt to find out otherwise. I'm good friends with
several males in this system who have aspirations similar to mine. And
from our talks, they go through the same process I do.

(Assistant Principal, Southeastern city)

A few women who worried about discrimination in the past, now believe
that times have changed and discrimination is no longer an issue.

I'm pretty woman-oriented, but I don't have any horror stories to tell.
My experiences have been positive all the way through my career. But
partly, that's because of who I am. I am willing to go in and work for
what I get. My attitude is "Here I am," rather than "I'm a woman."
Seven or eight years ago, I read the women's lib literature and thought
about some things that happened to me in the past. I got depressed, but
I worked things out in my mind. I try to be conscious of how women
are doing, but I can't afford to get depressed. I do the best I can, but
I'm also in a good environment.

(Student, Midwestern city)

A department head concludes:

I'm not as worried about discrimination against women as those who
have been trying to get into administration longer than I have. They
seem hyper-conscious of the problem. But maybe those who broke
trails for women in administration need to be that way.

(Southern metro)

A few women admit there is some discrimination at the secondary level,
but they do not think the bias will affect them personally.

I don't happen to feel the way some women in this district feel. I don't
believe that I was ever denied a position or was held back because I am
a woman. There's no question or debate that women are not placed in
the high schools at the same rate as men. But I probably still have as
good a chance as any male in the district of getting assigned to a
secondary principalship.

(Assistant Principal, Western metro)

Although these few respondents doubt that discrimination negatively
influences their career opportunities, Timpano alleges the results of
discrimination are undeniable. Even though "the discriminator [may be]
unaware of his offense and the victim unaware of the offense committed

against her, the practice of sex discrimination in the selection of educational leaders continues—subtly, insidiously."[8] Most of the respondents in this study agree that the reality of discrimination remains undeniable. Weber et al. conclude "sex was the only factor which had any significant relationship to the hiring process. Other variables such as age, length of experience, size of school district and background, and type of position had no relationship to the hiring process."[9] Most female aspirants realize discrimination will continue to affect their careers in school leadership. A student (midwestern city) sums up the feelings of this majority: "I think people are still unsure of hiring women—they hesitate, there's discrimination, the whole gambit." Although eighty-seven percent realize they have to be better than men to get hired, seventy-six percent also believe that school boards still prefer to hire men. The following example remains typical of administrative hiring:

> Everyone knew who the two new principals would be, because the two men hired had gone hunting and fishing with the "powers that be." The women don't get that chance, and the district doesn't even bother to hide the fact. I find it hard not to get discouraged by that.
> (Library Specialist, Northwestern town)

*Summary*

Most female administrative aspirants believe their careers are negatively influenced by discriminatory practices. While some women speak at great length about the problem, others have appealed to the courts to establish the veracity of their claims (see Chapter Thirteen). Female aspirants, however, are more than what discrimination may or may not make them. They are active and complex people, not just passive victims of discrimination. For the most part they pursue school leadership with an understanding that biased hiring practices will influence their chances of success, and that the higher they attempt to go in administration, the more likely they will experience discrimination.

# 13    Litigation

After several years of negative experiences, I
finally filed a grievance. I could no longer
remain in or attempt to do my role as a
professional woman while I was expected to
be subservient to the male principal. I have
the ability to run the school maybe as well, if
not better, than he does. We have the same
qualifications. The reason he is the principal
and I am only the assistant principal is
because the district has systematically discriminated against women for years. I was
finally fed up with what had been done to me
and to other women over the years. I knew I
would lose my own professional integrity if I
sat back and allowed it to happen one more
time.

(Assistant Principal)*

FACED WITH REPEATED and blatant examples of sex discrimination, some women today consider taking their complaints to the courts
for litigation. Although there are new laws specifically designed to aid
women in such situations, choosing legal recourse continues to be an
individually difficult decision to make. In the past, women shied away
from using the courts for fear of negative repercussions upon their careers.
Timpano noted in the mid-1970s that "even when women are aware of
discrimination and have evidence of it and know how to prosecute it, some
of them hesitate to file complaints [fearing they will be] labeled 'trouble-
makers' and therefore [be] eliminated from future consideration for
positions in their, or any other, district."[1] Timpano concludes that women
do not wish to win the battle only to lose the war. Matthews finds that
similar sentiment still prevails in the 1980s. In her 1986 dissertation on
female administrators, she writes: "Some had reflected on what they would

---

*Geographical references for women who sued their districts are omitted to further
protect their anonymity.

204

do if they were discriminated against and, for most, it was something short of a lawsuit."[2] She describes her informants as "leery" of using the courts. Respondents in this study report similar feelings. An assistant principal (southern suburb) says she would not even consider suing if she is denied an upcoming promotion, because she does not want to "rock the boat" at this point in her career. Another woman, fearing ramifications in her personal life from a court battle, declined to prosecute what her local civil rights office considered a "strong" case. She describes her dilemma as follows:

Last May the high school principal resigned, and I, along with the male high school coach, applied for the job. The story is a typical one: I was the only one qualified, but without interviewing either of us, they hired the man instead of me. These people don't want me in administration because they don't think a woman can do the job. I asked the superintendent if the coach was certified, and after hemming and hawing for awhile, he said, "Not yet." Well, that's all I wanted to know. I went down immediately to the State Education Office, but I got the run around. Nevertheless, I continued to think and think about suing, and there's definitely a lot to sue about in this district because they don't advertise, interview or recruit minorities. All of the administrators are white males, and I am the only Mexican-American teacher here. In the end, I didn't pursue the case because of personal reasons. We were in the middle of trying to adopt a baby, and all of these people in the district were also our personal references to the adoption agency. I was afraid to create problems for fear of losing the baby. I know my decision disappointed the civil rights people who thought I had a great case. And, in a sense, I disappointed myself. My husband and family were behind me, and people in the street even stopped to tell me they thought I got a dirty deal. But a law suit would have split this community down the middle, and we might have lost our chance to adopt. I still feel very bitter about the whole matter.
(Department Chair, Southern rural)

An acting assistant principal sums up the concerns—both professional and personal—that women have had for years on the subject of suing:

If you go to the civil rights committee, honey, you probably won't *ever* get a good administrative position. Oh, you could win the case, but they can make life unbearable for you by giving you the worst school in the city. If you didn't have a hard time from then on, I'd be very, very surprised.
(Southern metro)

*Point of No Return*

Although many women still fear such reprisals, the decision not to sue is no longer as automatic as it once was. Some of the women interviewed now entertain the possibility of suing, and even the woman quoted above admits she might consider taking legal action—despite the ramifications— if years go by and she is not promoted. "If I see people placed over the next several years whose scores are lower than mine," she states, "I might consider suing—but I haven't reached that point yet." This notion of reaching a "particular point" suggests that some women are changing their attitudes about suing. Blandina Ramirez, a woman Ronald Reagan fired from the U.S. Civil Rights Commission in 1983, provides an excellent example. Ramirez decided to sue even though she could say "I never saw myself as one who would work that way." The federal courts ultimately reinstated her position. Ramirez goes on to state: " . . . there comes a time in a person's life when you almost have no choice. You cannot shirk the responsibility. You come to understand that the things you care about have much more to do with the process of history and development than with yourself."[3] A department chair (southern metro) agrees that there is a particular point in one's life when legal action becomes necessary: "I guess if year after year I didn't get a position and less qualified people were getting hired, I might get frustrated enough to sue."

With the support of equity legislation and affirmative action, respondents find themselves coming to that point of no return more frequently than the past. Furthermore, women who *do* go to court tend to give others hope and encouragement about their own situations.

> The same superintendent who continually rejected my own administrative applications was sued by another woman in the district who applied for principalships. She was a teacher-principal. Rather than place her, they hired a man who was a PE major with no experience as a principal. The coach finally pressured the superintendent to withdraw his recommendation and hire her instead, so they would not have to go to court. That woman's actions gave me a lot of encouragement.
>
> (Director, Midwestern suburb)

> Our county was slapped with a discrimination suit, and they settled out of court by promising to hire more women in administration. So now most of the schools have a woman assistant principal. That gives the rest of us some incentive to pursue educational administration.
>
> (Department Chair, Southern metro)

Some of these women believe there will be no significant changes in the hiring practices in educational administration unless districts are forced by the courts to hire women and minorities. Before her recent promotion to an assistant principalship, this woman considered suing her district:

> I'm thinking about suing, because I'm disgusted with the whole affair. The district is supposed to have a sex equity person and a grievance procedure in every building, but there's no commitment to equity at all. I know there are others who have been treated badly like me, but I don't know if they would be willing to risk suing. Since I'm looking for another job outside of education at this point, I don't feel like I have anything to lose. Until the district is forced to understand, that with seventy to eighty percent females in your personnel pool you ought to have seventy to eighty percent as your administrators, I think everything will stay the same. We ought to initiate a class action suit here like they did out West.
>
> (Southern metro)

As these women aspire to more responsible roles in school leadership, they know they will continue to experience some forms of discrimination. For many, repeated incidents of discrimination forces them—whether they want to or not—to reflect on legal resolutions. Women in this study report that they are more aware of their rights than ever before and more willing to register their displeasure with their districts.

> When I met with the superintendent, he told me that one big mark against me was that I was not in elementary education, and that women aspiring to leadership roles in this state should be in elementary education. I probably could have sued him for saying that.
>
> (Student, Southeastern city)

> This woman at the central office told me to be patient and I'd get this certain better position. Well, now she's been putting me off, and I'm beginning to see the handwriting on the wall. I could bring a law suit against her and the many people down at the central office who discriminate on the basis of sex.
>
> (Teacher-Administrator, Northeastern suburb)

> When I interviewed with other school districts, I was told over and over again to get into elementary education, because "we don't hire women at the secondary level." In one interview, someone used that rationale in a room full of people, and no one said a thing. Later I told the administrator, "That's illegal to say, you know." His response was: "Well, whose word are they going to take?" Another time I was asked all kinds of things that weren't related to the job: whether I was going to marry, whether I was planning on having children, and so forth. I

truly believe people don't know the legal ramifications of some of their questions.

(Assistant Principal, Midwestern suburb)

Although most informants willingly share stories of discrimination, the majority are still reluctant to do more than talk about possible legal action. Two women in this study, however, did seek legal redress for discriminatory practices in their districts. As the two cases illustrate, suing is personally and professionally stressful; however, the active pursuit of legal justice is also personally and professionally liberating. In both of these instances, the women won victories, if not for themselves, for other women in their districts. Because such cases are relatively few and often unknown to others considering legal action, they are presented here in some detail. The first case involves a single female plaintiff; the second stems from a personal grievance that grew into a class action suit.

*Marie's Case*

Marie is a soft-spoken, middle-aged woman who lives in the rural heartland of America. After thirteen years of teaching, she decided she was ready for a change. She applied for an administrative internship through a cooperative program her district had with a nearby university. She was the first woman ever in her district to seek such an appointment. In the previous year, two males were chosen who, by her evaluation, had less experience than she had. Initially the word went out that the board would accept whoever the superintendent and principal chose—"no questions asked." However, when Marie's name was submitted by the administration, she says the board "dug in their heels and said no." She explains further:

> My husband was an administrator in the district at the time. Although he would not have been my boss, they said they did not want two administrators from one family in the district. However, they had no written policy on the issue at the time. When I heard their objections, I was rather agitated and upset. The supervisor advised them that they were violating my civil rights by denying my request on such a basis, but they said: "Well, that's too bad." I guess they expected me to just roll over and play dead. Teachers don't have much of a reputation for being assertive, unfortunately.

Like others who sue, Marie reached a turning point when her daughter asked her what she intended to do about the district's decision.

> I told her I didn't know what I could do other than take some sort of legal action. She said, "Well, what they did wasn't right; they violated

your rights, didn't they?" She went on to say, "You've always told me if you believe in something, you should fight for it. So aren't you going to fight for your rights?" I felt like I had to live up to what I believe in and to what I'd taught my young daughter. So I said, "Yes, I am."

When the district found out she was not going to "roll over and play dead," and that she was seeking legal assistance from the State's Civil Rights Commission, their immediate response was to do away with the cooperative internship program itself. They also began to pressure Marie and her husband, but her husband encouraged her "to do what she thought she should do."

So began a long process for Marie and her family. She first obtained the tapes of her interviews with the board (all matters of public record), and she sent them to her caseworker. For two years, Marie and the caseworker moved "cautiously" to build a case without loopholes that the district could slip through because of some legal technicality. She describes why she persisted with the suit:

> To me, the situation was such an out and out case of discrimination. They never examined my employment records, university transcripts or my teacher evaluations. Nor did they interview me personally. They just turned down my request because I was married to my husband.

When the district received official notification that they had violated Marie's civil rights, they were ordered to reinstate the internship program as well as to admit Marie, or they would lose their federal funding. "This was quite a blow to a rural district," she explains. When the district immediately granted her the internship, Marie concluded: "The purse strings in this small district are very tight; withholding funds is a very effective carrot."

Reflecting back over the two-year process, Marie feels the hardest part was that she could not discuss the case with friends and colleagues. Once the case was resolved, many of these people came to her to express support and to offer congratulations: "A lot of people told me they were very glad I had chosen to fight it out." Although she felt she had the nonverbal support of both male and female teachers, she felt relieved to be able to talk openly about the case after the decision was made.

Still unsure about the long-range impact of the suit on her career, Marie states:

> Truthfully, I don't know what the ultimate impact of my case will be. As far as my internship, I've been very cautious, so I haven't had any problems. But I've had no contact at all with the board members who first denied my application for the program. I'd like to stay in this district because I've given quite a few years of my life to it, and I've

worked hard to establish a good professional reputation. But the
district has no female administrators, so I doubt if I will even apply for
a job here. (I'll apply within driving distance from here, though.) I
would like to continue my commitment to the district, but I don't think
they'll permit me to advance because I am a woman.

Even if an appropriate opening should occur in her district, she knows she
will hesitate before applying. She contends her relationships with board
members are still fractured, and she would not consider applying without
strong support from them. She explains her caution:

I don't intend to be embarrassed again. I am a person, and I deserve to
be treated as such. I won't initiate anything in this district that would
put me in a position to be humiliated again.

Despite these reservations, she wants to encourage other women who
may be considering legal resolutions to discriminatory practices. Although
suing is never an easy path to take, she describes the kind of individual one
needs to be to pursue a law suit:

You must have a total commitment, and not let anything stand in your
way. You've got to be ready to accept snubs, to see friendships vanish,
to have associations slide by the wayside. You need to know you'll get
a lot of criticism and peer pressure. The pressure can be subtle,
sometimes it's just a sly look or a giggle. You must realize that
whatever you do may affect you career forever—maybe even your
husband's career or someone else's in your family. You have a choice
to make: Either you stand up as a woman or lie down as a doormat.
And I was never very good at being a doormat.

Marie adds a further note regarding family concerns:

If anyone contemplates an action like this, they need to discuss it with
their family. A legal case affects your employment *and* your life. You
have to be prepared for the fact that nobody outside of your family
understands why you are suing. After all, no one goes against the boss.
When you say you're involved in a civil rights action, people will look
at you as if you are an animal that just crawled out from under a rock.
That's why we just told our families and our closest friends about the
case.

Even with these cautions, Marie is certain she would do it all over
again if she had to make the choice today.

Yes, I would. I found our governmental agency very supportive. They always treated me with courtesy, and I always felt they were very interested in my case. I hope others with good cases decide to pursue them. They must have proof and a commitment in their hearts to stick with it. The last two years were very difficult, and although I wouldn't look forward to living through that time again, I would if I had to. That's what makes this country great: You have the opportunity to say you were treated wrongly and that you won't be treated that way again. But you must prepare for the backlash, because there will be one.

Beyond the impact on herself and on her family, Marie sees her case influencing girls in her school district.

I've noticed a much greater consciousness on the part of little girls that they are equal to boys. In the years to come, I think that awareness will be a driving force in this county. I hope I contributed to that awareness. If I get an administrative position, then I will really be able to contribute. Incidentally, my own daughter has been one of my biggest supporters all the way through this.

In conclusion, Marie states she is not a "climbing woman's libber who would go out and burn her bra." She is, however, an individual who was pushed beyond a tolerable point in her life—pushed to question the assumptions and actions of a board who reacted to her gender rather than her qualifications. She feels good about what the case accomplished and positive about herself and the administrative experiences she's had since the ruling. When considering her future, she states:

If I can wait the necessary years, maybe I'll be one of the first rural female administrators in the area. But while I'm waiting, I'm going to get as much education, as well as all of the experiences, I can. If and when the time comes, I'm going to be as prepared as possible.

Only time will tell whether Marie's persistence pays off and whether she has the makings of a good administrator. In a way, her victory is a small one, and her prospects are dubious. Nevertheless, she believes that the case strengthened her personal and professional integrity. Her district went through an experience that will make the board at least pause before acting on a similar issue, and the female students in her district's schools have a new role model to attend to with interest. In Marie's mind, these positive changes, however small, were well worth the effort.

*Rose's Case*

Rose in an energetic woman with graying hair who belies the image of someone who would be at the center of controversy. She has worked for years as a secondary school assistant principal in a large metropolitan district considered "progressive" by people in other regions of the United States. What began as a personal grievance on her part, grew into a class action effort to stop her district from systematically discriminating against certified women who aspired to higher managerial positions. Although Rose was aware that the district continually failed to promote qualified women such as herself, she describes herself as naive at the beginning of the case.

> Initially, I didn't know what my rights were. Even after twenty-eight years of experience and many years of applying for assistant principalships and principalships, I didn't feel exploited. I think that's indicative of the trouble with many school people: We are, by nature, givers. We give more and get more inner satisfaction from our jobs than, say, people in the business world. I didn't want to sell shoes or jewelry; I wanted to work for an organization that did some good in the world. Because of my giving nature, it didn't occur to me to question those doing the hiring. But after a point, I began to read in the newspapers about sex discrimination, and I put two and two together about my own situation. After four years of being thwarted in my attempts to gain a higher administrative appointment, I finally filed a grievance.

What Rose describes about her experiences during the four years preceding her grievance would test anyone's credibility, if not for the fact that a national law center became interested in helping her win her case, and that much of what she relates is a matter of public record.

With good recommendations and several years of experience as an assistant principal, Rose transferred to an inner city school where the principal bluntly told her: "We don't want any white women in our school." While she sought to gain the acceptance of people in this new school through her usual dedication and hard work, she claims she underwent "all kinds of harassment and 'encouragement' from this man to quit." (Since her case was initiated, other women have made similar complaints against this same principal.) She reports that when she took her concerns to her superintendent and asked about filing a grievance, "the man literally treated it like a joke."

> The superintendent yelled across the office: "Ever hear of a girls' vice principal filing a grievance against a principal?" The staff relations man came in and said, "I've never heard of such a thing!" So that's all the advice I got. Back then I was too worried about my recommendations and my promotion to pursue my complaints further. If I could re-live that time, there is no doubt in my mind what measures I would take.

This comment, however, comes only in retrospect. At the time, she did not question the superintendent further, nor did she challenge district policies. In addition to feeling naive about her civil rights, she still trusted that her well-documented record of good performance would prevail against male principals who discriminated against female subordinates.

Rather than face continued harassment and threats in her job as an assistant principal, Rose decided to apply for principalship. Rose had always scored high in the promotional rounds when she sought new positions; however, this time her scores were lower. She reflects on the reasons:

> I didn't ask for my personnel file at the time, because I didn't know my legal rights. I was never told about Title VII and my rights relative to employment. When I asked at the personnel office what the problem was, they told me I needed high school experience. But I had that. Finally someone told me: "There is a person you need to outlive." Because of my personal life and where my kids were in school at the time, I decided to drop the application.

Rose remembers being afraid to face the fact that a principal was "blackballing" her. She now recognizes this reaction as one her attorneys call "the chilling effect." "When you don't make it," she explains, "losing has a chilling effect on you as an applicant."

After successfully requesting a transfer to a new school, she established a positive relationship with her new principal. Her improved working situation was shortlived, however, for a new male principal with a "poor reputation" for working with females moved into the building.

> He could not work with any woman in a collegial fashion. He was a former serviceman, and there was no way he wanted to work with a woman on his administrative staff. Within fifteen days of his arrival, he changed my assistant principal's job assignment to make me into the school bookkeeper. After building up my references once again, that's the kind of man who entered my life! I saw the red flag and knew I had to get out of the situation.

By this time, however, she had a greater understanding about her past experiences and began to fight back. She realized she was gaining a reputation as a troublemaker in the district, so she began documenting her activities with this new, "known sexist" principal. She wanted concrete evidence to refute any allegations this man might bring against her.

> I just felt trouble coming, and I knew I would need evidence. I had the feeling I needed to protect myself, so I intuitively began keeping records and documents. I could show his poor record of handling

black children, his lack of dealing with a teacher's sexual harassment of students, and so on. But rather than dealing with the principal's poor record, the area superintendent gave me an administrative transfer. Unfortunately, that kind of a transfer has a negative connotation in our district. Again, I got placed in a school with a principal who had a reputation for "doing women in." He had already gone through one highly competent woman, causing her to practically close up her office. She told me that the school was "hell." When I began to get critical memos from this principal, I called the central office and told them to get him off my back. I had put up with this kind of harassment before, but I wasn't going to put up with it anymore. When they reassigned me to yet another principal with a district-wide reputation for being abusive to personnel who didn't "kowtow" to him (particularly women), I knew I had trouble on my hands. He subjected me to unrelenting harassment and memos critical of my performance. After four months, he produced a packet of materials to substantiate his multiple allegations that I was "below standard in performance." Because I never received a rating during my entire career in education that was anything but "well above the standard," I felt I had to clear my record. And the only way I could do that was to file a grievance.

The district informed Rose that if she wanted to take her case to court, she must first utilize all the district's internal administrative procedures. She alleges that these grievance procedures work against an employee who wishes to file a complaint.

The grievant must pay half of the fees of the arbitrator, all the legal fees for representation, as well as pay for clerical, telephone and transportation costs connected with the hearing. The list of arbitrators is male-dominated, and the district can choose to strike out all the females. Because the cost of the transcript of the court proceedings is so high, most grievants cannot afford to request one; consequently, the arbitrator must rely on his own handwritten notes between hearing dates. Historically, the district provides one-hundred percent financial support to the principal being accused, for they consider him an agent of the district. He has at his disposal a highly trained, full-time legal representative, staff relations personnel, an unlimited budget and investigatory services—all provided at taxpayers' expense. An assistant principal such as myself, who files the grievance and who is *also* a management employee, has no protection or support from the district and must retain an attorney often unfamiliar with board rules. Furthermore, the district has the power to spread a three to fifteen-day hearing over two and a half years in an effort to wear down the grievant physically, emotionally and financially. While the grievance is taking place over this time period, the challenged information remains in the grievant's personnel file, thus diminishing the chances of applying for positions in another school district or of applying for a federal grant, special university program or sabbatical.

When Rose's intentions to file a grievance became publicly known, other women stepped forward to recount similar stories with some of the same male principals. No one, however, was willing to risk seeking a legal resolution to the problems. Rose listened and sympathized.

> They said, "As long as you're doing the suing, I will tell you what he did to me." They were afraid the district would retaliate, and they didn't want to put their professional futures on the line. I can't criticize them for that. For myself, I felt set up and like the district was after me anyway. After all my years of service, I was being sent from school to school, building a bad reputation and failing to get promoted. I felt like I didn't have much to lose.

Years of accumulated abuses, along with a growing awareness of legal rights, led Rose to her point of no return. She was unwilling to dismiss the problem any longer.

Only after her own hearing was underway, did Rose begin to think about a class action suit: "I read about the tremendous changes made by class action suits, and my lawyer thought the action was suitable." She wrote letters nationwide seeking support and financial backing, and found a public law center interested in the case. Rose believes the contact was a "happy coincidence," but another female administrator in her district (who is also in the study) calls it "destiny." The center quickly sought to mobilize women in the district and, although a well-attended meeting ensued and made headlines in the local news, only one other woman consented to place her name alongside of Rose's on the law suit. "Some very competent younger women, and some older women," she explains, "just didn't feel the case was worth the risk."

The efforts on behalf of a class action suit ran simultaneously with her own personal grievance. Rose initially hoped to recoup some of the costs of her own grievance via the group effort. She was advised, however, that class action litigation could take years, and that a quick, out-of-court settlement affecting all the women in the district should take precedence over her personal financial concerns. For Rose, the trade off became one of "getting something for women now—to open doors for the women today—rather than to worry about past personal wrongs that I had suffered alone." The threat of a class action lawsuit resulted in an agreement (consent decree) between the district and the law center—a settlement which precluded litigation. Goals and timetables evolved through negotiations between the parties' counsel, including annual and long-term goals designed to increase the representation of females in management positions throughout the district. Another assistant principal in the study comments on the implications of the decision:

> I now believe my chances might be greater because of the consent decree here in the district. Because the district is under the gun, more women must be hired. But I won't get all moon-eyed because some judge says the district has to change its hiring practices. I'll just assess things over a period of time, and hold my opinion in abeyance until I can see progress with my own eyes.

(This informant has since received a principalship, and thus, may have directly benefited from the decision.)

As for Rose's personal grievance, the outcome was not as positive. The arbitrator sided with the principal. Although a minority report was written and the matter was appealed to the Board of Education, the Board declined to hear the case. Understandably disappointed, Rose admits in her private moments that the financial burden of the grievance is "nerve-wracking." "I couldn't begin to tell you what my legal bill is going to be," she confides, "because I've been too afraid to add it all up." Despite the personal and financial costs, however, Rose's family has stood firmly behind her.

> We're a family, and we didn't have that much before this began. I've worked all my life, and so has my husband. Our children work as well. The case was a family issue, a matter of pride for all of us. There's an old proverb: "If you have no pride, you have no soul." Neither my family nor I was going to be beaten down by a system.

In reflecting on the grievance process, Rose is still surprised she lost. She felt she was right, that somehow justice would prevail and her former years of unflawed service would balance out her recent, more suspect experiences. She expected the board to intervene on her behalf to prevent male administrators from harassing her as well as other women. To this day, she believes her district keeps slapping her hands for bringing the whole matter to public light. And, despite her requests to eliminate from her personnel file the biased performance reviews written by one of the principals she complained about, that principal continues to negatively influence her career.

> On the last promotional round, he did not endorse me. Naturally he is not going to write anything good about me after I filed a grievance against him.

These problems aside, Rose continues to pursue a principalship in the same district. She takes heart from the fact that the consent decree holds promise for female administrative aspirants in the district. While she draws certain personal satisfaction from the energy she devoted to the case, she also realizes she is in a lonely position: "Only two of the recently promoted women principals told me they appreciated my efforts; the others were, and are, silent." She believes many aspiring women do not want to be seen with her for fear of being aligned with a "trouble maker." In fact, only a few women even privately acknowledge her efforts.

> Since the decision, the women who have gained promotions seem unaware of the efforts my coplaintiff and I went through to change district hiring practices. When they are informed of the changes we initiated, they tend to pooh-pooh the whole thing and pretend they didn't need any help in getting where they are now. These women used their own methods of getting ahead, I'm afraid—they cultivated the men in power.

Unbeknownst to Rose, another woman in the study did express gratitude for Rose's crusade. Now a newly appointed principal, she states:

> I'm grateful to the woman who sued—for all the suffering she has gone through and for the personal expenses she incurred. She brought something out into the open that a lot of us never thought about. In other words, we could all be in her position. I always thought management would stick up for management, but now I see how someone above you can really do a number on you. You have no way out, and that frightens me. I've seen what happened to her, and I know how capable she is. I wouldn't blame her if she is angry and bitter.

The results of Rose's legal battle, therefore, appear mixed. Although she still hopes to attain a principalship before she retires, she is realistic—but guardedly optimistic—about her chances. "I'm not going to be discouraged," she concludes, "because I don't think you can afford to be discouraged." She now believes she was "too patient" when she was younger, but she also admits she may not "have the strength to hold out" for a promotion now. She contends that many women in her district and elsewhere still remain unaware of what constitutes sex discrimination. And for this reason, she continues to tell her story. To some extent, telling her story is cathartic, but her larger concern is for educating other women about gender bias in administrative hiring. Realizing there is no central clearinghouse for information about legal cases such as hers, Rose believes she must continue to publicize her own experiences in an effort to inform others considering legal redress. For this reason, she is now a strong advocate of women's professional organizations, which she sees as one place where women can hear about court cases and can work for advancing female educators as a group. Would she sue again if she had it to do all over? She readily admits that the district's acceptance of the consent decree is somewhat validating, even though she has yet to benefit personally from the agreement. Thus, while she fears that the "district is not through with me yet," her sense of having made a stand—and consequently, a point— seems to balance out the ledger in her mind.

*Summary*

Legislation now exists to aid women who experience systematic discrimination or who face instances of bias that warrant legal action. The choice to seek legal redress, however, remains with the individual. O'Reilly notes, "It takes more strength than spite can give [to use the courts]; it takes commitment to a principle."[4] The two women in this chapter manifest the kind of commitment O'Reilly deems necessary for waging legal battles. First, Marie and Rose had the kind of individual fortitude needed to pursue court actions. They shared a personal conviction that the discrimination they experienced in their own careers could no longer be ignored without the loss of personal and professional integrity. Second, Marie and Rose developed strong, well-documented cases with proof to back up their convictions. Without careful record keeping and documentation, their cases would have been summarily dismissed. And third, their commitment steeled them to endure a long, drawnout legal process, regardless of the outcomes or costs to their careers and personal lives. Put simply, they risked everything.

Neither Marie nor Rose sees herself as a heroine, but others around them might. To date, neither one is yet a principal; however, although this goal still eludes them, their individual crusades have contributed to a growing awareness of how to legally combat sex discrimination in the workplace. Marie and Rose hope that women in similar situations find their stories constructive and that, at the very least, other women will seriously consider pursuing cases in the courts.

# Part Four

## Looking Ahead

# 14   Goals and
Expectations

Now that I've made up my mind to go into administration, I want to go as far as I can. I figure I will retire in the year 2000, so between now and then there are a lot of directions I could take. Although I am a "johnny-come-lately" to the field, I feel very young. Now that I am here, I believe there is no ceiling to my aspirations.

(New Coordinator, Western metro)

LIKE OTHER PROFESSIONAL FIELDS, education has been slow to open up its managerial ranks to women. Biklen argues that, "people, especially those in comfortable circumstances and sometimes even those at the bottom of one heap or another, adapt slowly and with resistance to movements to redress social grievances."[1] Despite a hiring pool replete with competent female educators, and despite legislation aimed at correcting past inequities in the field, school leadership in the 1980s remains predominantly male. In this post-women's-movement decade, Kaplan notes, "the sluggish, even decelerating, pace at which women and members of racial and ethnic minority groups are passing into the upper reaches of educational leadership remains a rankling sore spot."[2]

Although the numbers of women in educational administration remain essentially unchanged since 1980,[3] recent evidence suggests a significant change in attitudes on the part of female professionals in education. They no longer appear to accept the notion that males will "naturally" command the top administrative positions. As their concept of "women's work" expands to include these positions of authority, more and more women actively seek administrative roles. In a study of female aspirants in North Carolina, Woo found that the women had high motivation, expanded self-images and heightened career aspirations: "This new generation of women [are] more aware of themselves, of their expanded opportunities, and of their almost unlimited potential. The sky is the limit—or so today's American women are told."[4]

221

Like the women in Woo's analysis, female aspirants in this study reflect the changing attitudes women have about themselves and about administrative work. They no longer envision themselves merely as candidates for supportive management roles in education; rather, they desire line positions with all the accompanying authority and responsibility. Although Greenfield argues that administrative candidacies are full of ambiguities for any would-be executive,[5] informants in this study are at least clear about their desire for executive authority in public school management (if not necessarily clear on how to attain it). When asked to project their two highest career goals, very few (six percent) see themselves in the roles once considered appropriate for women within the managerial hierarchy of schools (i.e., specialist, coordinator, supervisor or central office staff member). In this study, forty percent of the women list principalships as one of their two highest career goals, forty percent seek full or assistant superintendencies, and thirty percent even mention hopes of reaching positions at the state or national levels at some point in their work careers. Minority women report higher aspirations than nonminority women, routinely listing superintendencies or beyond when queried about their ultimate career aims.

In case after case, women in this study illustrated the changing attitudes women have about their futures in school administration. One might argue that these women are exceptions, for they were nominated by educators across the country who knew they were highly motivated to succeed in school administration. On the other hand, countless other women were nominated who could not participate in the study, and one suspects that the 142 who did participate are not an unrepresentative group. Confident in their abilities and strongly focused on their professional goals, forty-four percent admit they are impressed with how far they have come in their careers to date. More importantly, however, fifty-three percent anticipate their future advancement to principalships and beyond.

### The Appeal of Administration

Why are women interested in the extra responsibilities and challenges of educational administration? An assistant principal explains:

> I could easily have gone for a supervisory role, but I don't want the traditional female role anymore. I decided the building level principalship with its power and influence is what I want to carve out for myself in the immediate future.
>
> (Southern city)

Another assistant principal (southeastern city) states, "I know the elementary school like the back of my hand, so I want a school of my own eventually." A third assistant principal (Southern metro) knows she "would welcome the challenge of a principalship." Although these women know their career goals to become principals run counter to traditional thinking, they contend that the challenges of administration are just too appealing to put aside.

Some aspirants do not believe they are challenging traditional role expectations in their desire to become administrators, as they have limited their aspirations to positions where women continue to enjoy some degree of acceptance. An administrative intern who seeks an elementary principalship explains:

> An elementary principalship is still a safe area for a woman. I was raised by parents who never put any limits on me—I could do anything my brother did. But in aiming for the elementary level, I won't be fighting a lot of tradition. I believe that I can prove myself and that my track record will speak for itself.
>
> (Western suburb)

Others are unwilling to settle for elementary positions, especially when their skills, interests and backgrounds lie elsewhere. An administrative assistant (southern metro) allows she might accept an elementary principalship while her son is still home, "but before I get through, my ambitions will take me into secondary administration."

Despite high levels of desire, women in this study are not naive about their prospects in school management. Although they have altered their aspirations, they know that the field of educational administration has not changed sufficiently to accommodate their heightened expectations. Aspirants remain aware of the many myths about female educators that negatively influence their opportunities,[6] and realize the numerous barriers they face—especially at the secondary level.

> I want to be a secondary principal, but the district may take a long time before they promote another woman to principal. The one we have does an excellent job, but it's going to take a long time before people change their thinking about female administrators.
>
> (Assistant Principal, Southern suburb)

> After a couple of years as an assistant principal, I was ready to move on. Sometimes I get bogged down and wonder why I keep trying to be a principal of a senior high school. I could go off into the back woods and be an elementary principal with 500-600 kids and have no headaches. But I only think that for a few minutes. I interviewed for a junior high principalship, but truthfully, all of my experience is at the senior level. Even though I could handle the job, I prefer to wait for a secondary position. Some people see junior high jobs as stepping stones, but I believe schools need principals who can provide

continuity, stability and devotion. I could not be that committed at the
junior high level.
                              (Assistant Principal, Southeastern town)

The pull between what a woman wants and what might be possible is
evident in the comments of several other aspirants:

My best bet is to get an elementary principalship and then to jump to a
high school. But I worry about getting stuck at the elementary level—
cast off there forever. That might be the end of the line for me, unless I
kept pushing and pushing. Getting stuck could easily happen to me; it
even happens to men.
                              (Teacher, Southern rural)

I don't want an elementary principalship. As a woman, however, I
don't think I'll be offered a junior high. That creates a paradox: I want
to be a principal, but I also think you should have appropriate level
experience and want to be with that particular age group of students.
                              (Assistant Principal, Southeastern city)

Commenting on the barriers women face, an assistant principal concludes:

A secondary principalship is my immediate goal, perhaps even my
ultimate goal. But with so few secondary schools here, I'll have to wait
for someone to move on or die.
                              (Northwestern town)

Despite the barriers, and in addition to the challenges and responsibilities, women want principalships in order to stay close to children—
something they would lose in central office support positions. In this
respect, women in this study have not changed their attitudes about
children as they seek executive roles. An administrative intern (western
suburb) cites "working with kids" as one of the primary reasons she aspires
to a principalship, rather than to a position in the central office. Others
agree that close contact with students remains one of the most important
attractions of administration:

I'd like a principalship, because I don't think I want to be that far away
from kids. Maybe after awhile I'd want that, but not now.
                              (New Principal, Northwestern town)

Personally, a principalship is as far as I want to go. I'm not very
interested at all in the county office level, because I don't want to be
that far away from kids. I think an administrator realistically needs
children nearby to do a good job—you need to reach out to them and

take a good look at what you're doing from time to time.

(Lead Teacher, Southern suburb)

I don't think I'd like central office because you lose touch with the kids when you move there. I went into education because I like kids. I must admit it's nice to send them home at three, but I'd miss them if I moved into the central office this early in my career. Maybe later I'll reconsider, but not now.

(Teacher, Northwestern metro)

*Aiming High*

Although some women claim to avoid higher levels of administration because they desire "to stay close to children," others in the study are not content with building-level management responsibilities. These women acknowledge greater bias against female executives the higher up the career ladder they go; however, many—especially minorities—talk about wanting superintendencies and other high-level administrative posts. Because their futures may be circumscribed by their gender—no matter how prepared or experienced they might be—they are hesitant to predict their chances for actually getting such positions.

I want to be a superintendent in some small place. People think I am being too ambitious for a woman, but that's what I want.

(Assistant Principal, Southern suburb)

My ultimate goal would not be a principalship, but a superintendency. That might be a bit unrealistic for a woman, so I will continue assessing my goal. But I'm not "ancient" at thirty-five years old; I still have lots of years of building my reputation and of politicking ahead of me. I don't think a superintendency is an impossible goal.

(Teacher, Northeastern city)

I haven't really decided how far I want to go. About every three years I start looking for somewhere else to grow, and maybe there's a lot of room for growth in a principalship. But my guess is I'll love a principalship the first year, find it terribly satisfying the second and by the third, begin to say, "Gee, I have done about all I can here. What would I like to do next?" When I retire at sixty-five, I'd ultimately like to be a superintendent. But that may not be realistic.

(Assistant Principal, Western suburb)

Some women admit surprise at their own seemingly lofty goals. Many never envisioned aspiring to top positions when they began pursuing entry-level positions in administration.

I don't know if I'll be content to stop with a principalship now. Here I am: I never intended to graduate from college, and few degrees later, I'm thinking about going beyond even a principalship!

(Teacher, Northeastern city)

Ultimately, I would now like to be a superintendent. But six months ago you couldn't have told me I would be interested in *this* role! Right now I'm enthused about the whole field.

(Student, Southern city)

In one interview, a principal asked me where I thought I'd be in ten years. I told him I wanted to be in a superintendency somewhere. Then I thought, "Did *I* say that?"

(New Principal, Northwestern town)

Other women show little surprise about their aspirations and view the superintendency as many men do: as the natural outgrowth of career progression. Because of their backgrounds and successful experiences, they express confidence and enthusiasm about their professional futures. One student (southeastern city) notes, "My ultimate goal is the superintendency; I know that clearly." A teacher (northwestern metro) professes similar confidence: "I may end up as a superintendent because I have no fears about going in that direction." Others share these sentiments about top-level roles in education:

I never intend to retire; I'm just not the retiring type. I'd like to work at the state level in administration, curriculum or whatever.

(Assistant Principal, Southeastern city)

Someday I would really like to be superintendent of public instruction for the state. I like to be in charge and would welcome the challenge. I need something bigger to do all the time. I "get off" on the fact that I'm the first woman administrator in the district. It's scary, but it's also neat. I'm still not even thirty, so there's lots of time to realize my hopes.

(New Principal, Northwestern town)

I don't know many creative people who survive in public schools, but for some reason I feel a strong tie to education. So I'm interested in trying to impact public education from a state or federal agency.

(District Planner, Southern metro)

Two women even talk of cabinet-level positions in Washington, albeit with a twinkle in their eyes:

I enjoy so many things, but eventually I would like to work at the state

level. I would *really* love to be a Secretary of Education, but I understand Ronnie is doing away with the position!
(Lead Teacher, Southern metro)

I joke about being the first female Commissioner of Education, but I guess Reagan fixed that!
(Department Chair, Southern metro)

Some women consider leaving public schools to seek careers on university campuses as professors or administrators. A desire to share their professional knowledge and practical experiences with others motivates their aspirations.

I would like very much to try my hand at college teaching. Maybe I won't like it as much as I think I will, but I've begun to make inquiries in that direction.
(Teacher, Southeastern rural)

When I entered the doctoral program, I had ambitions of being an academic dean. One day I might still pursue that.
(Assistant Principal, Southern metro)

My life's desire has really been to teach at the college level.
(Assistant Principal, Western metro)

After I'm an assistant superintendent, I think I will be ready to retire from public schools. When I do, I'd like to take all my experience and expertise to someone's college and teach future administrators.
(Assistant Principal, Southern metro)

Some women report that their interest in higher education stems from the fact that they had no female professors when they were in graduate school and that they would like to change the status quo on campuses for future women considering administration.

Overall, this study presents an image of female educators committed to their field and eager to pursue opportunities—whether at the district, state or national levels. A clearly articulated sense of career pervades their thinking and planning:

I want to be an assistant superintendent, so I need building administrative experience. I'd like to try an elementary principalship for two or three years—that was my original goal back in the 1960s when the field opened up at the elementary level for women. I'm trying to get a variety of administrative experiences, because I am a career-girl.
(New Assistant Principal, Northwestern city)

I see myself spending many years in a principalship, because I'm a career person. I wouldn't turn down something with a wider scope as well, say at the district level.

(Head Teacher, Western suburb)

A superintendency doesn't appeal to me—too many nuts, bolts and bus tires. Later in my career, I would like to be involved in some capacity in developing district policy.

(New Principal, Western metro)

## Long-Term Aspirants

Despite their hopes and dreams, a number of women are not optimistic about reaching their goals. In particular, many older and experienced women feel bitter about how their districts treat them.

After being turned down repeatedly for jobs where I was the more qualified candidate, my superintendent told me: "With so many good people, sometimes the truly good ones get passed over in the shuffle." I was supposed to be content with that consolation! Finally after twenty-four years in administration, I am now an assistant. But I should be *much* further along.

(Assistant Principal, Southern metro)

I'm not going to apply for any position for awhile, because I think I'm wasting my time. In this city, who you know—not what your qualifications are—gets you promoted. If they hired on the basis of experience (I've been an assistant for six years) and background, I should be a principal by now. I keep hoping maybe the hiring system will change, because a person has to have some hope and that's where I put mine. In seven more years, I'll have thirty years in education and will take early retirement if I'm not a principal by then. I'd rather keep working, but you don't always get what you want.

(Assistant Principal, Southern metro)

I hope whatever is happening with equity (or whatever this study does) helps other people. But for myself, I think I have just fallen by the wayside. I've been an assistant principal for ten years and have been trying for a principalship for six. I'm really very discouraged at this point. You get placed in this district either by who you know or by your ethnicity. I was really hurt when I didn't even make the placement list last year; but I'll bounce back and do my job better than ten other people, because that's the way I am. I like the kids, and I want to see them get ahead.

(Assistant Principal, Western suburb)

Discouraged by the rigid views held in many districts about women in the work force, these women begin to question their abilities and their aspirations:

> You get to the point of thinking something is wrong with you. And yet in my case, I had a former administrator write in my file: "Prime candidate for administration." But even with his encouragement and my aspirations, shaking the traditional views people hold about women is hard.
>
> (Teacher, Northwestern city)

Many women in the study share similar sentiments about the difficulties they have with stereotypes of female administrators. One assistant principal remarks:

> I know the women I have worked with who are head teachers or assistant principals don't feel their overall chances of getting principal-ships are very good. Yet many of them are as qualified, if not more qualified, than the men getting hired.
>
> (Southern suburb)

Only twenty-five percent of respondents believe the chances are generally good for female candidates seeking administrative positions. An intern (midwestern rural) admits she might not "even bother to apply" for openings, because she feels there is little hope of getting a job in a county with no female administrators. A counselor points to similar deterrents in her district:

> I am leery of applying, because there are only two or three female administrators in the whole district. The overall feeling from the board and from those at the top is not one of support for women. Despite the competence of women, they will go with a man at the secondary level.
>
> (Midwestern suburb)

A student (northeastern metro) agrees: "I would love to be a secondary principal, but I'm not sure that's ever going to happen with hiring as it is now." Whether in rural or metropolitan areas, hiring practices in school districts across the nation remain similar: Women want administrative positions, but few are hired. Before recently gaining an assistant principal-ship, one aspirant (southern metro) was repeatedly passed over for positions: "Men were always hired—some black, some white—and they were only working on the degrees *I* already had. Some weren't even going to school!" Clearly, just wanting a position does not guarantee success, but women contend that traditional hiring practices negatively influence their aspirations. Another new assistant principal remembers feeling "like the pits" whenever she was told in an interview: "Yes, you're qualified, and we'd love to have you in the job. But our board would not hire another woman; they want a man." She concludes: "I cannot imagine such a thing being said to a male candidate."

*The Economy*

In addition to traditional hiring practices that continue to discriminate against female aspirants, the poor state of the national economy during the past two decades also works against female administrative candidates. Although economic retrenchment affects men as well as women, female aspirants believe they will suffer most. A teacher describes her feeling of vulnerability:

> Our district received some federal money to encourage women to go into administration, and a lot of us got our first opportunities. Other women also became interested in management because they saw us in these roles. Now there are all these women competing for jobs, and there are so few administrative positions available. The women assumed there'd be positions coming up, because districts encouraged and trained them. During all this, however, the district had scheduled to close a dozen schools.
>
> (Midwestern city)

A specialist shares this concern:

> I'm worried about people—both men and women—who prepare to be administrators and then, with the closing of schools, fail to find any openings. They're all set to aspire with nothing to aspire to! The problem is an important one for their futures in education.
>
> (Western suburb)

In a northeastern town, an assistant principal states flatly, "The economic situation has certainly impacted *my* aspirations. I know there will be very few, if any, positions available." Many respondents in the Northeast, for example, express fears about tax limitation bills such as those initiated in the West and Northwest:

> I don't know where to go from here. People better get those jobs now, given the way the tax initiatives are going in this country. When the cuts come, blacks and women are the ones who will go—"last hired, first fired" kind of thing.
>
> (Assistant Principal, Northeastern suburb)

There are only so many assistant principals that can move into

principalships when a principal dies or moves away. Finding a job in times of economic hardship is very slow and tedious. There are a lot of people trying for very few jobs—and they're all doing it at the same time.
(Team Leader, Northeastern suburb)

While realizing the difficulties of securing immediate administrative employment, many women believe that opportunities will improve in the future. Several respondents believe that impending retirements of older administrators mitigates the otherwise gloomy job forecast. Thus, many adopt a wait and see attitude, as this State Department Coordinator indicates:

The economic situation is devastating to education. But they will still need people with my background and experience in education. Hopefully in the years to come, I will be able to find an administrative position that allows me to use the skills I've acquired.
(Northeastern metro)

*Alternative Careers*

Believing that school administration may never offer widespread opportunities to female candidates, some women contemplate leaving education altogether. These individuals stress their unwillingness to sit by and wait until either the economy improves or until the educational profession fully opens its managerial ranks to women. "School administration is no longer an attractive choice to many people," Thomas maintains, and many women are now choosing "law, medicine, [and] business...rather than education."[7] Should new options arise, many female administrative aspirants may indeed look elsewhere for careers.

I am very disillusioned with our school system right now, because they fail to hire women for leadership positions. The typical choice for an administrator is either a male coach or someone who looks like they are big enough to break up fights. I don't know if I'm willing to wait until *they* think a woman is ready to run a public school.
(Assistant Principal, Northeastern metro)

For those who have devoted a major part of their lives to education, however, moving to a new field presents a difficult choice:

I look at my background and think, well, I could leave education. But because I've invested so much in my training and now have years of experience, I'd hate to lose it all. I also believe that the school system is an important part of our society, and I would like to help education

become more responsive to people's needs. It's really a difficult
decision.

(Teacher, Northeastern town)

My husband keeps urging me to look into business and get out of
education entirely. But I really love the field. Besides, I'd have to go
through the ranks all over again.

(Assistant Principal, Midwestern city)

Many aspirants believe that their skills and experience will transfer to
jobs outside education. An assistant principal (southern city) states: "The
skills I have from education will transfer to a business of my own." A
district planner (southern metro) believes her staff training skills will assist
her if she needs to search for a job: "People think I am pretty cocky, but I
know I can support myself outside of education, say in sales, if I need to do
so." An assistant principal reaches a similar conclusion:

The reality of our statewide situation makes me think a bit about
where else I might use my skills. I always thought my niche was in public
education, but now I see that my skills are marketable in any field.

(Northeastern town)

Some women take classes to explore ways of utilizing their talents in other
professions.

With the declining number of principalships because of school closures,
I began to wonder why I was bothering to advance in education. I
thought about what else I could do, and I took a couple of women's
management courses. In those classes, people from different industries
came in to talk about their jobs and the potential for future employment. That's what prompted me to think about personnel work.

(Teacher, Northeastern rural)

I'm taking courses in business administration and math research, so I
don't have to stay in education. Managing is just solving problems,
and I think it's a transferable skill.

(Assistant Principal, Midwestern suburb)

In their search for other employment opportunities, several respondents
developed separate resumés for different fields—highlighting how their
skills and experiences in education could be applied in different settings.
Because of the limited opportunities in educational administration, others
have initiated career seminars to aid themselves and others in thinking
about new careers. One teacher (northeastern rural) describes one such
gathering in her area: "People come together and talk about how to change

direction, how to rewrite resumés and how to deal with all sorts of practical aspects of looking for new jobs."

For many women, the frustration of being unable to progress in educational administration has solidified their resolve to explore other options. Several aspirants anticipate seeking principalships only for a specific number of years, and if they do not succeed within that time, they plan to leave education. A teacher states:

> I have a six-year limit in mind. By then, I will have been in the district twenty years. If I don't get a position with growth potential in that period of time, then I will get out of education and go into something else. Otherwise I would feel like I was just hitting my head against the wall. I don't want to leave education, but I certainly will if I have to.
> (Western metro)

Other aspirants already feel they are at the point of total frustration and realize they must face some hard decisions in the next year or so. An assistant princial (northeastern metro) reports, "I feel very, very stuck in education, and I need to find a way of stepping out of this uncomfortable position." In districts facing cutbacks in management positions, administrative aspirants must face the possibility of returning to classrooms. A district planner (southern metro) claims she would rather "sell supplies and make $50,000 a year than go backwards." A specialist summarizes:

> I have thought a lot about exploring other fields, even though I have invested so much in becoming a principal. On the other side of the coin is the fact that I am not getting any younger. There are other things I can do, like personal relations work in a big company, but I'm scared.
> (Western suburb)

At the secondary level, aspirants allege they feel even more pressure to seek employment outside of education. An assistant principal talks about one of her colleagues:

> My friend took an assistant principalship at a junior high, thinking she would get her foot in the door. But now she's locked into that position, and she isn't happy at that level. She is trying to get into industry now, because there are just no openings for women in high schools.
> (Midwestern suburb)

Business is the first field female aspirants think of when they consider employment opportunities outside education. A teacher notes with a smile, "If I don't get a school, I think I'd cry for awhile." But she goes on to say:

> However, I wouldn't remain here as a public school teacher because I'd

be too discouraged. I might go into private industry, but I don't know how easy or difficult that would be. I know it's easy for men to jump from teaching into some sort of business administration, but I think it's less easy for a woman.

(Southeastern rural)

Women think of business first because they believe that field is more receptive to women than education.

I think it's easier for women in the business world. If you've got the initiative, you can even go out and start your own business. If you fail, so what. Try again. Each failure makes you stronger.

(Administrative Intern, Southern metro)

I think business is open to women because more businesses than school districts have been sued by women. They have spent more time in the court rooms, and they seem more aware of what the legislation says about sex discrimination.

(Coordinator-Intern, Southern metro)

Many view the business world as the new frontier for women. A state coordinator advises:

I certainly wouldn't recommend anyone going into education now. If I were going back to school—and I've thought about going back—I would get a Master's in business administration. That is the only degree that makes any sense to me now.

(Northeastern metro)

Women also find business an attractive alternative to educational administration because they believe they can command higher salaries. An administrative assistant (southern metro) believes some women "can't afford to stay in education" because they head their own households and need more income than education can offer. An assistant principal concurs:

Money is a big factor to me now. After twenty years of experience and a Ph.D., I just feel like I shouldn't have to spend so much time budgeting scarce resources I would like a salary comparable to women in the business world. One of my friend's daughters makes more than I do, and she's only been two years in her job! I have worked hard, and I want to enjoy some of the rewards. So I may go into business where I think there is a lot of money.

(Southern metro)

For others, the money is secondary: they feel stuck in education and just want the chance to use their skills in some other profession.

> I want to see how far I can go in a career. To get a principalship in this town as a female, you have to be fifty years old and politically "in" with the right people. The other day, my assistant superintendent referred to me as "that little girl." When he said that, I realized that I didn't have much of a chance here.
>
> (Supervisor, Southern town)

> I will probably leave education because I want to see if there is something else I can do. I would like to have some totally different experiences.
>
> (Teacher, Midwestern city)

A teacher (who later left education), relates:

> I don't feel locked into education because I know I can do something more important in the work world. I was never terrifically interested in education in the first place; it was just a field open to women with children. If I had been a man, I would have gone to law school or done something besides teaching, and that bothers me. I was once a buyer in business and can remember thinking that the last thing I'd do was teach! Business is scary, but I'd like to be a manager somewhere. I figure I have twenty years left to work, and I'm motivated by what I am *not* presently doing. I've got to make it as an administrator in education or switch paths.
>
> (Northwestern city)

Some women are less sanguine about employment opportunities in business. They believe the adjustment from the public, service-oriented sector to the private, profit-oriented sector will not be as easy as some might predict.

> Some of my friends who were teachers and who then changed fields are successful in terms of money, but they are not happy. They're having a hard time adjusting, and they miss a lot of the aspects of teaching.
>
> (Teacher, Northeastern rural)

> I taught and then went into business management for two years to gain some administrative experience. But the business world is not for me, because I am not a profit-motivated person. I'm people-oriented, and that's not the attitude people need to succeed in business.
>
> (Teacher, Northwestern city)

In sharp contrast to the optimism of those who believe that business will provide greater opportunities for women than education, one respondent reports choosing an educational career *because* of the discrimination she experienced in the business world:

> Back in the early 1970s, I worked as an engineer, wore a hard hat and drove the company car. I took a lot of heckling over that, but I learned to cope with the discrimination. I was next in line for a promotion, but they had no intention of hiring a woman to oversee the men, so I left. I still have female friends who are in the same jobs and who have not been promoted yet. Business isn't more liberal than education. I found the education world (as it is in this part of the state, at least) a little more open.
>
> (Assistant Principal, Southern metro)

The debate about which field is more open to women will likely persist as long as women are barred from advancement solely because of gender. One counselor (southern metro) cautions: "Change is slow—like watching the growth of a child—it doesn't happen over night." Because of this, she concludes, "We can't all run away to business; there is too much that needs to be done here in education." Other women express a similar commitment to the field:

> Work is extremely important to me, just as my family is. I want to do satisfying things, and if I can't do them in education, I'll try something else. But no one has proven to me that I can't do satisfying work in education. A lot of people say to me, "Why bother? Go into the corporate field." But that's not what I care about; what I care about is education.
>
> (Student, Northeastern metro)

> After teaching several years, I was in some turmoil about whether I wanted to stay in education or not. I looked for other things to do, but came to the realization that I am truly an educator and will probably always be in education because I enjoy it.
>
> (Teacher-Student, Midwestern metro)

Finally, in addition to this feeling of commitment to education, long-time educators cite their many years of service as the reason they decided to remain in the field. After twenty-two years of experience in education, one assistant principal (southern metro) concludes: "I have too much to lose to even think about changing careers." Another assistant principal notes:

> At my age (forty-eight), there is probably not very much out there for me in another field. I don't think anyone in a corporation is going to

hire me. So I probably need to stick with education.

(Southern metro)

*Maintaining Hope*

Despite the barriers in education and the possibilities of more lucrative employment elsewhere, most of the women interviewed still consider school administration as the focus of their career efforts. Forty-four percent of the respondents believe their own chances of finding administrative positions within the field remain good. Even with the many problems they face, sixty-five percent continue to describe themselves as "extremely interested" in finding leadership positions in public schools. Although they sympathize with women who feel discouraged, they remain determined to succeed.

> After a four-year build up in administration, my superintendent told me not to count on anything. I felt depressed for two weeks. I can understand how women get to the point of saying they don't want to put themselves through this. After coming out of my depression, I seriously considered the private sector myself. But here I am, continuing to pursue the channels open to me and spending my time growing and learning.
>
> (Teacher, Northwestern city)

> I can see why all the talented women with Ph.D.s get discouraged. I, myself, will probably put off looking for a principalship for ten years or so. But I'm a task-oriented person, and will continue pursuing my goals.
>
> (Supervisor, Northwestern town)

> The political scene is a disaster now. So what does that mean? Do we all give up and go home depressed? That doesn't work. You can get depressed, but then you have to figure out where you go from here.
>
> (Student, Northeastern metro)

An assistant principal agrees:

> I'm certain discrimination will continue, but I'm still going to work towards a principalship. I'm not going to be discouraged, because I don't think you can afford to be discouraged.
>
> (Western suburb)

From their long-term perspective, these women advise other aspirants to fight the discouragement that comes from their unsuccessful attempts to secure executive positions in a male-dominated field. "The waiting is terrible," an assistant principal (midwestern suburb) acknowledges, "but we have to keep a balance and not give up or turn bitter." Some women maintain their vision and perspective by discussing their problems with others.

> I experience the barriers, all right. But for that matter, there are now barriers for white men as well. A lot of these men believe it is much easier for a woman or a black to get ahead, and in some cases, there is some truth to that belief. There are barriers for everybody, but I think people in education tend to become overwhelmed and passive. We can all find reasons why things can't happen. I'd like to convince people that there are a lot of reasons why things *can* happen, regardless of where you are.
>
> (Student, Northeastern metro)

Other informants suggest that women must learn to live with the difficulties they encounter and try not to let problems deflect their career goals.

> You have to live within the system, and I learned early on that fighting doesn't really help. I don't necessarily like that, but you have to live in the real world and that's the way it is. For example, a male elementary teacher is looked upon with more authority and credibility than a female. "Oh, my, aren't we lucky to have a man teacher," that sort of thing. A lot of things used to bother me, but I've learned to live with them.
>
> (New Principal, Midwestern suburb)

An assistant principal reluctantly agrees:

> They pay the male assistant principals $6000 a year extra, while the female deans (or lead teachers) get only $200—and the duties are shared. But anyway I can get to be an administrator is the way I will do it. The dean's job is still an entry point, despite the pay discrepancy. If you want the job that comes later, you go this route. You take what you can get.
>
> (Southern metro)

Like this last respondent, many women express a willingness to do almost anything to advance in administration—especially when faced with the possibility of returning to the classroom. Although they place high value on teaching, these women are ready to move on to something else.

> Despite the cutbacks, I was determined not to go back into the classroom, because I saw that as a step backwards in my career. All of a sudden, the district offered me a new position in a new program. So I

feel justified in that I waited and didn't go back into teaching. I just had the feeling something would open up, and I wasn't willing to settle for less than what I wanted.

(District Planner, Southern metro)

I love administrative work. To get me back into the classroom or the counselling office would be difficult; I may chain myself to the principal's chair.

(Acting Assistant Principal, Southern metro)

Finally, a teacher (northwestern city) admits she feels pushed towards administration "simply because I cannot go back to teaching, or I will go bananas!"

Clearly, these women believe in themselves and in their potential to become good administrators. Like this recently hired principal, these women are determined:

I am personally very confident in myself. I know clearly what I want, and I know I am capable of doing administrative work. I think I can make some special contributions to education, and I will keep trying to get the chance to show that.

(Northwestern city)

Others make similar comments:

I feel secure in my ability and my training, and the people who make the decisions know my qualifications. When a school opens up, I could be placed there. I don't believe this is conceit or false modesty on my part; it's just a realistic assessment of my abilities and strengths.

(Coordinator, Western metro)

Every step is a stepping stone, because I intend to be an administrator. There might be some delays on the way, but I expect to take every opportunity and use it positively to do something important. Wait and see.

(Counselor, Southern metro)

A new principal (northwestern suburb) summarizes her confidence stating, "I have been successful in everything I've done before, and I know I can do the job."

As noted in an earlier chapter, these determined women recognize the existence of discrimination in the field. Unlike those who are discouraged with their chances of attaining principalships, these optimistic aspirants believe they can overcome the barriers that threaten to block their career aspirations. A recently hired principal (midwestern suburb) says her strength comes from her conviction that she will "do what has to be done."

She adds, "I really want this principalship, and I've sacrificed to get it." Acknowledging continued discrimination, other aspirants share a similar determination:

> I feel I have been discriminated against quite a bit because I'm female. In one interview, for example, someone said I didn't look fierce enough to be a principal, sitting there in my yellow dress. I countered that I was fully capable, however I was dressed. The problem is getting your foot in the door so you can demonstrate your ability to do the work. Now that I'm in an assistant's position, the initial stumbling block is out of the way and I can go places.
>
> (Assistant Principal, Southern metro)

> I figure there's discrimination out there, but regardless of that, I'm still competing with topnotch people. Some of the jobs I didn't get I'm sure were because of discrimination; but some of them were because I wasn't good enough. Despite discriminatory attitudes, I think people recognize that I'm more qualified than a lot of men.
>
> (New Principal, Northwestern town)

Although the women describe themselves as "enthusiastic," "conscientious," "dedicated," and "dependable," most of them believe they must be "more determined" than male aspirants if they are going to succeed in administration. "You just have to want it badly enough not to let anyone stop you," one new principal states. She goes on to say:

> Job hunting can be frustrating, but I'm sure it is frustrating for men, too. Even though its rough out there, you just can't give up.
>
> (Northwestern town)

An assistant principal (western metro) explains, "I'm not resigned to being a failure, so I will keep trying until I'm sixty-five." And finally, a teacher describes these feelings just prior to gaining a principalship:

> This year I will ask for clarification if I am not placed. I won't fade back into the woodwork again. I've had too many positive things happen to just say: Oh well, it wasn't meant for me to be a principal. I feel like it *is* meant to be, and I intend to get there, no matter what.
>
> (Midwestern town)

### Summary

As of 1979-1980, the career goals and expectations of these 142 women range widely and do not conform to any traditional notion of what is "proper" work for women in education. If they seem highly motivated, it is because they believe they must be to succeed as women in a male-dominated profession. They know if they are to gain any of the top-level positions they seek in school management, they must have superior determination as well as superior credentials.

For some at this stage in the study, life circumstances (such as rearing children) or specific district practices (such as bias in recruiting and hiring) impinge on their dreams—temporarily in some cases, with more lasting consequences in others. The cost of choosing to delay career advancement while caring for children, for example, has yet to surface for the more recent aspirants in this study. Likewise, those who have pressed on with their careers while having children have yet to see the consequences of their decisions. Several trends from the first phase of this longitudinal study bear repeating: those in career-holding patterns because of childrearing, experience more conflicts in their work lives than those women without such familial obligations; those who have aspired longer without attaining a principalship are more discouraged and more often cite barriers to their careers than those just beginning to seek management positions; and the longer a woman aspires, the more likely she is to claim discrimination as an issue and affirmative action as an ineffective antidote. Some of these early concerns, like delayed careers or slow advancement, may end up benefiting female candidates in the long run. For the longer a woman aspires, the more educational experience (both practical and possibly academic) she is apt to have. If and when she does advance, she may be less likely to face comments about her lack of experience and training that female candidates typically receive when seeking administrative positions.

In this initial research phase, important differences surface between aspirants with more years of experience and those with less. Women in their fifties (who have been pursuing principalships for years) are more likely to cite the elementary principalship as their highest career goal. A coordinator explains why:

> Men in the field don't have the same problems as women. Men are free to pursue career mobility, while women are trying to be wife, mother and worker—all things to all people. Often we don't have mentors, even from among those few women administrators in the field. I saw many men go directly from my school into administration, because a principal—either male or female—would immediately push them. I didn't get that kind of pushing and neither did the other women I know. We got praise for doing a good job, and we had lots of responsibilities. But no one encouraged us to go up the ladder.
>
> (Western suburb)

Although many of the younger and more recent aspirants have the same double burden at work and home that this woman speaks of, they do not circumscribe their career aspirations in the same way. As a result, they are more open to any level of leadership responsibility than are the older aspirants. Minority women, in particular, set their sights high. Such an enlarged world view brings the women just beginning to aspire into direct contact with some of the same struggles that men have faced for years. Many are contemplating the effects such pressures might have on them. A student reflects on her own battle to maintain her original motivation—that of doing something for children in schools—while at the same time advancing in the field:

> Men in this society have been pushed to achieve and to earn money. They've been told their self-esteem is dependent on how far up the ladder they can go and they're the ones killing themselves trying to get to the next higher rung. It's so easy to lose sight of why you are in education—which is because of the kids. Ever since I was ten years old, I've been told I'm too idealistic, and that one day I will grow up. People say I'm going to want children, a house, a dog and a station wagon, and that somehow I will lose sight of my ideals and just go for power and money. But I'm hoping I don't buy into the achievement game. Women naturally want to achieve, too, but the male version of that game isn't so terrific.
>
> (Western metro)

Finally, this first phase of the study highlights numerous problems that female aspirants face in educational administration. Whatever the problems, however, these women speak confidently of their commitment and eagerness to become school managers. Certainly desire alone does not insure success; there are too many factors, whether personal, institutional or societal, that determine career outcomes. But the will to at least try is evident throughout the stories of these women—whether young or old, and regardless of race or geographical setting. In an enterprise replete with difficulties, women hope to bring new imagination and courage to education. Many, like one student (southeastern rural), believe "administrators must go out and slay some dragons." This student concludes, "I hope to have the chance to be the kind of administrator who has the guts to do courageous things." Inherent in this kind of thinking is the will to push the limits within themselves as well as the limitations set upon women within the field. And although the numbers of women hired in educational administration in 1979-1980 are not high, significant changes are occurring in how female aspirants view their abilities to influence the future of education. Brownmiller concludes: "For things do improve, and progress is made, and [women] are, in their awareness if not yet their freedom to choose, a little closer to being themselves."[8] Only time will tell whether or not this awareness, coupled with hard work and determination, will bring the women in this study any closer to fulfilling their dreams.

# 15    Outcomes and Advice

There are not a whole lot of women out there in administration, and their numbers are declining. That scares me. But I do feel if you want something badly enough, you shouldn't give up. You should try to maximize on whatever you can. I think the key is to get a lot of support and then channel that support in the right direction. In other words, you must set things up, because they don't just happen. You can't sit around and wait for a job offer to drop into your lap.

(New Principal, Midwestern metro)*

## PART ONE: OUTCOMES

The preceding chapter detailed the aspirations and hopes of female aspirants at the beginning of the study in 1979-1980. During the 1984-1985 school year, 139 of the original 142 women responded by mail or telephone to a career update (of the three who were not contacted, two were deceased and the third was reported by her former employer to have left education). The aspirants answered a brief set of questions on their career progress, their current thoughts about the field of educational administration and what, if any, advice they had for other women (and minorities) considering administrative careers in public schools. Despite the grim statistics of women hired nationally in school administration, those in this study have fared quite well. A full third are now principals, reaching in five years the initial career goal held by all of the aspirants at the start of the study. Another third are now in positions higher than when first interviewed, though short of principalships. And roughly another third still hold their

---

*From this point on, women who have moved up in administration since the beginning of the study are so noted. Where a specific title is used alone, a woman has held that position for several years; "new" or "recently hired" in this chapter means that the woman just moved into that position during the 1984-1985 update.

same of similar positions. The success rate of minority women approximates that of nonminority women: nearly one quarter of the minorities are now principals.

Among those women who have achieved principalships, the majority (approximately sixty-seven percent) are at the elementary level, and the remaining thirty-three percent are at the secondary level. Only four of the women placed in elementary schools had secondary experience in middle or high schools, suggesting that most of the women who have advanced did so at levels appropriate for their experience. Although these successful aspirants had an average of six years of teaching experience (ranging from one to seventeen years), only six had no administrative experience prior to gaining a principalship. Among the majority who had administrative experience, the average was just under six years, but some had as many as twelve years. Four of the women with no previous administrative experience were promoted directly from their classrooms or after receiving their Ph.D.s. Indeed, a quarter of the new principals hold Ph.D.s, suggesting that advanced degrees may be helpful to women advancing in the field. And finally, these successful aspirants took on the average six years to reach their first principalship. Some advanced after only one year, while others have been trying for as long as seventeen years.

The two respondents who took legal action have not yet attained principalships. Marie (who sued over an internship program) completed her internship and her Master's degree in 1981. Subsequently, she retired from teaching because of poor health. She believes her current health problems "are due to hypertension, which I believe to be a direct result of the anxiety I felt during my civil rights action against the Board of Education." Rose (who lost her own grievance, but succeeded in getting a consent decree from her district to set goals and timetables for advancing women in administration) works in the same district, but still as an assistant principal. Although she feels discouraged, she states: "I didn't go through all that to give up." Other women in her district have fared well since the legal battle. According to her local newspaper (October 1, 1985), "the percentage of women appointed to administrative posts in [her district] has far exceeded the long-range goals set by the district . . . The report, required annually under terms of the suit's agreement, shows the percentage of assistant principal, principal and administrator jobs given to women each year since 1980 has outstripped the [percentages set]." Rose's assessment is that "they have changed the system of selection, but it still seems to have many flaws." On a related note, another woman in the study—in part because of Marie and Rose—reports that she is contemplating suing her former district.

Those in the study who now hold principalships are understandably enthusiastic about their progress. One middle school principal (southern suburb) notes: "I am pleased to have reached a goal I set for myself years ago when I was a teacher." Other successful aspirants concur:

I am very pleased to have my own school, and I want to stay with it for a number of years. Being a principal is the most challenging job in education. I believe I am right where I should be.

(Principal, Northeastern metro)

I feel validated as a school leader by my recent assignment to one of the district's largest elementary schools. The superintendents confidence in leaving the school with a female principal and two female assistants not only breaks an "unwritten" rule in this district, but has helped to build my confidence.

(Principal, Western metro)

To improve career opportunities, many women in the study returned to graduate school for advanced degrees. They believed a doctorate would give them an edge in the job market, and help to balance the scales when they competed with men. At the beginning of the study, only eight percent (eleven women) had doctorates; now seventeen percent (twenty-four women) hold doctoral degrees. Nearly twenty percent of the minority women hold Ph.D.s or Ed.D.s, while slightly less (sixteen percent) of the nonminority women do. Of the twenty-four women who now have doctoral degrees, six are principals. One new elementary principal, who chose a doctoral program to improve her own chances for advancement, reflects on the progress women are making:

The majority of women who do aspire and obtain administrative positions are quite competent and are generally more thorough than their male counterparts. Many, like myself, postponed entry into administration until they got doctorates and felt they were really "ready." This may be a waste of women years on one hand; but on the other, it may account for women's competence once in their positions.

(Northwestern town)

Some in the study would argue with this principal about whether they personally chose to postpone their careers or whether it was done for them. For example, six of the eight who held doctorates at the onset of the study (four of whom are minority women) still do not have principalships.

Although sixty percent of those in the study still consider themselves active aspirants five years into the study, others no longer aspire to principalships or have had to temporarily put their careers on hold. Some women are content with their current attainments or are deferring their quest for further advancement while their children are young. Still others, mainly older aspirants, express frustration at being blocked—either by the economic climate in the country or by discrimination. Minority women continue to find racial discrimination a major obstacle, as this counselor indicates:

> I see white females given the opportunity to advance in educational administration, while continuing barriers deny me equal opportunity for upward mobility in the public school system. Opportunities should be extended and opened to minority females. I am strongly disappointed and frustrated with the educational field.
>
> (Northwestern metro)

Rural women also express concern about barriers they perceive in their districts: inadequate advertising of job openings, few opportunities to gain practical experience, lack of mentors and general sex discrimination. One elementary principal states:

> I don't really want to admit it, but I'm afraid this is as high as I'll go in this rural district. They would never hire a woman superintendent. Talk about a dead end. If I do change jobs, it will probably be to something outside of education and that's difficult to admit to myself. I do think the doors are opening more easily for the ones coming in now. In fact, I am currently grooming my sixth grade teacher to become an administrator. I would certainly hate to think she has to plow the same ground I did.
>
> (Midwestern town)

Nearly a quarter of the original 142 informants are planning to leave education or have abandoned their administrative goals altogether. A state department employee (northeastern metro), who has given up on a principalship, believes politics and sexual "hanky-panky" play too big a part in administrative hiring. She confides: "All my aspirations have been crushed. I'm not wired to anyone to help me politically, and I don't feel like 'fooling around.'" Although this woman happens to be a minority, a nonminority woman (northwestern rural) came to the same conclusion. Many of those discouraged with education turn to business to utilize their management skills. "The bottom line is it is still easier for a woman to get ahead in the business world than in education," claims a former assistant principal (northeastern rural) who is now a vice president of a business. Perhaps because more women are looking for options outside of education, there is a greater interest among aspirants to earn degrees in business or psychology. At the onset of the study, none of the informants considered disciplines other than education. In a southern city, an elementary principal expresses her concern about this exodus: "I worry that we will not attract talented women into the profession, because so many business opportunities are available to them now and they provide greater financial incentives than education." Thomas would concur with her observations: "Should the pool of trained women in education decline, it is even more likely that men will dominate leadership positions."[1]

For women leaving education or giving up their administrative goals, as well as for those continuing on, three major concerns influence their decisions: discrimination in the field, unsupportive female educators and family conflicts. Informants report they have greater concern about discrimination in educational administration today then they did five years ago. In part, this may stem from a political climate in the country today that emphasizes fiscal, rather than equity, issues. Or, perhaps as the aspirants move further up the administrative career ladder, they meet more resistance in this typically male profession. Whatever the root of the belief, many now admit sexual discrimination and its impact on their careers has increased, rather than lessened, over the years. They contend that not only is the "good old boys' network" alive and thriving, but that women still have to work doubly hard to get half the distance. Furthermore, they believe that many male administrators still feel threatened by female "movers and shakers." A secondary assistant principal concludes:

> While more opportunities are now available, most of the decisions are still made by men for men. The issue of power and control is evident in almost all situations.
>
> (Northwestern suburb)

A newly hired principal (northeastern metro) agrees: "My recent experiences in securing the principalship prove to me that a significant bias exists against women as high school leaders." Several women offered evidence of this ongoing problem:

> I interviewed for a junior high principalship, and I thought the interview went well. They were looking for a disciplinarian, and I tied with a 6'4" man who resembled Frankenstein. Need I say more? By all standards, he turned out to be a lousy disciplinarian and left education altogether after two years!
>
> (University Coordinator, Southern rural)

> The female principal at my school is doing some hiring, and everyone asks her if she is going to hire a woman. No one ever asks a man if he is going to hire another man! The same old issues seem to be present: The sex of the candidate, not the qualification, count in hiring.
>
> (Assistant Principal, Northeastern suburb)

> I'm not a radical when it comes to women's rights, as is obvious by my recent choice to temporarily abandon my career to take on a more traditional mother role. But I was amazed by a comment from a male principal asked to consider me for an assistant principalship. He said they were not interviewing women, because they had one once and she hadn't worked out!
>
> (Teacher, Southern city)

For a recent opening, I was told they hired a male at a substantially higher salary than mine, because "he's a family man, after all." When we discussed my salary, I was told by a board member that because my husband was employed and I loved my job, I should be happy to work for nothing!

(Principal, Midwestern rural)

An interviewer told me once: "You're lucky. You have several things going for you: You're a woman (true), you're young (I was thirty-six) and you have an ethnic surname (my husband is Italian)." I stood up and said, "I'm sorry you've neglected to see such attributes as enthusiasm, intelligence and leadership capabilities. You've only focused on minor elements which have nothing to do with anything!" Needless-to-say, I did not get the position, nor did I want it after that!

(Administrative Intern, Western suburb)

In assessing the incidence of discrimination, women in every region of the country admit, like one principal (northwestern town), that "sexism may be more subtle, but it is still rearing its ugly head." According to the informants, this phenomenon alone accounts for many of those leaving education for other fields. As a coordinator sums up:

We're not getting a fair shake. Women have been prostituted, used. We pay our dues, but we don't get the pay-off. We are still threatening to men, and I feel angry and bitter. I felt like a seasoned educator when I first interviewed for this study, and yet I'm still not getting anywhere. Despite my extra schooling and skills, and my working what feels like a forty-eight hour day at three positions, I'm still not advancing.

(Midwestern city)

Clearly, many forms of discrimination are next to impossible to prove; however, when a profession such as education has a large pool of female employees at the lower levels, logic would suggest that a representative group of those qualified and experienced women would move up into the managerial ranks. The fact that they do not, and that men do, points to a continuing problem in the field.

A less prevailing, yet decided concern among many of the respondents today, is the failure of other female educators to support female administrative aspirants. Although many women praise female administrators for their excellent performance and for their role modeling, others seem concerned with the jealousy, competition and lack of support shown them by female educators. Labeled by several as the female aspirants' "worst detractors," there continues to be a serious distrust of women in the field today. A coordinator explains:

I'm concerned about the harm that successful women do to other women in this district. The men are supportive; the women are jealous and sabotaging. Now that a few women have made it to higher levels, they seem to relish the opportunity to "do in" other women. At least the men who were in power before were more innocent about it.

(Northwestern city)

A teacher (northwestern city) is no longer considering a principalship because she says her self-esteem could not handle it at this point. She states: "I would be paranoid if I thought my staff was talking and thinking about me as my colleagues do about our female principal." Older women feel especially betrayed by more recent female aspirants who disassociate themselves from those women who struggled for years to pave the way for women in administration. A secondary assistant principal says:

Unfortunately, I feel the kind of women aspiring today are not the same caliber as those who preceded them. Most of us believed hard work and extensive experience would get us recognition and promotion. Now women are getting in that aren't that competent. They pretend they didn't need any help getting where they are because they have their own methods of getting ahead. And those methods usually mean cultivating the men in power.

(Western metro)

Although most aspirants admit that compromises are necessary along the way, many resent female colleagues who turn into "pseudo men" to advance in the field. Yet some in the study who might be accused of fitting such a label, would defend their actions:

When I was an assistant principal in junior high, I *had* to come up with ways of conveying my ability to deal with discipline above and beyond my skill to do so. Symbols are important. I had to walk tough and appear as if I could eat nails.

(State Department Employee, Southeastern city)

To counter the perceived lack of support from some female educators, most informants in the study agree on the importance of women networking together for support. As Weber et al. note, " . . . encouraging other women to aspire to positions in educational leadership . . . place[s] the responsibility for action in the group with the vested interest—women."[2] Through networking, women receive encouragement for their aspirations, while simultaneously breaking down barriers that exist between female educators which militate against the advancement of competent female aspirants. For isolated women in management, meeting other women can make a significant difference, as this assistant principal (midwestern suburb) indicates: "There is one other female administrator in my district and we do get together—time permitting, of course—to blow off steam. Though such occasions are rare, they help tremendously."

The third major area of concern for all of the aspirants today is how to balance the demands of work and family. Many who thought they could juggle both roles at the beginning of the study, find themselves questioning that assumption in 1985. A secondary principal explains:

> I'm in my early thirties with two small children and, although my husband is very supportive, it appears that perhaps at some point in the near future I will have to make a choice between *my* children and the time I spend at work with *other peoples'* children. I used to think it was simply a matter of organizing time wisely. Now I am uncertain. Increasingly, my own children seem to suffer from the lack of time I spend at home.
>
> (Midwestern metro)

A department chair who earlier believed she could manage a school while parenting, has now delayed her administrative aspirations to raise her small children:

> I know there are women who can do it all, but they are few and far between. They are to be admired. But the pressure is still there to be wives and mothers first and *then* hold jobs. Those expectations are awfully hard to break out of for women.
>
> (Southern rural)

Another aspirant confesses that she, too, has had to reassess her earlier beliefs about her ability to assume a principalship and raise a family as well:

> I interviewed for a principalship and an assistant principalship, but I didn't get either one. After my initial sense of disappointment, I found I didn't mind. I felt comfortable with the challenges of those positions, but I didn't know how I would cope with caring for my baby girl. The uncertainty of the hours, of when I would get home, and of the whole child care issue is very perplexing to me.
>
> (Department Chair, Northeastern rural)

Nevertheless, although these women question their original timelines, they have not abandoned their hopes to become principals.

Women who successfully fuse career and family are often labeled "superwomen" by their colleagues, yet these women experience many of the same difficulties as those who choose to slow down or delay their administrative careers. "I resent the fact," relates a secondary assistant principal, "that my principal can leave to take care of his daughter while his wife has her hair done." She goes on to say:

> But when I go to do something for *my* child, eyebrows go up around the building. My principal doesn't mind, but those subordinates who are privy to such information are critical. We women are judged on entirely different standards.
>
> (Midwestern suburb)

A director (northeastern suburb) believes people take her less seriously as an administrator, now that she has taken several maternity leaves. A personnel director concurs:

> I thought my career would move faster, but apparently being pregnant didn't help. I didn't slack off in my work while I was pregnant, but somehow being pregnant hurt my image. I got the message that personnel directors don't have babies.
>
> (Southeastern city)

The conflicts these women experience when trying to balance career and family responsibilities are well-documented in our society. An assistant principal (midwestern metro) reasons: "Women have the same duties at work as the men, but they also have the responsibilities at home." Although women in this study do not view family responsibilities as momentous a barrier to their careers as discrimination, they conclude that deciding how to balance role demands gets increasingly more difficult as they move up the administrative career ladder.

## PART TWO: ADVICE

In both the original study and the career update, female aspirants make it abundantly clear that they know what they want and are working hard to achieve their individual goals—whatever their personal timetables. They acknowledge that they are constantly learning from their colleagues, their mentors and their bosses, as well as from their own mistakes. In the last career update, they were specifically asked whether they had any new or different advice to offer other female aspirants in educational administration. Although these women do not statistically represent all of the female aspirants in the United States, their advice to other female aspirants seeking school leadership positions is informative. Some of their advice may be specific to their own school districts or states and needs to be assessed with that in mind; however, much of what they have to say has broad relevance to all aspirants—both female and minority—who seek administrative positions in professions dominated by nonminority males. The advice from those who have successfully advanced in the last five years may be particularly relevant to aspirants, and may aid them in making informed choices about their personal lives and careers.

### Attitudes and Choices

There is no disagreement among the women in this study that aspirants must possess a seriousness of purpose about their career goals and have the ability to articulate their resolve to others. Aspirants should leave no doubt in anyone's mind that they are earnest in their desire to become administrators and will not be deterred from achieving that goal. One administrative aspirant relates:

> No one got serious about supporting me until *I* got serious about management. When I made the commitment to go back to school and to pursue administration, I finally got the support I needed.
>
> (Southern metro)

In addition, informants stress that aspirants should not assume that others know of their strong desire to become administrators. Individuals interested in becoming school managers must actively promote their candidacy, as one program director illustrates:

> I was groomed for the position by my mentor, and when he left I assumed I'd be asked to take the position. Instead, the staff began discussing what kind of person should fill the position. Suddenly I thought: "I *am* that person! Tell them; don't wait to be asked." When I talked to the assistant superintendent, he said they were waiting for me to come in. If I hadn't made the move, they felt I wasn't the right person for the job.
>
> (Midwestern town)

Once a woman decides to pursue administration, she needs to understand that there is a big difference between making that choice and eventually securing a position. A newly hired elementary principal offers this advice:

> Advancing in administration takes a lot of hard work, perseverance and dedication to *want* to get there. You can't expect to just walk into jobs. You have to prepare yourself and work hard to be successful.
>
> (Northwestern rural)

Informants suggest that one of the things aspirants must work on is gaining the acceptance of their male colleagues. Despite hopes of being hired for their skills, backgrounds and experiences, many acknowledge that gender still has a great impact on hiring committees. An assistant principal recommends:

> You must be comfortable with men and come across as someone who listens. I don't call it playing up to them, but some might. I let them know I appreciate their experience and that I want to learn from them. That's all the male ego needs to hear. Sometimes I've said some things to men that weren't even true, but it becomes a self-fulfilling prophecy. Once they know someone is watching them and trying to learn from them, they improve themselves.
>
> (Southern metro)

Women also indicate that aspirants must expect to work in positions they dislike or find boring if they are to achieve their career goals. Plateaus, delays and detours in their careers are inevitable; however, keeping sight of their ultimate objective will help aspirants to maintain their momentum and stay on course. A district office employee observes:

> Although this isn't the position I originally aimed for and it may not look like much on paper, it's a tremendous position if you take advantage of it. A lot of women don't do that. In this job, I travel, make presentations and get to know people throughout the district and state. I'm sure the contacts and experience will help me to get a principalship at a later date.
>
> (Western metro)

One strategy to increase opportunities for future administrative employment is "getting into someone's debt." A new assistant principal explains:

> Basically I operate with the idea that it's good to get people indebted to you, because somewhere along the way they will return the favor. I always offer help when someone needs that little extra thing done. In other words, I build points for the future. Although it may not sound nice, that's what the men do, and I wish I learned the technique earlier. That's what you have to do to get ahead. The people I help are all looking to get ahead themselves and when they do, I come by to say hello. Alternatively, I send them articles with my comments to give us a reason to meet again once they leave the building.
>
> (Southern metro)

Rather than seeking to accrue debts, some informants counsel aspirants to simply "make themselves indispensable" by "working like Trojans." One woman (northeastern city), who has gone from being a graduate student, to a principal, to a state department employee over the course of the study, remembers "frantically" trying to learn as much as she could in graduate school: "I wanted to have something to bring back to my principal when I returned, something he specifically needed and would be grateful for later on down the line." She believes her principal valued the contributions she made and that they have paid off in several of her recent placements.

An essential ingredient of any career-building strategy is perseverance. Because of school closures and the attendant decline in administrative positions, women in this study caution that if aspirants are to succeed in school management they must be patient. An elementary principal (southern metro) claims patience is a necessity, "because there are only so many positions to fill now." Another woman who now works in higher educational administration agrees:

> Women, as well as men, need to aspire without *urgency*. For so long, all I heard was women can't make it. We can. But we have to show the ability not to panic.
>
> (Southern town)

Patience of this kind means trying again and again, and resisting the inevitable depression that occurs when someone else is chosen for the job. A new high school principal offers an example:

> A lesson I have learned is that persistence and patience *do* pay off. The same men who refused my promotion in 1980 are the ones who supported me in 1984. It was worth the wait.
>
> (Northeastern city)

Deciding on an individual strategy about when or when not to move to another position remains problematic for most women. Those who go back to graduate school, for example, face the decision of whether to return to the classroom or to hold out for an administrative job once they complete their schooling. In making such choices, aspirants should be aware of the traditional career ladders in their districts, as they vary from region to region. A woman (who later became the director of a parochial school) recalls she was told *not* to take a teaching job when she finished her graduate degree if she wanted to advance in administration. In 1980, she said:

> Perhaps I would go back to teaching temporarily if I had some sort of agreement it would not be a permanent arrangement. I don't think I could get anywhere, however, if I went back to teaching hoping my principal would realize my capabilities and pull me out of the classroom. If you're doing a wonderful job at teaching, you will *stay* teaching.
>
> (Midwestern metro)

When she finished her graduate work, she was unsuccessful in her quest to attain a public school management position and, rather than returning to the classroom, she accepted the leadership of a private school. She has since become an elementary principal in a public school.

Other aspirants face the decision of whether to take one of the more plentiful elementary principalships when their career goals are clearly at the secondary level. Today, as in the past, women report being counselled to move into "appropriate" elementary principalships—even if their experience and interest is at the secondary level. Despite the attraction of gaining building-level responsibility in an elementary school, many seeking secondary positions fear the possibility of being locked into that level. An assistant principal offers this advice:

> I would not encourage women who aspire to a secondary principalship to take elementary positions. As long as we settle for elementary schools, they get us out of the way. I'm not saying elementary schools aren't important; they are probably *the* most important schools. But in terms of spreading our wings and flexing our muscles, we have to fight for what we want and for what we are certified to do. So I'm hanging in there.
>
> (Southeastern city)

Because this woman is still in the same position five years later, questions surface about her strategy to attain a secondary principalship. It is possible that experience at the elementary level might have enhanced her possibilities for a secondary position; nevertheless, because her qualifications and desires are in secondary education, she is willing to wait rather than to risk changing levels. Others might find more success using alternative strategies, especially if their districts have a history of transferring elementary principals to secondary schools.

### Background Experiences

Successful careers require careful planning, suggesting that aspirants should coordinate their educational and work experiences with an eye toward future goals. For a variety of reasons, particularly those related to family responsibilities, women often remain present-oriented in their work and fail to plan adequately for their future careers. A district coordinator (western metro) comments: "We settle for staying in a position, rather than moving on like most men do." Many women in this study understand this shortcoming and recognize the need for more thorough planning if they are going to achieve their career goals. A teacher describes the importance of the planning process:

> I outlined a plan for myself as to what steps I needed to take to get into

administration. As job opportunities came up, I began taking those steps. I didn't always get the job, but I went through the process. Sometimes my heart was in my mouth during some of those steps, but I grew more and more comfortable with the process.

(Northeastern city)

She advises that aspirants should study the pattern of administrative progression within their districts and then develop a long-range strategy for meeting the intermediate steps to their administrative goals.

Successful implementation of a career plan requires great flexibility. Some women comment that they eventually achieved their career goals by accepting intermediate management positions that were less desirable. Others actively seek a broad range of experiences which will increase their flexibility as different opportunities for advancement arise. Now an elementary principal, one woman followed this successful strategy:

I think women and men can get themselves in a real bind if they don't have some options. You can feel trapped. So I got certified as a teacher, a specialist and an administrator.

(Northwestern metro)

Some of the essential experiences an aspirant needs are the same, no matter what administrative level or career path an aspirant chooses. Clearly classroom experience is critical, as this assistant principal notes:

A common question asked in administrative interviews is: How many years has it been since you were in the classroom? I know some women who had their education and administrative certification, but had very little time in the classroom. That's a big drawback. To work with teachers, it's critical to have some years of teaching experience under your belt.

(Northwestern suburb)

Frequently, classroom experiences for male administrative aspirants are not scrutinized as carefully as they are for females. Recognizing this disparity, women in this study advise that female aspirants should pay close attention to the quality and quantity of their teaching experience as they prepare for their careers. In 1980, a specialist (western suburb) anticipated how she might respond to the question of "whether or not she could identify with teachers." She remarked, "I'm getting back into the regular classroom next, so I will be absolutely prepared for a principalship. When I interview, I don't want them to say I've been out of the classroom too long." She is now an administrative assistant, a position equivalent to an assistant principalship in her particular district.

After teaching experience, the next step toward a management career is administrative certification. A department chair (southern rural) comments on the importance of keeping her certification current because "that's what gets you into the first paper screening." Likewise, a middle school assistant principal states:

> Have your certification in your pocket and sit on it. Don't leave a question in anyone's mind about how you got the job or why. It's not because you are female, but it's because you were prepared.
>
> (Northwestern city)

Many women in the study simultaneously pursued internships while obtaining their administrative certification. These women believed that such experiences would introduce them to a variety of school leadership roles, enabling them to make informed choices about future possibilities. More importantly, perhaps, they assumed that internships would serve to counter arguments that they lacked administrative experience when applying for jobs. At the onset of the study, a student (southern city) described her thinking: "I still don't know which direction I want to go in administration, so I designed my internship to give me experience at both the building and district level." She has since successfully interviewed for a secondary assistant principalship. Hired to open a new school in 1980, a teacher (northwestern metro) credited her graduate advisor for making her internship meaningful. He correctly assessed that she knew few administrators, and arranged for her to work with other administrators who had opened new schools as she was slated to do.

Because of the great variation among internship experiences, women in the study counsel aspirants to be assertive and to insure that their time is spent in a worthwhile manner. Interships often fail to materialize as planned; therefore, students—those who have the most to gain or lose— should be prepared to actively intervene in the process. An assistant principal describes how she shaped her internship:

> I went to the administrative meeting and said: "Please put me on the agenda so we can talk about how I'll be used during my internship. I *need* these experiences." People are supportive in my district, but you need to push them to pay attention.
>
> (Northwestern city)

Many of the women in the study believe that advanced degrees in administration (or in related fields) will not only provide the important intellectual foundations for their future careers, but will enhance their immediate employment opportunities as well. With a doctoral degree in administration, they contend, it is difficult for school districts to casually dismiss their administrative aspirations. One new principal counsels:

My years as a doctoral student and my total immersion in study have already proved invaluable to me. I feel much more mature in my outlook, and I find myself sitting back and asking the right questions before I allow myself to be swept along with the latest trends. I would wholeheartedly recommend going back to school to other practicing administrators who are equipped with the necessary scholastic ability.
(Northwestern city)

A student (midwestern town) urges aspirants to "take time off to take part in university life; it is refreshing, and you get so much more out of it than if you commute or piece it together over summers." Others suggest that aspirants should expand their academic horizons beyond the field of education.

Diversification is the answer. Make sure you do more than just get certified in administration. If I could do it over again, I would get a degree in business. Even with my math background and my administrative experience, I'm still not accepted in other fields outside of education as an expert. We need *more* than education degrees.
(Assistant Principal, Southeastern rural)

I encourage women to seek further education outside schools of education, such as business and psychology, to help broaden their knowledge base.
(Director, Southern metro)

Many women in the recent update speak of the importance of joining professional organizations and of reading professional journals. Participation in such organizations and associations exposes aspirants to important current issues, provides a forum to discuss the daily work of administration, and gives administrative candidates an avenue to gain the visibility among other administrators that is necessary for career advancement. To determine which organizations are most worthwhile, one teacher (southern suburb) recommends: "Ask your university professors or your administrative bosses to list the administrative organizations and journals you should be familiar with as an aspirant." According to several informants, active participation in professional organizations proved to be indispensable for their career success.

Aspirants must also critically assess their career preparation, with particular regard to gaps in their backgrounds. If they lack experience or training in some central aspect of administration, it is imperative that they initiate steps to correct the deficiency. For example, a specialist explains why she took her current position:

I was attracted to this position because it deals with the business end of education, rather than with curriculum and instruction. I think it's an area where women, including myself, chronically lack experience. Now I deal with budgets, equipment and personnel in sixteen different schools. I think it fills a void I had in my background.

(Southern metro)

Another specialist took a similar course of action, recognizing that she lacked expertise in two important areas:

I went back to graduate school to learn more about educational law and finance, because I knew those were two areas that I needed to understand if I was going to be an administrator. Now I can say I have that knowledge.

(Western metro)

Another, and often-forgotten, strategy for strengthening background experiences involves taking advantage of serendipitous occasions which may arise within their buildings or districts—opportunities that may seem trivial at the time, but which may result in a significant increase in responsibility. A woman, who is now an assistant principal, remembers volunteering to help her department chair in an effort to gain administrative experience:

Our department chair was a real educational leader, but incredibly disorganized. So I made a deal with him. In exchange for teaching one less class, I organized the department and helped him to run it. I got some valuable administrative experience by being his assistant.

(Northeastern suburb)

A teacher, who has since moved into the district office, recalls seizing another kind of opportunity:

District money was tight, and we were losing our assistant principal. So I went into the district office and said I would like to assume some of the responsibilities because I wanted to become an administrator. I explained how it would save them money, while at the same time, give me some much-needed experience. They agreed, and that's how I became an administrative assistant.

(Northwestern city)

Finally, an assistant principal believes she got her management position because of her willingness to "go the extra mile" when her district got in a jam:

The district asked me if I would be willing to help out my principal, and I said "fine." If I had been a man, I'm not sure they would have phrased it like that. Maybe a lot of people would not think it worth the hassle to respond positively to such a request, but I was willing to do anything to get some experience then. I'm not sure I would have gotten this job if I hadn't been willing to help out back then.

(Southeastern city)

Informants in this study caution that depth and breadth of experience alone will not insure career success. The best of experiences, they argue, can go unnoticed if aspirants fail to document those events by building strong personnel files. A specialist describes the care she takes to look as good as possible on paper.

I've written a concise one-page application, which I am finding is probably the most important part of what you send to a personnel director. I remember to document each of my responsibilities, and I have my principal look it over each time before I sent it out with a job application.

(Western suburb)

Another way to improve a personnel file is to include letters, especially unsolicited ones, that document special capabilities or experiences. A teacher, now a principal, found this strategy useful:

Several years ago, I interviewed for a job in a private school. I didn't get the job, but I did receive a nice letter describing how tough the decision had been for them. They hired the man who had temporarily filled in for them and, until I applied, there had been no serious competition for the job. Because it was such a nice letter, I decided to use it in my dossier. I think it has helped me.

(Northwestern suburb)

Finally, although careful planning to gain and document the necessary background experiences may lead to achieving an identified goal, informants in this study stress that when planning a career an aspirant must be willing to entertain alternative goals. The best-laid plans may fail to materialize because of shifts in district priorities or because of administrative cut backs resulting from a lack of funds. Faced with these possibilities, aspirants must reassess their career goals and timelines and, in some cases, redirect their energies toward other administrative positions. An assistant principal recalls that when she learned of pending administrative cut backs in her district, she realized the necessity of moving from her satellite program to a more secure position as a building administrator.

Even though I would have liked to stay another year at the center where I was, I threw my hat in the ring for an assistant's position. I hadn't planned to apply at that time, but you can't always pick your moment.

(Midwestern suburb)

A director agrees that aspirants must have flexible goals:

I have some opportunities in this job that I wouldn't have if I had gone into a building as I first planned. That's why I always say, if you don't gain a specific goal, make some alternative ones. There is no guarantee you'll achieve the goals you first set for yourself, but with options you can still move. I didn't get into the administrative ranks the way I expected, but now I'm in.

(Western metro)

Maintaining flexibility and openness towards alternative career goals in school management is essential for aspirants. Indeed, several informants admit that apparent detours from their original plans turned out to be extremely helpful in the long run.

*Making Significant Contacts*

The importance of mentors for aspirants is well documented, especially for women and minorities in male professional arenas such as educational administration. Women in this study recognize the value a mentoring relationship can have on their careers; however, just as with internships or any other administrative experiences, they realize aspirants must actively initiate contacts with those in a position to help. These women advise aspirants not to leave such vital connections to chance; wishful thinking that some informed, well-established educator will automatically respond to their need for sponsorship seldom produces desired results. Aspirants must seek mentors, as a teacher explains:

I know you need a sponsor to make it, and I don't have one at this time. So I'm going down to the district office and *find* one! I know the assistant superintendent, and I'm going to tell him I need help.

(Southern metro)

Some women in the study find it hard to accept that their skills and talents are not always sufficient to get them jobs. An assistant principal expresses her frustration:

Mentoring is a necessity, at least from where I stand, because my only hope for advancement is through the sensitivity and understanding of our new male superintendent. He is not afraid to recognize female potential and ability. But isn't it sad that the hope I feel is based only on the moral goodness of another person, rather than on my skills and qualifications?

(Northeastern suburb)

Once aspirants find mentors, they should seek to involve them with all aspects of their career plans. A woman (northwestern metro), who is now a principal, recalls her hesitancy to "bother" her principal when she was a teacher. When she began interviewing for administrative positions, however, she began asking for his advice. She realizes that for years she "wouldn't have thought to ask him such things." Another woman, who is now interviewing for assistant superintendencies, recalls using her superintendent as a sounding board whenever she received a job offer:

When I was offered an assistant principalship, I called my mentor to ask about his perceptions of the district. If you can find a friend that has that kind of knowledge, you'll learn things that you couldn't possibly have learned in the classroom.

(Northwestern suburb)

Mentoring relationships can have surprising results. A department chair recounts how a university professor urged her to initiate an important contact from which she has benefited in unexpected ways:

One of my professors suggested I talk with my superintendent about urban education and current trends. So I set up an appointment with him for my whole study group. Now, every time I run into him at a meeting, or just see him across a room, he will wave at me or ask how things are coming. That contact hasn't hurt a bit!

(Southern rural)

Because finding a mentor can be difficult, many women in the study instruct aspirants not to limit their search solely to their principal or superintendent. A teacher considers university professors as potential mentors:

Since my own administrators don't give me feedback or support, I think I will make an appointment with one of my professors at school and ask him about my future in school administration. I want to know if he thinks I'm going in the right direction.

(Midwestern metro)

University placement offices offer another source of mentors, a former teacher (now a director of a private school) relates:

The placement director is a fan of mine. He is probably the most honest of any of the people who advise me . He is an active member of the old boys' network and close to the selection process. He agreed to solicit feedback about me and then tell me what he learns. He's going to say: "Hi, Joe. So and so is an advisee of mine, and I think she has a lot on the ball. I want to know what you thought of her when you talked to her."

(Northwestern city)

Likewise, a district personnel director became a mentor to a specialist in the study:

After two years of applying and not getting hired, I met a personnel director from another school district. I mailed her the application papers I'd submitted for jobs and asked her to be as harsh, blunt and critical as she could be. She said that *she'd* hire me if she had a job and that I should not give up. Her advice was invaluable, because I was on the verge of doing just that. I was losing my confidence.

(Northwestern suburb)

According to many informants, direct appeals for an objective evaluation of their credentials and future possibilities in administration proved beneficial. A teacher describes this approach:

I would like to sit down with someone in administration who has power and who I respect. I want to say: "This is where I am, and that's where I want to go. From your objective point of view, what do you see standing in my way? Is it my appearance, my background, whatever? Tell me." Maybe I'm batting my head against the wall, or maybe they're just not hiring short people this year. Either way, I want to know so I can redirect my goals if I need to.

(Western suburb)

Along with gaining the support of a mentor, many women suggest that aspirants establish networks with individuals who have similar interests and who face similar problems. In a midwestern city, a coordinator stresses: "We need other women to develop support groups wherever we are, so we can help each other and talk things out. To do this, we need women, not men." On the other hand, a coordinator counsels aspirants to utilize all available networks, regardless of their gender composition:

In this climate of decreasing resouces, women might get squeezed out if we don't continue to network and to nurture one another. We need both men and women to do that, because we can't do it alone.

(Western metro)

Strong female networks exist in some regions of the country, and informants believe their impact has been beneficial for female aspirants. Among other contributions, these organizations systematically remind school districts that qualified women *are* available for leadership positions and deserve to be considered when vacancies occur. "With support systems such as our local, county and state women's organizations," notes an administrative aide (western suburb), "we have an effective network to promote our interests." In addition, these organizations often furnish a wide range of services: from a clearinghouse for job opportunities to a place of solace and renewal for discouraged aspirants.

Establishing contacts with mentors and networks requires considerable effort and persistence. Those efforts will go for naught, informants admonish, if aspirants fail to assiduously cultivate and maintain them. In 1980, a student (southern city) recontacted numerous supporters when she applied for principalship: "I'd be a fool not to do so." She is now in her fourth year as a principal and credits much of her success to staying in touch with those who could support her candidacy. A teacher, who was later successful in her quest for a principalship, offers a different strategy:

> My goal is to walk into any state meeting where people will know me just by my reputation for the inservices that I conduct. And the recognition is beginning to happen. People now say to me: "Oh, I've never met you, but I know your name." I think connections like these are the only way I'll get anywhere.
>
> (Northwestern suburb)

A teacher recommends that aspirants maintain contact with their professors in graduate school:

> It's hard to hear of jobs in this rural area, so I always keep in touch with my former professors. I know some of them frequently get called about job openings and are asked to suggest names of potential candidates. So when I finished my certification, I went around and asked all of them to let me know if they heard of a good job in my area.
>
> (Southeastern rural)

Another woman, now employed at a state department, recalls how she made use of her time on a university campus to maintain and expand her network:

> I used my GTF position as a means of networking all over the state. Whenever we did a presentation, I made sure the superintendent knew me by my first name. I'm a hustler, and it paid off.
>
> (Southeastern city)

A specialist said in 1980:

Everyone *knows* I am looking for a principalship, because when I meet them I say: "Hi, I'm so and so, and I'm looking for a job as an elementary principal." I think I get called a lot more about jobs, now that I constantly remind people of my interest. Maintaining a high level of visibility is important for women seeking administrative jobs today.

(Northwestern suburb)

Although this woman has yet to attain a principalship, others concur that female administrative candidates must aggressively promote themselves. An assistant principal (since hired as a principal) shares her technique for maintaining important relationships:

I pestered our superintendent every time I saw him, reminding him not to forget that I was still aspiring. I told him I needed his help in my weak areas and, that with his support, I expected to get promoted. Everyone told me I was going to make it, so I made up my mind to keep badgering the decision-makers.

(Southern metro)

Establishing and maintaining visibility as a potential administrator requires confidence, imagination and persistence. A principal offers this recommendation:

Be persistent and sell yourself. If *you're* not confident you can be a leader, it will be hard to convince a superintendent or a school board that you're capable. I believe a healthy philosophy is: "What I don't know, I'm certainly willing to learn."

(Southern metro)

An administrative assistant (southern metro) advocates: "Bluff your way in and *then* go and figure out how to do the job. Otherwise, you will never get the chance." Persistence and imagination is particularly important for aspirants moving into new districts where their abilities are unknown. In 1980, a student (now a personnel director) described her active approach when she moved to a new district:

I made an appointment with the superintendent because I knew that no one would know I could do other things besides teach unless *I* told them. I went to the meeting prepared and started by saying, "Let me tell you some of the things I've done." After detailing my administrative experiences, I showed him letters and other documents to substantiate what I had said.

(Southeastern city)

In advising aspirants to take a direct, personal approach with their superintendents, women in this study agree that written communication is as important as personal conversation.

> In my university program, I was trained to state my intentions in writing. So I wrote a letter to my superintendent, stating my interests, background and goals. Apparently, not many people do that. People talk all the time, but they usually fail to put anything down on paper. And then they wonder why their name never comes up. I used to think someone was out there watching to promote those who were doing well. I soon found out otherwise. The buddy system doesn't get you there; *you* get you there.
>
> (Southeastern city)

> I am going to write the superintendent a letter to say "Here I am." I don't enjoy having to sell myself to others; however, I can do it and I have done it before. It appears to be necessary. After writing the superintendent, I'm going to get others to talk to him about me as well. I don't think most women in the country seek positions as aggressively as this. They don't use all the resources available to them.
>
> (Lead Teacher, Southern metro)

> I tried to get our personnel director to see me in a sensible light and to know that I was aspiring to become an administrator. I wrote to him and met him a couple of times to get career counselling. I wanted to be sure he knew I was pursuing administration. I also kept up my contacts with people who work for him, so if my name came up they would all know something about me first hand.
>
> (Principal, Southern city)

In the recent update, a new consultant (southern city) suggests: "You must get very politically involved to succeed—and don't think of it as 'brown-nosing' when you do so." Self-promotion may be difficult, but the recommendation to aspirants from the women in this study is clear: "If you don't promote yourself, who will?"

*Further Leadership Experience*

Because women often have difficulty obtaining necessary administrative experience within their own schools or districts, informants counsel aspirants to consider gaining that experience in organizations outside of the public school arena. One woman, who is now interviewing for assistant superintendencies, notes:

> I used opportunities in the state education association, the American Association of University Women, and in church and communtiy

organizations to learn how to lead people without them hating you. I took advantage of these opportunities to hone my leadership skills, and it helped.

(Northwestern suburb)

Likewise, a director relates:

I got involved outside of the classroom in community and church affairs. I made a concerted effort to know the things men know so I could talk to them. The average teacher doesn't know those things, because they just teach in classrooms. Now the men are the ones who promote me for jobs.

(Western metro)

Some women find serving on school boards a good way to gain valuable administrative experience.

I am now serving on the school board, and I'm getting some good experience there. I am able to observe the whole system from the top level of management down. The experience is invaluable in terms of administrative preparation. Being part of a negotiating team and actually being on the side of administration has benefited me greatly.

(Coordinator, Northeastern metro)

Others, while not sitting on school boards, cultivate relationships with board members and volunteer their services. A principal (who was an assistant principal at the start of the study) recalls her earlier strategy:

I worked very hard to get my first assistant principalships. I did all the appropriate things such as attending meetings, doing in-services and getting to know the board members informally. In other words, I got involved with important people in our district. I often volunteered to go to meetings no one else wanted to go to, because I wanted to stay visible and improve my skills. I wanted to be seen as one of *them*, rather than one of *those*. That's the politics of administration.

(Southern city)

Joining school and community organizations not only allows aspirants the opportunity to develop their management skills, but also increases their visibility among those in positions to positively influence their careers. A woman, who is now a principal, remembers a suggestion she received:

A woman principal told me not to bother with curriculum resource positions because they only expose you to other teachers. And teachers are not the people who measure your abilities or who give you administrative opportunities. You have to demonstrate your ability to be a change agent. She told me: "Get political and join every organization under the sun that will get you entry into the old boys' system. Do the best you can in places where people who ultimately write recommendations can see you doing your work. Everyone is perfect here and only the super-perfect make it."

(Western suburb)

Visibility, however, can be a two-edged sword. Active participation in a wide variety of organizations, while providing aspirants with excellent training and greater visibility, can sometimes prove to be a liability. A newly appointed principal cautions:

There's a fine line about how much visibility a classroom teacher should have when branching out into administration. We have some top level administrators—male and female—who are insecure and who feel threatened by anyone appearing to have a great deal of support or visibility.

(Northwestern suburb)

*Interviewing*

Careful career planning and preparation will enhance an aspirant's opportunities of being interviewed for administrative positions. Women in this study underline the importance of becoming comfortable with the interviewing process and suggest that aspirants should practice their interviewing skills by scheduling interviews even before actively seeking administrative positions. If aspirants are concerned about any risks inherent in interviewing in their own district, respondents suggest they apply to other districts. A counselor explains the advantages of this tactic:

I applied to some other school districts to gain a background in interviewing. Besides finding the process interesting, the interview forced me to crystallize some of my thoughts and my philosophy of education.

(Midwestern metro)

Interviewing in one's own district serves as a means of gaining greater visibility. A teacher recalls her strategy when she arrives in a new district:

I decided to interview just because no one knew me in that district. It gave me a professional way to introduce myself and allowed me to tell them I was interested in administration. They told me they appreciated my interest. I really didn't expect much to come from the interview, other than getting some experience with their process.

(Midwestern rural)

In this case, her efforts paid off. When a principal got ill later in the year, the interviewing committee remembered her eagerness to get into school management and hired her to finish out the year. What began as an exercise in getting acquainted, ultimately resulted in a permanent principalship. Although few practice interviews end with jobs, they are a valuable way to build confidence and learn more about what is expected in an interview. Another woman (midwestern metro), who later gained a directorship in a private school, recalls the advice she received from a personnel director: "Go out and let people know you are available. Get your foot in the door and to let them know that whenever an opening comes up, you're interested."

In the recent update, women strongly enjoin aspirants to apply for all administrative openings. The only exception came from an assistant principal (northeastern metro) who cautions: "Don't apply for any position where there's an acting principal, because they always get it—but apply for *everything* else." A woman applying for superintendencies found out the hard way that she needed to pursue a wide range of positions:

> When I left my principalship to go to graduate school, I thought I could easily find what I wanted later. But when I finished my doctorate, I only applied for a limited number of positions. By the time I saw the handwriting on the wall, even the principalships were filled. I learned a lesson: Seek a variety of positions—you can always turn them down.
>
> (Northwestern suburb)

By applying for many administrative positions, aspirants enhance the possibility of being granted more interviews. In turn, more interviews allow aspirants to develop confidence and helps them to improve their interviewing presence. A lobbyist recalls some feedback she received from a friend after one interview:

> He told me he was surprised at my nervousness (So was I!). He said I had all the right answers, but I needed to work on my confidence and learn to express assurance about myself.
>
> (Western city)

Rather than waiting to interview until they see a position they truly hope to get, aspirants who lack confidence should seek as many practice interviews as possible. An assistant principal (now a principal) recalls instructions given to her by a personnel director:

You need to be hungry and really push for a position. Every time you interview, you should act as if you want that job, that you are the best person for it, and that you're sure you will get it. If you do this when you're interviewing, you never really know you *aren't* the best person for the job!

(Western suburb)

On the other hand, another assistant principal (now also a principal) cautions aspirants not to be too hungry:

When I went in for my interview, I felt very good and secure. I knew I was ready to move, but I didn't feel desperate. I still liked my current job, but I didn't want to delay interviewing until I couldn't stand it anymore. So I felt like I was in the best position of all.

(Northeastern metro)

Aspirants should carefully prepare for interviews and develop strategies for improving the quality of their interview. For example, a new principal describes how she sets a congenial tone in her interviews by shaking hands with everyone at the beginning. She offers another suggestion:

I ask if I may take notes during the interview. That request usually blows their minds, even though it's legal. As they ask me questions, I jot things down about what I want to go back and ask them. They always ask you at the end of an interview if you have any questions, and you should be prepared. Taking notes puts you in an active role during the interview. It's a cooperative approach: *You* need to find out about the district as much as *they* need to find out about you.

(Northwestern town)

She also recommends avoiding educational jargon, because such language can be a "real 'put down' for some people and most of it is just junk anyway."

Women in the study offer other techniques for successful interviewing. An assistant principal (southeastern city) believes in asking interviewers to talk with people she works for, rather than relying on the recommendations of central office personnel "who hardly know me." According to a new principal (western suburb), another strategy for preparing for interviews is to read the school plans thoroughly and then articulate, during the interview, how your own strengths relate to those plans. A teacher (southeastern city) cautions aspirants not to say "you know something if you don't, because you might misunderstand what it is they are after." She also recommends reading local newspapers when applying in other districts, and stresses the importance of remaining

current with relevant professional journals. Thorough preparation for
interviews can build confidence, for in expanding their knowledge,
aspirants will be ready for a wide range of questions. A teacher-coach in
higher education comments on her growing confidence in interviews:

> In earlier interviews when people asked me to tell them something
> about myself, I used to say there wasn't much to tell. Now that I'm
> prepared, I can pull out my list and say, "Where do you want me to
> start?" I'm also no longer afraid to say what my accomplishments are.
> (Southern town)

In preparing for an interview, aspirants need to anticipate how they
will respond if sexist comments or questions come up during the process.
Regardless of what the laws say, women continue to face illegal and even
offensive questions during interviews. Two female principals illustrate
different approaches aspirants might consider. The first uses humor in her
interviews:

> When I got my first assistant principalship, I was asked in my
> interview how I thought I'd get along with a younger man as my
> principal. I said, "Well, so far I don't have trouble with younger men."
> They laughed, and I got the job!
> (Northwestern town)

The second principal, however, approaches such problems differently:

> After awhile, I decided that being polite when asked sexist questions
> wasn't getting me any jobs. So in the next interview I said, "I resent
> that question, because my babysitting arrangements have no bearing
> on this." I was honest, and I was hired. I just got tired of people prying
> into my private life. Usually they are surprised at first, but then the
> sexist questions stop.
> (Northwestern town)

Alternatively, other women advise aspirants to ignore sexist comments, or
at least dismiss or minimize them. Whether aspirants respond with humor,
hostility or silence, they must be prepared for the possibility that sexist
questions might arise. Aspirants who fail to foresee such inquiries in
advance run the rise of becoming suddenly confused during the interview.

Would-be administrators should also anticipate how to deal con-
structively with feelings of disappointment following unsuccessful interviews. The task is difficult, as this teacher (northwestern city) attests:
"Once you've been turned down and gotten discouraged, it's hard not to
come across bitter when you apply again." Some frustration is inevitable
when aspirants discover that a less-qualified candidate or a male received

the position. A counselor (midwestern metro) warns women "not to get frustrated and disappointed when they interview for a job and ascertain a man got the position—we must not give up!" Some women exhort aspirants to think about unsuccessful interviews as opportunities—thus lessening their feelings of frustration and disappointment. A director of a federal program (midwestern metro) suggests writing a letter to discover why someone else was offered the position. Requests for this kind of feedback, she argues, may resolve some of the candidate's doubts about the hiring process and assist the aspirant in preparing for the next interview. A teacher (western suburb) recalls the counsel of her superintendent: "It is ridiculous not to call for feedback after an interview." Likewise, a department chair (southeastern rural) acknowledges the importance of receiving feedback from interviews: "You don't want to make the same mistake twice." Many of the women in this study report that personnel directors or building administrators gladly give unsuccessful candidates such information, especially when asked in a non-defensive, "what-can-I-do-to-improve" manner.

Informants advise aspirants to proceed cautiously following interviews, suggesting that there are still positive things candidates can do to influence the hiring process. After an introductory interview in one district, a supervisor (now a principal) recalls:

> I wrote the superintendent a follow-up letter after our interview to reiterate my interest in the job. Later I found out he was very impressed with people who wrote letters after an interview.
>
> (Midwestern suburb)

An assistant principal (northeastern rural), who is now the vice president of a private business, recommends that aspirants further prepare themselves following interviews by listing the pros and cons of the position should it be offered. A woman, currently interviewing for a superintendency, recalls how her advanced planning paid off:

> When I was offered my first assistant principalship, I didn't jump at the salary they first presented. I had decided to bargain like a man. I told them it wouldn't hurt my feelings if they added another $1000 to my salary, and they did!
>
> (Northwestern suburb)

Finally, informants caution aspirants not to make premature judgments about their performance in interviews. Candidates are often not the best judges of how they did, and it is easy to misinterpret the concerns of those conducting interviews. A new principal reminisces:

> After my interview, I chastised myself about how I answered this or

that question. Then I just decided to go home, take a shower, bag out in front of the TV and watch a good movie. The phone call offering me the job came at ten p.m.

(Northwestern suburb)

*After Promotion*

After receiving administrative appointments, successful candidates should continue to proceed cautiously. Female administrators, like female aspirants, are frequently judged more critically than males in identical situations. Because of their minority status within administrative ranks, women usually face more questions about their management capabilities than their male colleagues. Informants recommend that successful aspirants anticipate the close scrutiny they will receive on the job and to prepare themselves in advance for the duties they will assume. One woman, now in her fourth year as a principal, recalls working over the summer to ready herself for a new supervisory position:

> I wanted to do a good job, so I prepared myself for my new responsibilities. At the first meeting in the Fall, everyone could see I had done my homework. They didn't have to say, "Oh, they hired another incompetent woman."

(Southeastern rural)

A new principal shares a similar approach:

> I proceed cautiously, because the staff often proceeds cautiously with a woman. When I got my first assistant principalship, I didn't lose any sleep over the fact I was the first female administrator in the school. However, I was scrupulously careful about even the most simple memorandum.

(Southern metro)

A teacher (now a principal) remembers how deliberately she acted when temporarily filling a principalship:

> I was assigned to the school in the middle of the year, and they hadn't had a woman there in many years. The school had severe discipline problems, and they were concerned whether a woman could handle things. I went around to every room and introduced myself as the acting principal. I even asked the kids if they had ever had a woman principal. I think that was important to the kids.

(Midwestern rural)

On the other hand, informants suggest that successful aspirants should temper their caution with confidence, for some people will associate caution with weakness or even incompetence. A new college level administrator explains:

> When a man is given a job and he doesn't know what to do, he finds out. He's expected to do just that. Women have to weigh the consequences of seeking help at a higher level. Women need to say they will do the job, regardless. We may make some mistakes, but we'll learn. The image of female administrators is damaged when we have to ask men to help us all the time.
>
> (Southern rural)

Because respondents believe school administration is not a gender-specific profession, they note that women must be confident and willing to assume *all* of the duties of an administrator. An assistant principal recalls how she handled the gender issue in 1980:

> At first, they didn't want to bother me with night duties, buses, et cetera. But I didn't allow that, because I didn't want to be accused of being pampered. Also, you don't get the experiences you need to move on.
>
> (Southeastern city)

Another assistant principal relates how she overcame the tendency of her male colleagues to exclude her from certain duties:

> The first couple of months as an administrative assistant, I just hung right with the three male administrators. I wouldn't let them out of my sight and did everything they did. Pretty soon, I just became part of them. Other women administrators before me just resorted to finding out things from the secretary!
>
> (Southern suburb)

Finally, in the recent update, a new principal explains how she overcame her initial difficulties as a female administrator:

> In my first year as principal, a key male staff member got angry with me and left the building forever. The other male old timers openly bragged about being able to "train" all the previous principals and essentially run the school themselves. My advice is don't tolerate male temper tantrums or power plays. You must be the leader of the building, even if it hurts like hell.
>
> (Northwestern town)

*Summary*

Despite the special problems women face in educational administration, women in this study believe that if aspirants are prepared and persistent they can surmount the difficulties. That two-thirds of the original 142 respondents have succeeded in attaining higher positions, suggests that their beliefs may be accurate. While underscoring the need to be aware of female stereotypes, they continue to emphasize that hard work is often the best antidote for the barriers they face. In 1985, a new secondary principal offered this advice to female aspirants:

> You must be careful as a woman, because if you are the least bit emotional you will get criticized. You should be conscious of the stereotypes and attend to them. As women, we have a responsibility to keep things together and to model carefully. We have to be perfect; there is no room for error. In our administrative meetings, the men used to jump all over any suggestions I made. Now they *ask* for my opinions. It took time and a lot of hard work to get where I am now.
>
> (Midwestern city)

Informants know that the demands of school leadership are great, yet they counsel aspirants to relish the opportunities that administration provides. A new principal (midwestern city) concludes that "you must like what you're doing as an administrator, because you will be doing it for so many hours of the day." To enjoy administrative work, a director of a private school instructs aspirants to prepare themselves thoroughly for the tasks ahead:

> I would encourage women to not only prepare themselves with credentials and internships, but to prepare psychologically and emotionally for administrative work. The stress of the job is immense, and more so for women who must constantly do their best. Even being a success in the job is stressful.
>
> (Northwestern metro)

Except for a few older women still holding assistant principalships, the women in this study are eager to take on these challenges. Indeed, the lure of professional stimulation and the promise of subsequent growth is what enticed these educators out of classrooms and into the management arena in the first place.

# Afterword

I'm shocked at the figures showing how few
women administrators actually get hired. I
thought there were more opportunities for
women today. I feel somewhat optimistic,
however, because I can see *some* improvement. So far, I've been lucky. Every interview I've had, I've gotten the position. But at
the slow rate women are progressing, it's
going to take a long time for women to get
ahead in this field.

(New Principal, Northwestern city)

At the conclusion of her 1981 literature review of women in educational
administration, Adkison challenged future researchers to provide "studies
of new generations of women moving into administration [that] can
provide evidence of changed attitudes toward women and raised aspirations among women." She believed then that "the careers of women who
have entered the market more recently may reveal different patterns" from
those studied earlier.[1] Although this longitudinal study commenced prior
to Adkison's observations, it details the missing voices of that new
generation of women actively seeking careers in public school administration. While other scholars debate whether the female voice is unique or
superior, this study focuses on documenting their words. Shakeshaft and
Novell argue: "An approach that allows the female voice to be heard from
the conceptualization of the research questions to the interpretations of the
data will help us to better understand all of human behavior and,
hopefully, will allow us to work from gender-inclusive theories."[2] The 142
voices in this study may contribute to those researchers planning new
studies and developing new theories, training programs and textbooks.

This study focused on why women want to be school managers,
rather than on documenting the reasons women do not want to be
administrators. Specific information about aspirant's lives and work may
assist researchers, practitioners, trainers and aspirants to raise new

questions about women and educational administration that transcend the generalizing tendencies of traditional statistical analyses. "[H]umanity is denigrated," Mead concluded, "when human beings are treated as interchangeable ciphers in monolithic schemes in which . . . the distinctiveness of the individual being is ignored or denied."[3] To achieve these goals, we must listen to our informants and trust their accounts. Descriptive data, such as is found in this study, may help to "demystify" many of the incorrect notions about women in education.[4]

Clearly the 142 women in this study demonstrate the "raised expectations" Adkison hinted at in 1981. Their successes far exceed those of women in general. Throughout the country, women continue to make minimal, if any, gains in school leadership ranks. During roughly the same time frame of this study, Jones and Montenegro tracked the progress of women and minorities in educational administration: In 1981-82, women comprised twenty-five percent of all school administrators nationwide; in 1984-85, the figure stood at only twenty-six percent.[5] When the data are analyzed in terms of administrative levels relevant to this study, only slight increases appear at the superintendent, assistant superintendent and principal levels (see figure on next page). In the case of the first two levels, there is only a little over one percentage point averaged each year, and at the superintendent level, women gained only one percentage point in four years. As the figure graphically portrays, despite slight gains by women, men continue to hold the majority of positions in all three categories.

But statistical analyses alone fail to capture the whole story of women in educational administration, just as a single, statistically-contrived portrait fails the test of reality. Individual women, who share a common commitment to education and a common determination to push the limits placed on women seeking leadership roles, instruct us by their very diversity. These women believe they have untapped potential as school executives and only require the opportunity to demonstrate their abilities. In a recent study of female administrators in Wisconsin, Schneider found that the attitudes and qualifications of upcoming female educators "directly contradict the long-held belief that women will be less available and committed to their work than men . . . [and dispels] the notion that the hiring of women will result in employing administrators with inferior qualifications . . . ."[6] Aspirants in this study are not only schooled, they are experienced—in classrooms as well as in administrative offices. By describing their world, these aspirants furnish researchers with concrete experiences that challenge some of the assumptions about women in administration. In turn, these examples will hopefully promote "research which questions rather than merely documents the world around us."[7]

In addition to anticipating that future studies would reveal women's raised aspirations, Adkison hoped that new research would find changed

# DISTRIBUTION OF U.S. PUBLIC SCHOOL ADMINISTRATORS
## by Sex, Position and School Year

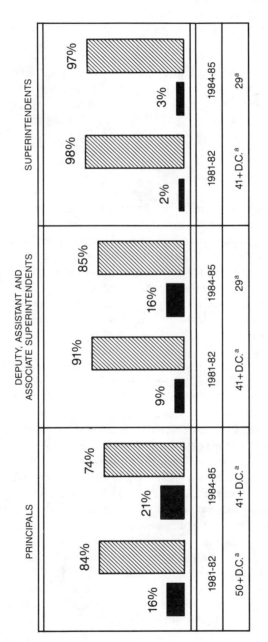

Source: E. Jones and X. Montenegro, *Women and Minorities in School Administration* (Arlington, VA: American Association of School Administrators), 5-15.

[a]Only this number of states (and Washington, D.C. where indicated) responded with information broken down by sex.

attitudes toward women in administration. With few exceptions, however, women in this study still find discrimination an ongoing concern and gender bias—especially at the secondary level—a continuing barrier to their advancement. They can not necessarily prove discrimination; but, as this newly hired elementary principal writes, they can sense it:

> I recently applied for the principalship in my junior high after being the assistant principal for nearly seven years. I was given, instead, the job as principal in an elementary school and *its* male principal was transferred to *my* junior high school. I cannot measure the discrimination in this move (there may have been *none*), but I *feel* there was some.
>
> (Northwestern town)

Although these women confront barriers similar to those other women and minorities face, their strong motivation to succeed helps them to overcome the discrimination they experience. As a secondary assistant principal (southern metro) observes: "Though our numbers nationwide are limited, I believe there is a future for women who have the strength to persevere."

Since the inception of this project, there has been a shift in national priorities relating to issues of equity. During the last ten years, the issue of sex equity in public school administration—fueled by legislation and the countless efforts of concerned individuals all over the country—moved from the exciting forefront of national concern to the obscurity of the proverbial back burner. Tetreault and Schmuck believe much of the past decade's scholarship, action and legislation concerning women is either being ignored or dismantled. "We are fearful," they conclude, that "we may be seeing the end of an epoch of educational history—where the scholarship and research on women were coupled with federal mandates— one which, for the first time paid attention to females in schools . . . . "[8] In the recent update, one elementary principal (northwestern city) remarks, "The urgency to hire women is gone, if, indeed, it was ever there to begin with." Fauth contends that we have entered a period of history where economics, demography and politics overshadow equity issues, producing "hazardous times for the principle and practice of equity in public education."[9]

Deterrents aside, many women continue to strive and to prepare themselves for school management. According to Wong et al., these women "are 'survivors' whose lives deserve our attention."[10] Although some districts have changed their hiring practices, Johnson and Douglas find the change "is not so dramatic that it promises correction of our history of inequity."[11] They conclude that there is still a "plethora of reasons for not promoting women, all of which are couched in the belief by many that it would be more efficient to hire a man."[12] Survivors in this study face similar obstacles, as a high school principal reflects:

There are definitely more sacrifices required of the female educational administrator—publicly and privately. For example, there is little local support for women in administration and even less for minority women. There are fewer opportunities for women who also want to be good homemakers and parents on top of it all. Although there are more women administrators in my district now, they usually got their jobs because of a crisis or because the school was at its lowest ebb. Women don't get the plums; we get "the challenges."

(Northeastern metro)

An elementary assistant principal (southeastern city) agrees, claiming that the women who advance in her district get "their promotions by fluke, midyear openings, sudden changes and the need to find someone fast." Thus, Ortiz maintains that "organization members are not provided with a clearly legitimated reason for placing the woman in an administrative post."[13] Given such obstacles, the strides made by the women in this study seem all the more important—for in their stories, are seeds of hope. A middle school principal notes:

I am more realistic now than before I got into this position. The work is hard, the hours long, the challenge great. I'm striving to improve the balance I have between job and home. I continue to note the loneliness of the administrative role, the greater difficulty in supervising women than men, and the strength of the old boys' network in educational administration. But I'm encouraged, because in several cases where I was a finalist for a position, the other woman got the job.

(Northeastern town)

These women do not want an advantage over their male peers, rather they seek only the chance to compete as equals for leadership roles in schools. Perhaps some who read this study will gain insight into how to help able female aspirants succeed. Smith et al. believe that those persons responsible for hiring and promoting "must understand the situation, how it got that way and how it can be changed."[14] They believe educational leaders must be aware of the problems women and minorities face so they can offer support, both to those who aspire and to those who succeed in gaining administrative positions. Smith et al. conclude: "If the path seems blocked, [women] need to know there is some hope. If the path seems easy, they need to know that others still face obstacles."[15]

Those interested in women's progress must find renewed energy to celebrate the small, individual victories, while pushing for the larger social ones. As Greene urges, "It is up to us, if we stand together, to tell our truths, to bring the severed parts together, to countervail, to transform."[16] Any woman in educational administration—whether an aspirant or an office holder—is a pioneer to some extent, and being a pioneer takes its toll.

Those so-called "superwomen" who balance administration and family, not only face a lonely battle at the office, but often a maximum load at home. Equally in need of support are the other women who find themselves waiting in the wings for an opportunity to further their careers. Unlike the pathbreakers, these women often have greater difficulties in securing administrative positions because, as Bell points out, the successes of a "first" woman or minority can become a barrier, rather than a bridge, for those who follow. He argues that those responsible for hiring continue to compare and wait for someone "as good" as the first few successful pioneers; consequently, they fail to see how more recent aspirants may even exceed the abilities of those chosen earlier.[17]

In the 1970s, some people argued that there would be equity in school management when there were as many mediocre women in the field as men. However, just as all male aspirants do not make good administrators, neither do all females who may wish to manage—and this book should not be misconstrued to assume otherwise. Identifying and promoting the best school leaders—regardless of race or gender—is the desire goal. Where equity legislation aids this end, it should be applauded; where it creates artificial barriers which help neither the aspirants nor the schools they seek to serve, it should be rejected. Legislative mandates aiding women and minorities are a step in the right direction, but an equal number of people of either gender or of all races is not a goal in and of itself.

Because school improvement remains a major goal of these female educators, the question remains: Can women change the nature of school administration in ways that will lead to the betterment of public education? Because educational administration emanates from a male model, these women face a difficult task. Marshall contends strong undercurrents in both the informal and formal structures of schools "promulgate practices that force on women the added burden of learning to 'pass'—to gravitate toward male postures, male practices, and even male clothing in order to gain acceptance in the field."[18] Possibly, such uniformity adversely affects school climate. "A school culture that is hostile to female . . . administrators," writes Shakeshaft, "is not a place that is conducive to their best efforts. If schools are to be hallmarks of excellence, they must provide environments that allow female . . . professionals to grow, to achieve, and to develop self-esteem, in their own, not necessarily male, ways."[19] In an environment that encourages everyone to develop their own potential to address educational issues, school improvement becomes possible.

We cannot accurately assess whether the women in this study are capable of transforming schools. But because they must examine their career motivations and educational philosophies more thoroughly than men, they may well alter the face of school administration—and perhaps schools as well. Kaplan predicts that "leadership may wear different clothing and serve different purposes in the coming years."[20] The women in this study, regardless of race, age and geographical region, confirm

Kaplan's prophecy. Although many admit they want success, school improvement—not personal gain—motivates their aspirations. A secondary assistant principal states:

> Male or female, I hope people aspiring understand the importance of administrative positions. Leadership in schools is fundamentally a moral act that requires one to possess sound values and which places the needs of society and others ahead of personal needs for power or control. Moral leadership and direction for youth has been sorely lacking in education recently.
>
> (Northeastern suburb)

Finally, although the numbers of female administrators remain low, the commitment and enthusiasm of these 142 female aspirants provides a message of encouragment to women and minorities considering similar career goals. Cautious at times about their own eventual success, they urge willing and able women to aim high. Most of the women in this study would agree with this advice:

> Get the background and the experience, and then *go* for those positions! Administration is time consuming and frustrating, and it requires above average stamina. But although I get frustrated at times, I can honestly say I am never bored. Educational administration is an exhilarating and rewarding field.
>
> (Principal, Southern metro)

Public schools need administrators—whether female or male—who describe their work in such exiting terms. The female aspirants in this book represent individuals who not only seek challenges, but who believe they *can* make a difference. Early in the study, a graduate student (now a principal) described her optimism which continues to characterize the stance of these women:

> I have experience in schools, financing and coaching, and now I'm working on my Ph.D. Thus, I should be able to answer all the stereotypes that arise in interviews about women in administration. Hopefully, all a hiring comittee will have left to say to me is: "OK, when can you start?"
>
> (Midwestern metro)

# Notes

## INTRODUCTION

1. S. Diaz, "The Aspiration Levels of Women for Administrative Careers in Education: Predictive Factors and Implications for Effecting Change" (Paper delivered at the Annual Meeting of the American Educational Research Association, San Francisco, 1976), 61.

2. F. Ortiz and J. Covel, "Women in School Administration: A Case Analysis." *Urban Education* 13 (July 1978): 214.

3. L. Valverde, "Succession Socialization: Its Influence on School Administrative Candidates and Its Implications to the Exclusion of Minorities From Administration" (Unpublished paper, National Institute of Education, Washington, D.C., 1974), ii.

4. L. Larwood and M. Lockheed, "Women as Managers: Toward Second Generation Research," *Sex Roles* 5 (October 1979): 659.

5. Ibid., 662.

6. L. Larwood, M. Wood, and S. Inderlied, "Training Women for Management: New Problems, New Solutions," *Academy of Management Review* 3 (July 1978): 592.

7. For complete descriptions of the barriers women face in the field, see: K. Lyman and J. Speizer, "Advancing in School Administration: A Pilot Project for Women," *Harvard Educational Review* 50 (February 1980): 25-34; P. Schmuck, *Sex Differentiation in Public School Administration* (North Arlington, VA: National Council of Administrative Women in Education, 1975), 64-113; and H. Beck, "Attitudes Toward Women Held by California School District Board Members, Superintendents, and Personnel Directors Including a Review of the Historical, Psychological, and Sociological Foundations" (Ph.D. diss., University of the Pacific, 1978).

8. E. Jones and X. Montenegro, *Recent Trends in the Representation of Women and Minorities in School Administration and Problems in Documentation* (Arlington, VA: American Association of School Administrators, 1982).

9. E. Jones and X. Montenegro, "Sex and Ethnic Representation in School Administration" (Unpublished report, American Association of School Administrators, 1982), 2.

10. M. Weber, J. Feldman, and E. Poling, "A Study of Factors Affecting Career Aspirations of Women Teachers and Educational Administrators" (Paper delivered at the Annual Meeting of the American Educational Research Association, Boston, 1980), 2.

11. For further discussion of women's administrative aspirations, see: S. Diaz, "A Study of Personal, Perceptual, and Motivational Factors Influential in Predicting the Aspiration Levels of Men and Women Toward the Administrative Roles in Education" (Ph.D. diss., Boston University, 1975); and S. Wyant and P. Schmuck, "The Oregon Network: A Research and Service Activity of the Sex Equity in Educational Leadership Project" (Paper delivered at the Annual Meeting of the American Educational Research Association, San Francisco, 1979).

12. For a portrait of the current female administrative aspirant in Oregon, see: S. Edson, "If They Can, I Can: Women Aspirants to Administrative Positions in Public Schools," in *Educational Policy and Management: Sex Differentials*, ed. P. Schmuck, W. Charters, Jr., and R. Carlson (New York: Academic Press, 1981), 169-185.

13. E. Dubois et al., *Feminist Scholarship: Kindling in the Groves of Academe* (Urbana: University of Illinois Press, 1985), 7.

14. Ibid., vii.

15. Ibid., 197.

## CHAPTER 1

1. For additional reading on the barriers and problems women currently face in the field of educational administration, see: J. Adkison, "Women in School Administration: A Review of the Research," *Review of Educational Research* 51 (Fall 1981): 311-343; and C. Shakeshaft, "Strategies for Overcoming the Barriers to Women in School Administration," in *Handbook for Achieving Sex Equity Through Education*, ed. S. Klein (Baltimore: The Johns Hopkins University Press, 1985), 124-144.

2. Schmuck, *Sex Differentiation*, 34.

3. P. Schmuck, "The Spirit of Title IX: Men's Work and Women's Work in Oregon Public Schools," *Oregon School Study Council Bulletin* 20 (October 1976).

## CHAPTER 2

1. For further discussion about female graduate students in educational administration, see: P. Silver and D. Spuck, eds., *Preparatory Programs for Educational Administrators in the United States* (Columbus, OH: The University Council for Educational Administration, 1978); M. McCarthy, G. Kuh, and J. Beckman, "Characteristics and Attitudes of Doctoral Students in Educational Administration," *Phi Delta Kappan* 61 (November, 1979): 200-203; and S. Oller [Edson], "Female Doctoral

Students in Educational Administration: Who Are They?," *Sex Equity in Educational Leadership Report* 7 (Eugene, OR: Center for Educational Policy and Management, 1978), 1-2.

2. *National Research Council, Summary Report, 1982: Doctorate Recipients from U.S. Universities* (Washington, D.C.: National Academy Press, 1983), 29.

3. G. Sheehy, *Passages* (New York: E. P. Dutton, 1976), 294.


CHAPTER 3

1. J. Grambs, "Women and Administration: Confrontation or Accomodation?," *Theory and Practice* 15 (October 1976): 294.

2. B. Harragan, *Games Mother Never Taught You* (New York: Warner Books, 1977), 152.

3. Grambs, "Women and Administration," 294.

4. Schmuck, *Sex Differentiation,* 112.

5. M. Lee, "Tough Questions and Hidden Tests Revealed," *Ms Magazine,* June 1983, 51.

6. Ibid., 75.

7. M. Patterson and L. Engelberg, "Women in Male-Dominated Professions," in *Women Working: Theories and Facts in Perspective,* ed. A. Stromberg and S. Harkess (Palo Alto, CA: Mayfield Publishing Company, 1978), 269.

8. I. Settles, *Marketing Yourself—A Handbook for Educational Administration Applicants* (Olympia, WA: Washington Association of School Administrators, 1983), 31.


CHAPTER 4

1. R. Kanter, "The Impact of Hierarchical Structures on the Work Behavior of Women and Men," in *Women and Work—Problems and Perspectives,* ed. R. Kahn-Hut, A. Daniels, and R. Colvard (New York: Oxford University Press, 1982), 236.

2. S. Krchniak, "Entry into School Administration by Women in Illinois: Facts and Dynamics" (Report to the State Board of Education, Illinois Office of Education, 1977), 18.

3. S. Paddock, "Male and Female Career Paths in School Administration," in Schmuck, Charters, Jr., and Carlson, eds., *Educational Policy and Management,* 157.

4. Harragan, *Games,* 157.

5. J. Cronin and S. Pancrazio, "Women as Educational Leaders," *Phi Delta Kappan* 60 (April 1979): 586.

6. K. Crandall and D. Reed, "Career Patterns of Female Administrators in Public Schools" (Paper delivered at the Annual Meeting of the

American Educational Research Association, San Francisco, 1986).
    7. Ibid., 9.

CHAPTER 5

    1. *Webster's New World Dictionary*, 2d ed., s.v. "role model."
    2. Grambs, "Women and Administration," 297.
    3. C. Wolman and H. Frank, "The Solo Woman in a Professional Peer Group," *American Journal of Orinopsyhiatrics* 45 (January 1975): 164.
    4. M. Smith, J. Kalvelage, and P. Schmuck, *Women Getting Together and Getting Ahead* (Newton, MA: Women's Educational Equity Act Program, U.S. Department of Education, 1982), 3.
    5. *Webster's New World Dictionary*, 913.
    6. For further discussion of the lone female in a work group, see: M. Lockheed and K. Hall, "Conceptualizing Sex as a Status Characteristic: Applications to Leadership Training Strategies," *Journal of Social Issues* 32 (Fall 1976): 111-123.
    7. D. Socolow, "How Administrators Get Their Jobs," *Change* 10 (May 1978): 43.
    8. J. Speizer, "Role Models, Mentors, and Sponsors: The Elusive Concepts," *Signs* 6 (Summer 1981): 714.
    9. M. Horner, "Toward and Understanding of Achievement-Related Conflicts in Women," *Journal of Social Issues* 28 (Summer 1972): 157-175.

CHAPTER 6

    1. R. Kanter, *Men and Women of the Corporation* (New York: Basic Books, 1977), 181-182.
    2. M. Hennig and A. Jardim, *The Managerial Woman* (New York: Pocket Books, 1978), 62.
    3. Kanter, *Men and Women*, 181-182.
    4. Ibid., 183.
    5. B. Pavan, "Mentors and Mentoring Functions Perceived as Helpful to Certified Aspiring and Incumbent Female and Male Public School Administrators" (Paper delivered at the Annual Meeting of the American Educational Research Association, San Francisco, 1986).
    6. C. DiBella, R. Eckstrom, and S. Tobias, "No Room at the Top," *American Education* 13 (June 1977): 23.
    7. Kanter, *Men and Women*, 184.
    8. DiBella et al., "No Room," 23.
    9. S. Oller [Edson], "Male Teachers: Early Childhood Education or Administration?" *Sex Equity in Educational Leadership Report* 3 (Eugene, OR: Center for Educational Policy and Management, 1977), 3-4.

CHAPTER 7

1. J. Pleck, "The Work-Family Role System," in Kahn-Hut, Daniels, and Colvard, eds., *Women and Work*, 109.

2. M. White, "Women in the Professions: Psychological and Social Barriers to Women in Science," in *Women: A Feminist Perspective*, ed. J. Freeman (Palo Alto, CA: Mayfield Publishing Company, 1979), 365.

3. Pleck, "Work-Family," 103.

4. Paddock, "Male and Female Career Paths," 191.

5. H. Papanek, "Men, Women and Work: Reflections on the Two-Person Career," in *Changing Women in a Changing Society*, ed. J. Huber (Chicago: University of Chicago Press, 1973), 108.

6. White, "Women in the Professions," 365.

7. G. Sheehy, "The Mentor Connection," *New York Magazine* 5 April 1976, 36.

8. Pavan, "Mentors and Mentoring," 13.

9. Patterson and Engelberg, "Women in Male-Dominated Professions," 287.

10. P. Bourne and J. Wikler, "Commitment and the Cultural Mandate: Women in Medicine," in Kahn-Hut, Daniels, and Colvard, eds., *Women and Work*, 117.

11. Ibid., 115.

12. Pleck, "The Work-Family Role," 108-109.

CHAPTER 8

1. Jones and Montenegro, *Recent Trends*, 18.

2. E. Jones and X. Montenegro, *Women and Minorities in School Administration* (Arlington, VA: American Association of School Administrators, 1985), 21.

3. For further explanation of the fluctuation in female elementary principalships, see: J. Stockard et al., *Sex Equity in Education* (New York: Academic Press, 1980), 84-87; and S. Howard, "Notes on Women and Minorities in Educational Administration" (Unpublished report, Resource Center on Educational Equity, Washington, D.C., 1984).

4. For further discussion of sexual harrassment in the workplace, see: "Put Out or Get Out," in Harragan, *Games*, 365-370.

5. J. O'Reilly, *The Girl I left Behind* (New York: Collier Books, 1980), 119.

6. Ortiz and Covel, "Women in School Administration," 220.

7. Ibid.

8. S. Tibbetts, "Sex-Role Stereotyping: Why Women Discriminate Against Themselves," *The Journal of NAWDC* 38 (Summer 1975): 181.

9. Ibid.

10. Larwood, Wood, and Inderlied, "Training Women," 587.

11. P. Caplan, *Barriers Between Women* (New York: SP Medical and Scientific Books, 1981), 44.

12. G. Will, "The Cold War Among Women," *Newsweek* 26 June 1978, 100.

13. Kanter, *Men and Women*, 158-159.

14. Ibid.

15. For further studies confirming this theory, see: Kanter, "The Impact of Hierarchical Structures," 238-239.

16. G. Staines, C. Tavris, and T. Jayaratne, "The Queen Bee Syndrome," *Psychology Today* January 1974, 55.

17. Caplan, *Barriers Between Women*, 65.

18. Staines, Tavris, and Jayaratne, "Queen Bee," 60.

19. J. Berry and R. Kushner, "A Critical Look at the Queen Bee Syndrome," *The Journal of the N A W D C* 38 (Summer, 1985), 117.

20. G. Huws, "The Conscientization of Women: A Rite of Self-Initiation With the Flavor of a Religious Conversion Process," *Women's Studies International Forum* 5 (1982): 406.

21. Harragan, *Games*, 33.

22. E. Goodman, "Women's Movement Lacks Movement," [Eugene, OR] *Register-Guard*, 8 April 1986.

CHAPTER 9

1. B. Pope, *Factors Influencing Career Aspirations and Development of Women Holding Administrative Positions in Public Schools* (Palo Alto, CA: R and E Research Associates, 1982), 66.

2. Adkinson, "Women in School Administration," 322.

3. For a detailed discussion on women and men in educational positions, see: Stockard et al., *Sex Equity*, 80-91.

4. R. Carlson, *School Superintendents: Careers and Performance* (Columbus, OH: Charles E. Merrill, 1972).

5. Stockard et al., *Sex Equity*, 107.

CHAPTER 10

1. For a detailed description of these forces and laws, see: P. Jacklin, "The Concept of Sex Equity in Jurisprudence," in Schmuck, Charters, Jr., and Carlson, eds., *Educational Policy and Management*, 55-72.

2. *Federal Register* 36 (December 1971): 131.

3. Ibid., 132.

4. Kanter, *Men and Women*, 134.

5. P. Schmuck and S. Wyant, "Clues to Sex Bias in the Selection of School Administrators: A Report from the Oregon Network," in Schmuck, Charters, Jr., and Carlson, eds., *Educational Policy and Management*, 55-72.

6. Ibid.

7. Ibid.

8. C. Marshall, "Organizational Policy and Women's Socialization in Administration," *Urban Education* 16 (July 1981): 219.

9. Ibid.

10. Larwood and Lockheed, "Women as Managers," 664.

11. Ibid., 660.

12. M. McCarthy and A. Zent, "Affirmative Action for School Administrators: Has It Worked, Can It Survive?," *Phi Delta Kappan* 63 (March 1982): 461-463.

13. Schmuck and Wyant, "Clues to Sex Bias," 75.

14. Harragan, *Games*, 189.

15. Adkison, "Women in School Administration," 321.

16. Ibid.

17. Hennig and Jardim, *Managerial Woman*, 15.

18. Ibid.

## CHAPTER 11

1. Adkison, "Women in School Administration," 331. See also 331-335 for a brief discussion of recent studies on minority women in the field. For detailed analyses of minorities in educational administration, see: F. Ortiz, *Career Patterns in Education* (New York: Praeger Publishers, 1982), 84-117; L. Valverde, "Succession Socialization"; and A. Contreras, "Spanish-Surnamed Administrators," *Emergent Leadership* 3 (Spring 1979), 33-47.

2. Jones and Montenegro, *Recent Trends.*

3. Jones and Montenegro, "Sex and Ethnic Representation," 3.

4. Contreras, "Spanish-Surnamed Administrators," 33.

5. Ortiz, *Career Patterns*, 94.

6. Ibid., 91, 94.

7. Ibid., 189.

8. J. Stockard, "Why Sex Inequities Exist in the Profession of Education," in Stockard et al., *Sex Equity*, 106.

9. C. Epstein, "Positive Effects of the Multiple Negative: Explaining the Success of Black Professional Women," in Huber, ed., *Changing Women in a Changing Society*, 169.

10. Ortiz, *Career Patterns*, 106.

11. R. Doughty, "The Black Female Administrator: Women in a Double Bind," in *Women and Educational Leadership*, ed. S. Biklen and M. Brannigan (Lexington, MA: Lexington Books, 1980), 165-174.

12. Ibid., 169.

13. Valverde, "Succession Socialization," 15.

14. C. Epstein, *Woman's Place* (Berkeley: University of California Press, 1970).

15. Ortiz, *Career Patterns*, 93.

16. Ibid., 93-94.
17. Valverde, "Succession Socialization," 138-140.
18. Ibid., 143-144.
19. Ibid., 148.
20. Epstein, "Positive Effects," 152.
21. Stockard, "Why Sex Inequities Exist," 106.
22. Ibid.
23. S. Paddock, "Careers in Educational Administration: Are Women the Exception?" (Unpublished paper, Sex Equity in Educational Leadership Project, University of Oregon, 1978), 6.
24. Epstein, "Positive Effects," 169-170.
25. G. Lerner, *The Majority Finds Its Past* (New York: Oxford University Press, 1979), 111.
26. Ibid., 94-95.
27. Epstein, "Positive Effects," 170.
28. N. Payne and B. Jackson, "The Status of Black Women in Educational Administration" (Unpublished paper, National Council on Women's Educational Programs, Department of Health, Education, and Welfare, 1978), 19. See also: N. Payne, "The Status of Black Women in Educational Administration" (Ph.D. diss., Atlanta University, 1975).
29. Payne and Jackson, "Status of Black Women," 20.
30. Paddock, "Careers in Educational Administration," 6.
31. Ortiz, *Career Patterns*, 112.
32. Ibid., 94.
33. Epstein, "Positive Effects," 170-171.
34. D. Coursen and J. Mazzarella, "Two Special Cases: Women and Blacks," in *School Leadership: Handbook for Survival*, ed. S. Smith, J. Mazzarella, and P. Piele (Eugene, OR: ERIC Clearinghouse on Educational Management, 1981), 56.
35. Ibid.

CHAPTER 12

1. DiBella et al., "No Room at the Top," 21.
2. M. Weber, J. Feldman, and E. Poling, "Why Women Are Underrepresented in Educational Administration," *Educational Leadership* 38 (January 1981): 322.
3. D. Timpano, "How To Tell If You're Discriminating Against Would-Be Women Administrators and What To Do About It If You Are" *The American School Board Journal* 163 (June 1976): 19.
4. M. Thomas, "Why Aren't Women Administering Our Schools?," *N A S S P Bulletin* 70 (March 1986): 91.
5. I. Frieze et al., *Women and Sex Roles* (New York: W. W. Norton, 1978), 287.

6. C. Safilios-Rothschild, "Women and Work: Policy Implications and Prospects for the Future," in Stromberg and Harkess, eds., *Women Working*, 430.

7. Thomas, "Why Aren't Women Administering," 91.

8. Timpano, "How To Tell," 21.

9. Weber et al., "Why Women Are Underrepresented," 321.

CHAPTER 13

1. Timpano, "How To Tell," 21.

2. E. Matthews, "Women in Educational Administration: Support Systems, Career Patterns, and Job Competencies" (Ph.D. diss., University of Oregon, 1986), 190.

3. C. Paige, "Life Is What Happens When You're Making Other Plans," *Ms Magazine* April 1986, 69.

4. O'Reilly, *The Girl I Left Behind*, 136.

CHAPTER 14

1. S. Biklen, "Introduction—Barriers to Equity—Women, Educational Leadership and Social Change," in Biklen and Brannigan, eds., *Women and Educational Leadership*, 1.

2. G. Kaplan, "Shining Lights in High Places: Education's Top Four Leaders and Their Heirs," *Phi Delta Kappan* 67 (September 1985): 15.

3. In roughly the same time frame as this study, Jones and Montenegro report the total number of female administrators in this country has risen from 25% to 26%, see: Jones and Montenegro, *Women and Minorities*, 21-22.

4. L. Woo, "Women Administrators: Profiles of Success," *Phi Delta Kappan* 67 (December 1985): 286.

5. W. Greenfield, "Administrative Candidacy: A Process of New Role Learning—Part Two," *The Journal of Educational Administration* 15 (October 1977): 170-193.

6. For a recent review of the literature on the four most strongly held myths about women in administration, see: G. Fauth, "Women in Educational Administration: A Research Profile," *The Educational Forum* 49 (Fall 1984): 66-74.

7. Thomas, "Why Aren't Women Administering," 90.

8. S. Brownmiller, *Femininity* (New York: Simon and Schuster, 1984), 237.

CHAPTER 15

1. Thomas, "Why Aren't Women Administering," 91.

2. Weber, Feldman, and Poling, "Why Women Are Underrepresented," 322.

AFTERWORD

1. Adkison, "Women in School Administration," 339.
2. C. Shakeshaft and I. Novell, "Research on Theories, Concepts and Models of Behavior: The Influence of Gender," *Issues in Education* 2 (Winter 1984): 200.
3. Quoted in J. Howard, *Margaret Mead—A Life* (New York: Fawcett Crest Books, 1984), 270-271.
4. M. Greene, "The Impacts of Irrevelance: Women in the History of American Education," in *Women and Education*, ed. E. Fenema and J. Ayres (Berkeley: McCutchon Publishers, 1984), 36.
5. Jones and Montenegro, *Women and Minorities*, 5-6, 10-11, 14; and *Recent Trends*, 12. Both reports give a further breakdown of the statistics of women and minorities in the field and delineate the difficulties in getting consistent and valid statistics from the states. The latest report documents a decline in the number of states that breakdown their data by sex. There appears to be a trend of reversing the keeping of such records, making it difficult, once again, to track the success or failure of women in the field.
6. G. Schneider, "Career Paths and Mobility Differences of Women and Men in Educational Administration" (Paper delivered at the Annual Meeting of the American Educational Research Association, San Francisco, 1986), 12-13.
7. M. Scherr, "Women as Outsiders Within Organizations" (Paper delivered at the Annual Meeting of the American Educational Research Association, San Francisco, 1986), 12.
8. M. Tetreault and P. Schmuck, "Equity, Educational Reform and Gender," *Issues in Education* 3 (Summer 1985): 64.
9. Fauth, "Women in Educational Administration," 65.
10. P. Wong, G. Kettlewell, and C. Sproule, "On the Importance of Being Masculine: Sex Role Attribution, and Women's Career Achievement," *Sex Roles* 12 (April 1985): 767.
11. M. Johnson and J. Douglas, "Assessment Centers: What Impact Have They Had on Career Opportunities for Women?," *NASSP Bulletin* 69 (November 1985): 110.
12. Ibid.
13. Ortiz, *Career Patterns*, 71.
14. Coursen and Mazzarella, "Two Special Cases," 39.
15. Ibid.
16. M. Greene, "Women's Vantage Points and New Realities: A Philosophical Viewing" (Invited address to the Annual Meeting of the American Educational Research Association, Los Angeles, 1981), 17.

17. D. Bell, "*Brown v. Board of Education* and the Black History Month Syndrome" (Unpublished address to the Eighth Annual Conference for Facilitators of Organizational Development, Eugene, OR, 1985), 10.

18. C. Marshall, "The Stigmatized Woman: The Professional Woman in a Male Sex-Typed Career," *The Journal of Educational Administration* 23 (Summer 1985): 150. See also: Matthews, "Women in Educational Administration," chapt. 7; Matthews analyzes four distinct styles women adopt as a means of coping with their minority status and finds a significant link between a woman's point of view regarding sex equity issues and their career experiences.

19. C. Shakeshaft, "A Gender at Risk," *Phi Delta Kappan* 67 (March 1986): 502-503.

20. Kaplan, "Shining Lights," 16.

# INDEX